KEEP *THIS* QUIET TOO!

Praise for Keep This Quiet!

"Margaret Harrell's *Keep This Quiet* offers an illuminating look at Hunter S. Thompson in full throttle trying to make it as a Top Notch prose-stylist. Harrell fills in many important biographical gaps. A welcome addition to what is becoming the HST cottage industry. Read it"

—**Douglas Brinkley**, editor of *The Proud Highway* and *Fear and Loathing in America*

"The reader comes to feel an affinity with the trio of writers in their attempts to achieve their iconoclastic visions of success, glimpsing them as individuals beyond their work, seeing how they think"

—**Kirkus Indie Reviews**

"If you want to know what the Sixties were really like, read *Keep This Quiet: A Memoir*. It's all there: the openness, the hope, the ideals, the risks, the highs and lows, the travel, the love"

—**Robert Morgan**, author of *Gap Creek and Terroir*

"Keep This Quiet? Not likely. Margaret Harrell's K*eep This Quiet!* is a feast for the Gonzo soul. It's all new and a valuable addition to my collection. . . . Highly recommended"

—**Martin Flynn**, owner of hstbooks.org

"This book is a joy to read, particularly for anyone that has that urge to express themselves through the creative arts in all their forms. In terms of its importance to the Hunter S. Thompson world I would have to say that there are not many other books out there that have the same intimate understanding of the man behind the myth"

—**Rory Feehan**, owner of totallygonzo.org

"Thompson loved Harrell's work as the line editor on *Hell's Angels* and she here details the nature of their relationship"

—**William McKeen**, *Literary Journalism Studies*

"Harrell's writing is crisp and easy to follow. I found it nearly impossible to put the book down"

—Isabel Escobar

"*Keep This Quiet!* is a moving read and much recommended to any literary studies or memoir collection"

—Midwest Book Review

"While the job at Random House did offer her the opportunity to meet a lot of writers and famous people, it is Hunter that became her secret office romance. . . . A great deal of the book is personal letters from Hunter to Margaret, with Margaret's inside emotions written in the theoretical margins. Harrell is an excellent storyteller, in a story that is never about the narrative, but about the real people. Every person in the book is bold and well defined"

—San Francisco Book Review

"*Keep this Quiet!* is a riveting, soul-baring honest look into Margaret Harrell and the inner workings of one of the world's greatest writers"

—**Nick Storm**, owner of Storm Generation Films

"Harrell beautifully tells the story of how her relationships with the three men, predominantly Thompson, progressed, sharing intimate moments and keeping the reader turning the page"

—Portland Book Review

"*Keep This Quiet!* is at once noisy, sensual, and word-drunk, as well as quietly intimate and full of Harrell's wonder at her luck. While most readers will come to this book for the Thompson content, in truth all the portraits here—all four of them—are compelling and often touching"

—**W. C. Bamberger**, *Rain Taxi Review of Books*

"*Keep This Quiet! My Relationship with Hunter S. Thompson, Milton Klonsky, and Jan Mensaert* by Margaret A. Harrell is a masterpiece! I never expected to say that about a memoir"

—**Ron Whitehead**, author of *The Storm Generation Manifesto and on parting, the wilderness poems*

Praise for Keep This Quiet Too!

"Margaret's life is, as always, more amazing than any book. If I didn't know Margaret, I wouldn't believe her incredible life story. But I know her and I can tell you: all of it is true."

—Frank Despriet, author of *Communication Psychology: From Reptile to Robot*"

"A passionately written memoir that doesn't sit around being fit and proper and straight laced . . . As a key to the lives of these three writers it is idiosyncratic and in age where blandness is the norm, it is a pleasure to go on her journey and find out a little about what made these men tick and what drove her to them."

—Eric Jacobs, *Beat Scene* (UK)

"At times adventurous, at times sensual, *Keep This Quiet Too!* hinges upon the complexities of human relationships, especially the challenges posed by the heart-wrenching feelings of love that may or may not be fully requited. Highly recommended."

—***Midwest Book Review***

"Deep and provocative . . . insightful . . . unique, for sure!"

—Russell D. Park, licensed clinical psychologist, coauthor of *The Power of Humility*

"In her brutally compassionately explicitly honest second autobiography, KEEP THIS QUIET TOO! More Adventures with Hunter S. Thompson, Milton Klonsky, Jan Mensaert, Harrell manages to repeatedly pull the rug out from underneath the reader . . . From depth psychology to dream analysis to hangoutologies to ecstatic love making to out of body astral travels to spirit guides, adventures and misadventures, she guides herself and is guided ever homeward, to her own heart and soul."

—Ron Whitehead, US Beat Poet Laureate

"With an eye for surprising detail, Harrell conjures a charged and vivid milieu, even as the story she tells is often painful . . . A journey with grand destinations throughout the globe and within the author's consciousness."

—***BookLife Review***

KEEP *THIS* QUIET TOO!

More Adventures with Hunter S. Thompson, Milton Klonsky, Jan Mensaert

---

Margaret A. Harrell

Saeculum University Press
USA Romania

For bulk discount or signed copies, e-mail orders@hunterthompsonnewbooks.com

A particular thanks to Hunter Thompson Literary Executor Douglas Brinkley, Professor of History at Rice University, for permission to reprint from the Hunter S. Thompson letters and other materials.

Cover design by Gaelyn Larrick of wakingworld.com
Cover HST image © Alan Becker

Publisher's Cataloging-in-Publication Data
Harrell, Margaret A. (Margaret Ann).
Keep this quiet too! more adventures with Hunter S. Thompson, Milton Klonsky, Jan Mensaert / Margaret A. Harrell; illustrated by Hunter Thompson and Jan Mensaert.
p. cm.
"Volume 2"

Includes bibliographical references.

ISBN 978-0-9837045-3-9 (pbk.)
ISBN 979-8-9871061-1-2 (hard cover)
ISBN 978-0-9837045-5-3 (epub)

1. Thompson, Hunter S.—Friends and associates. 2. Man-woman relationships. 3. Thompson, Hunter S.—Biography. 4. Self-actualization (Psychology). 5. Harrell, Margaret A.—Travel. I. Title.

E169.12.H37 2012
306/.1097309046—dc22

2011909464

Saeculum University Press
5048 Amber Clay Lane, Raleigh, NC 27612

A division of Saeculum U. P. S.
Didi-Ionel Cenuşer, publisher
B-dul Victoriei 5–7
550024 Sibiu, Romania

For Virginia Parrott Williams
A champ among champions

All reckoning is to a certain extent futile when it has to do with one who possesses originality of soul.

KIERKEGAARD

The world is the great gymnasium where we come to make ourselves strong.

VIVEKANANDA

The Roster

Hunter Stockton Thompson: July 18, 1937–February 20, 2005

Milton Klonsky: November 26, 1921–November 29, 1981

Jean-Marie Eugene Carroll Mensaert (Jan): September 3, 1937–December 27, 1990

Contents

PART TWO

Foreword

Keep This Quiet Too! More Adventures with Hunter S. Thompson, Milton Klonsky, Jan Mensaert by Margaret A. Harrell races along, a fast-paced trans-Atlantic crisscrossing of Belgium to Morocco to Egypt to Switzerland, on the one side, New York City to Aspen, writers' retreats to lucid dream lab on the other side, interspersing stops in Harrell's native North Carolina.

This book is a masterwork memoir of four writers' lives—the author's as well as the title characters'. It is a literary study of the interplay of conscious and unconscious action—the external romantic escapades, and the symbology and synchrony of the dreamlife of the woman who matched wits against three who emerged into prominence.

A Jung Institute alum, Margaret Harrell produces a study of her historic marriage to Belgian poet Jan Mensaert, tempered by two others: Hunter S. Thompson, creator of Gonzo Journalism, and her mentor, New York poet Milton Klonsky.

All three figures supply the medium of her psychological evolution. She measures and tests herself amongst them, giving as good as she gets. She in turn becomes their medium for communications to us: she helps to set their record straight.

The book is by turns pure riveting storytelling of larger-than-life public figures and effortless theory exemplified: Jung's "Confrontation with the Unconscious" as Harrell's personal confrontation with the unconscious.

Assuredly entertaining, assuredly eye-opening, the story bounds along, shockwave after shockwave—integrating real-life dream-life characters in a compelling personal narrative.

For the Hunter Thompson followers, this is your story. For the literary icons, Klonsky and Mensaert, this is also their story. And for the novice to all three, Harrell gives a good ride.

Mary Paul Thomas

Author's Note

Crazy Wisdom teachers come in all sizes and packages. Hunter told me once, late in our relationship: "You talk the craziest of anyone I know." "I'm not crazier than you," I objected, profoundly astonished. "No," he said. "But you *talk* crazier. That's why I invented Duke [his alter ego]."

Crazy Wisdom teachers can be wrapped in cloaks, hidden in forms they might not realize. I first encountered the term in a Swiss friend's memoirs on the great Eastern teacher Swami Muktananda. While he personified love, she said, he startled his students by, for example, rattling pans in the ashram kitchen in the middle of the night. The illogical act shook up their rational egos. I heard the term applied to Hunter by outlaw poet Ron Whitehead and thought: *yes, plant that at the start.*

Prologue: Clueing the Reader In

It was February 25, 1970. The red carpet was unrolled outside the soot-darkened two-story neo-Renaissance town hall. The neoclassicist façade—with MDCCCXXXVI (1836) above its columns—faced a Gothic church, Our Lady of the Pool, on the market square. The small European car stopped. I stepped onto the cobblestones in a floor-length white satin American wedding gown with veil and started walking on the carpet to the town hall door. I was getting married in Tienen, Belgium, in Dutch, with the words translated but spoken first in the official language of Flemish Brabant. Belgium has two main languages: Dutch and French. How I came to be in this situation takes us back to the end of the first volume.

What I was about to do—marry Jean-Marie ("Jan") Mensaert—was a dangerous step by many measures. He had a pixie smile that went with his *enfant terrible* imagination, that went with his still being a child in terms of lack of restraint. I was bound and determined to marry Jan Mensaert, once I got the idea, which was several years in coming. I had met him in an enchanted coincidence in Marrakech, Morocco, during four months of travel in 1965, just before beginning a job as copy editor at Random House. In Morocco he seemed a happy, wildly creative poet and visual artist. (He was then unpublished.)

And though he was only in the background in my copy editing days in New York City, he made a big impression as a quaint, faraway, unbelievable storyteller who wrote me the most exaggerated, daring tales, all of which he swore had happened to him. Which they had, though he told them with added flair. But the real high drama came after he quit his French-teaching post in Morocco and moved back to Belgium. From there he wrote me after the fact about having attempted suicide on a trip to Santorini, which he took for that purpose.

Whenever he lived in his birthplace, Tienen, he collapsed into a suicidal alcoholic. Yet he described that breakdown with fictionlike tales of comedy and woe.

Finally, in 1969, after four years of letters—from both Morocco and Belgium—I flew to Belgium for our first reunion, having gotten the brilliant brainstorm that he was so unusual, why not turn him into my next big fictional character for a new novel? Instead, I unexpectedly fell head over heels in love.

By then a recognized poet—he had been published by the most reputable poetry house in Belgium—he translated to me from his second book, *Slow Night on the Meander: Libretto for a Baroque Opera.* The locales were exotic—such as Bagdad 1367 and Babylon. A sample: "There is a god who lives in me / like all the gods his cruelty / sometimes he goes that I would know / what I would give uncrowned to be."

A few months later he moved to Freiburg im Breisgau, Germany, pursuing his parents' wish that he be a diplomat. He was studying German at the prestigious Albert-Ludwigs University founded in 1457, affiliated with nineteen Nobel laureates. But internally he rejected this career plan. In no time I flew in—on a surprise rescue mission (his suicidal thoughts had returned).

To really understand the starting point of this story, however, we have to backtrack further, because during the four years while Jan and I exchanged letters, a lot else of great significance (to me) had happened, which I described in the first volume. And that is essential to setting up the parameters of this tale.

There were two other males involved. The first was "the older man," or fount of wisdom, Milton Klonsky, who attracted me but not in a physically passionate way. I was so bewitched by his mind and profundity that on the spot, when I first met him, it was a kind of love at first sight. The type that might lead a writer—and did lead me—to use him as a model for the protagonist in a novel.

I put him onto a pedestal of what a quicksilver mind could be—what wisdom and integrated walking, talking totality could be. He was an amazement to me every time he spoke. I captured his words like water drops or huge stones that had been used to build great temples of knowledge, and I ran to some secretive place (leaving a restaurant table or scribbling on a directory if we were talking by phone), and in this way got his words down live, not for posterity in the usual sense but as a human tape recorder who would use his brilliance for my character Robert in my first book.

It was only when I thought, erroneously, that that book was nearing completion that I had gone to Belgium for the reunion with Jan Mensaert. That was in June 1969. By the following February I was married.

The third in my trio of very important, fascinating males who hovered around the point of my marriage and some periods after was Hunter S. Thompson, whose book *Hell's Angels* I'd copy edited at Random House in 1966. That tale is at the heart of the first volume of this memoir, *Keep This Quiet!*—a book about strong, outrageous, unpredictable males who before all else insisted on their authenticity. Their own ways of planting their feet in the ground, their hands onto my inner Hollywood Walk of Fame. I'd possibly passed the real Walk—certainly nearby—with Hunter during his press appearances just after the publication of *Hell's Angels*, when I flew out to L.A. to join him incognito.

In many letters in the earlier volume, Hunter vents and sagely explains what he was feeling at the time. But Hunter was married. And I hadn't thought marrying him a possibility. I hadn't thought anything. Being with him was so "in the moment."

Just before I left for Freiburg, Germany, Hunter was gearing up for his second book. Wanting me to be part of the crew, he asked me to contact his editor, Jim Silberman, for whom I'd copy edited *Hell's Angels* at Random House. It was Jim who, surviving handily the ups and downs of Hunter's early experience with book publishing, was waiting out Hunter's infertile period before his next book materialized. Jim loved a good story.

He'd said, when he gave me Richard Fariña's manuscript, *Been Down So Long It Looks Like Up to Me,* to copy edit, "Do you think I'm crazy?" He didn't mean it, but he wondered if the book would sell, catch other eyes as it had his. No matter. He put it onto the list.

And a good thing because though it didn't immediately take off, it's now a cult classic.

So Hunter was off in Woody Creek, Colorado, at his compound, Owl Farm, trying to write his next book—on The Death of the American Dream—and had been complaining that he couldn't get his arms around such a shapeless topic. He had nothing tiny to get his teeth into and pull and tease out the story. He had no "Grain of Sand," as he put it, referring to William Blake's line "To see a World in a Grain of Sand." That is, have a minutely particular perspective to see through.

Hunter was struggling, the manuscript hadn't materialized, and unknown to him, I'd flown to Germany. His forwarded letter began, "Ho-ho, and late again." Here it is, as it touches me so:

> Dear MA…
>
> Ho-ho, and late again. Not much to say either, except in terms of madness & bad scheduling on all fronts. I seem to have let everything drift for too long. Recently I spent 10 days in LA,* running totally amok in every way, crazed on rum and mescaline. Before that it was a savage election here. I ran a campaign that amounted to a takeover bid, and we lost by six votes.
>
> Now I'm back here at this rotten machine, trying to hash together enough bullshit to satisfy Silberman and get that contract off my back. He no longer answers my letters. I'm convinced they think I've gone mad. Which may be true—although it only seems to come out when I sit down to write this thing I have no use for. On other fronts, I still function like a human being. But running out of money tends to narrow a man's vision some-

* With his wife, trying to get her over a painful miscarriage, a baby girl they'd both wanted who lived a few hours. This wrenching experience, one can put into chronology now. But at the time, he swallowed his grief and kept it to himself quite rightly.

what, and that's my gig for now. Stone broke and flapping around like a jangled beast.

Are you off to Algeria yet? Where will this gibberish find you? [In Germany, perhaps in a *bier-stube*.] Your talk (in an old letter) of pine trees and crickets got hold of me in a weird way. I keep remembering that line I quoted somewhere, by somebody—"All my life my heart has sought a thing I cannot name." Maybe it never existed. To be homesick for a myth is a form of madness, I guess. So maybe they're right. All I know, for now, is that I have to put a string of words together, in order to pay my bills. But I can't get too excited about it. Neither the writing nor the bills. What I'd really like to do right now is spend about two weeks alone on a golf course, with nobody else in sight… armed with a putter and two irons, maybe a 3 and a 7… why not?

Anyway, I'm tired of this goddam locked-in winter. Tired of the death and craziness in this landscape. All of it. Everywhere I go people are cracking and breaking and crumbling. Backing off and hunkering down. My only real hope is that things are really as bad as they say. That should give us some action. The more I think about your "second life" notion, the more I think maybe you're onto something. Let me know how it's working out.

Ciao, H

—Merry Christmas

PART ONE

— 1 —

One Proposal Stuck

> Surely all art is the result of one's having been in danger, of having gone through an experience all the way to the end, where no one can go any further
>
> —Rainer Maria Rilke

One proposal stuck. After asking for my hand in a café at night, then canceling the next morning—several times in Freiburg—Jan at last didn't retract the proposal. Just before Christmas 1969 we were traveling from Germany to his parents' home in Belgium, engaged.

Riding the train through the dense forests and mountains of the Ardennes, I was thrilled as he sang songs and arias in French and Italian—such as Edith Piaf's "*Ils sont arrivés se tenant par la main*" / "They arrived holding hands"; or "*O, Mimi, tu più non torni*" ("O, Mimi, will you not return?" from *La Bohème*). Piaf goes on, in "Lovers for a Day": "The sunshine of love was deep in their eyes, so young, oh so young—too young to be wise."

I was enthralled by this dashing, delicate man beside me, so cultivated, fast-thinking, attentive. The very foreignness made my heart skip beats. Beginning at fourteen, I knew, he'd learned eighteenth-century Italian by memorizing all the operas of Mozart. On a trip through Italy, invited into a palace where he played the piano for a gathering, he'd spoken that old Italian. It looked like the palace in Lampedusa's *The Leopard*, he recalled (talking about his youthful hitchhiking trip to the Orient). It spellbound me. All the culture I didn't have. And underneath everything, I expected his vast talent would thrive with the tiniest encouragement. Hadn't he already been published twice since we met—starting with poems he'd read me, pulling them out of a trunk.

He warned me, though, not to marry him: "You won't be able to accept that I'll never do anything, be anybody. You won't be able to live a life with no tomorrow."

He reconsidered: "With a tomorrow, yes. But no day *after* tomorrow."

In the wait before the wedding, he was often at his grand piano, playing classical and pop music with abandon. His fingers tripped through Mozart sonatas or concertos—sometimes presto, almost unbelievably fast. Also, I was captivated and flattered by his honky-tonk composition "Pretty Margaret."

To describe him as a character is an understatement. When my sister Norma flew in from Wellesley College with my wedding dress, he insisted on meeting her alone. My wonderful parents did not have passports and—on such short notice—were not coming.

At the airport, pretending to be Jan's relative, he told Norma the pitiful tale of how Margaret was marrying this flat-out-broke bum, this down-and-out no-gooder with disaster a likely prediction in his future: what pitfalls she was walking into. When my sister was terrified, he relented and charmingly, dazzlingly explained that actually, he himself was Jan. So glad to meet her. And they took the train with her head spinning.

Unclear whether this odd species (me) was an impoverished or a rich American (probably impoverished), Jan's mother and her housekeeper—to instruct me in domestic skills—poked my head over the bathtub, reminding me to scrub it with Comet after each use, which I considered primitive, coarse behavior. She hailed from peasant stock, Jan explained, while his dreamy, orphaned-young father was from upper middle class. Jan's mother (old-school Flemish) kept peeled potatoes in cold water in the cellar to make soup seasoned with fresh thyme (thickened with potatoes) twice a week, hand grinding nutmeg and ironing even Jan's underpants.

Between courses, she had herself and me hop up from the table and wash dishes—which spoiled my meal!

On the wedding eve, unlike with U.S. brides, she ordered me into the salt mines. With no one concerned about my fluttery stomach, I was told as night fell to arrange as many gifts as possible—such as a twelve-place porcelain setting from a closed abbey or a tall Val St. Lambert crystal vase—on the piano.

Happily, I slept at his rich uncle and aunt's. Fine paintings covered the walls and there were antique statues—including a large wooden pieta.

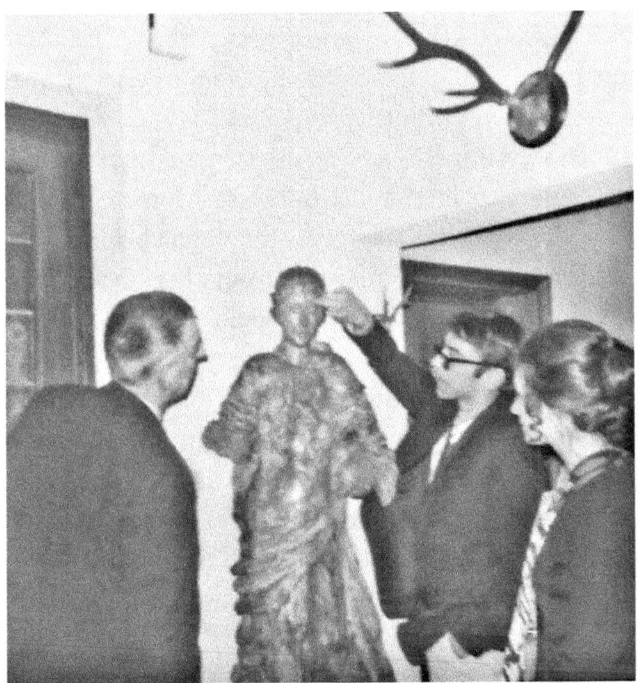

Jan and Margaret

At bedtime—celebrating his bachelor's night at local cafés with his Moroccan best man, Moulay—Jan rang up.

He said that to sleep, I should ask his aunt Isa for half a Valium and half a beer. As he put the receiver up to the Beaux Arts jukebox it played "I can't give you anything but love, baby."* Expressing his heart, cavalier, worry-free, happy about the big day, not to mention a honeymoon (his parents and mine had split the bill). Never mind the prospect of a penniless future.

Then we were in the Tienen town hall—with the red carpet out front. I could not have gotten married in a church without Catholic preparation. I was thirty. Jan was thirty-three.

We would honeymoon in Cairo (my idea; his had been Morocco). It would be a bohemian lifestyle—which I expected without fully understanding how I might react to cooking on charcoal in a small village that spoke primarily Arabic, communicating in broken Spanish or French. I expected—I don't know what, except that I would save him from suicidal thoughts because he would be safely at the typewriter or alternately in my arms.

In Hunter's eventually published letters he once referred to my having last been seen in a "toilet hole." In Morocco. But he stayed properly cryptic. No one would guess the drama behind those words, that should have told me the marriage would begin rocky and stay so. And in a sense finally, the whole point would be to get out in one piece.

Five years before, in '65, on my brief stay in Jan's Moroccan home in Larache shortly after meeting him in Marrakech, I had a nightmare in which I plunged down and down endlessly, in a bottomless fall—seemingly without sides or stopping point. But in February 1970, all warning thrown out the window, here I was, getting married.

I had left, fled Larache, after a ten-day stay in his home as a friend—breaking the deep attraction.

---

* Often Jan said something apt in a larger sense. The song was from the Katharine Hepburn, Cary Grant movie *Bringing Up Baby*. Baby, a leopard, loved the song. The leopard escapes, and a bespeckled, scholarly paleontologist, Grant, joins with heiress Hepburn to search for it in a zany comedy. He asks her to marry him as both stand on top of his pieced-together dinosaur reconstruction, which falls under the weight. He has lost four years of work, yet acknowledges that the crazy last few days (with her) were the most exciting of his life. Ahead of its time, the film lost at the box office but originated "machine gun dialogue" and was perhaps the definitive madcap comedy. The lyrics say he can't buy diamond bracelets and such at Woolworth's.

Would I be up to the challenges of such a marriage, have the strength not to be blackmailed but to stand two tall in an independent male/female artist relationship—American, at that, two strikes against me by his count?

Well, evidently, something in me thought so and needed to find that out. Anyway, I was too far gone to think of caution.

The city was in blackout as our plane hovered over Cairo, February 26. The Arab states had lost the 1967 Six Day War with Israel. And Egypt, under Gamal Abdel Nasser, was engaging in a War of Attrition that included heavy artillery fire along the Suez Canal, aerial warfare, and commando raids to recover territories in the Sinai Peninsula.

However, as we peered down during descent, the evidence of a blackout was scant. Below, lights glowed and twinkled. We stayed in style at the Nile Hilton (honeymoon-rate), frequenting the romantic rooftop French restaurant. The National Museum next door was sandbagged.

The locals whom Jan corralled liked Americans. He had an Egyptian reporter in tow as we visited the Sphinx and pyramids. We did not, as I later would have, bask in the thousands of years of esoteric history there. Instead, I found myself on a camel with a guide who began to gallop us deep into the desert.

This could have been innocent, but the Egyptian reporter took off after us—considering the dire consequences if I were kidnapped. It was the type of incident Jan relished. I have to say I did as well, as long as nothing really happened—besides being raced away on a camel followed by an Egyptian in hot pursuit. Life was never dull. All of it was fodder to his pen. And appealed to something in me as well.

In elaborate staging Jan converted to Islam (in equal parts from a belief in the Moslem culture and a desire to burn his bridges to a diplomatic career). It was a private ceremony before the highest Moslem religious leader in Cairo, the grand Imam of Al-Azhar (the world's second-oldest surviving degree-granting university)—in an ornate room. I was allowed to watch; he requested the name "Ahmed El Mehdi."*

Reporters waited outside the building to interview him. I don't remember how he managed to pull this off. Probably with the help of the journalist.

Then, leaving Cairo, we traveled to the site of ancient Thebes, on the east bank of the Nile, to the temples of Luxor and Karnak, the Valley of the Kings—the relics of centuries past: the pharaohs' burial chambers, the art, the towering statues along the way. The giant scale, the history and myth.

Back in Cairo, Jan told me with confidence, amusement, regret I'd need to return to Belgium alone; he intended to walk up the Nile—like Sir Richard Burton, the great nineteenth-century explorer who not only translated the *Thousand and One Nights* but had many dashing exploits, including expeditions to discover the source of the White Nile. Reading a biography of the ruffian Burton, an ordained Sufi fluent in twenty-nine languages, would be good preparation for understanding something of the complexity of Jan.

Though he didn't waver for days, he finally abandoned the idea because of the excruciatingly hot temperature.

When we arrived in Belgium with *two* of us on the plane, it turned out that his family had assumed he would *not* stick it out even through the honeymoon. His mother said, "sometimes sunshine, sometimes rain"; his father "good heart, bad character." That he only liked something "when it's new."

My mother, meanwhile, with whom I was very close, had not participated in my wedding. She was working in the yard in North Carolina, growing the beautiful boxwoods, roses, and other flowers she was known for. Someone riding past asked how she could do that. But what else could she do? Not sit still and worry. Not yet.

---

* He took "El Mehdi" from his friend Moulay El Mehdi. Moulay, the son of a religious leader, had a name with spiritual significance. In Islam the "Mehdi," or "Mahdi" ("the rightly guided one"), is variously significant in different traditions. Especially important in eschatology, he rids the world of evil preceding the Day of Resurrection.

I had married at thirty, sure we were a good match. I assumed that Jan would rate my potential as he did his—in spite of the fact that I could not figure out his psychology. Anyway, it was a compulsion, something I could not *not* do, once that far into it, destined as surely as our first meeting, when at a café terrace in Marrakech I'd sat down before an ownerless full coffee cup, desperately wishing that whoever came back to claim it would be a friend in that unruly country. And thus rescue me from the newly discovered perils of a woman traveling alone there.

Rather like a version of Cinderella and the slipper. That was springtime, the Djemma el Fna market square, Marrakech 1965.

In 1970 I walked into the temporarily tumultuous marriage, sure that just to establish a routine of writing would solve the detail of his unbalanced psychology. My parents had been behind me every step. His parents had in some instances sneakily tried to sabotage his artistic passion and set him into a practical lifestyle. It backfired. That's what I thought.

Just after Cairo we separated. At the urging of his family, I was to stay—for a short period—with my parents in North Carolina (to write). To set the stage for a diplomatic career, he would remain in Belgium to work on his thesis and prepare or pretend to prepare for the Brussels exams. Sure he would never be happy as a diplomat, I was set to support his rebellion. But I cabled him March 20 that there was a postal strike in New York: HAVE NOT RECEIVED AND CANNOT RECEIVE ANY MAIL FROM BELGIUM INDEFINITELY NOR SEND ANY. HOW'S YOUR SENSE OF HUMOR?

Finally, to my intense alarm, the strike ended, and I received this: "Four unfinished letters are lying on my desk and a fifth one that is finished but will never be mailed. You'd jump in a plane and dash off to Belgium if you read them. Another mood I had to go through. I counteracted it with a couple of cuts in my neck—available spots are getting rare."

He'd not met with his professor, but the latter had communicated that to pass the exams Jan had only to show up. He was still drinking—fairly moderately for him—but not remembering the next day: “It’s psychological of course, my subconscious wanting to forget everything that’s got something to do with Tienen.”

He went on—same letter, the next night: “Suicidal tendencies, brr! Tried—without any conviction—to walk under trucks.” He had noted on a beer card: “Let’s see: ‘Why should the mermaids have jumped off their cliffs after Ulysses’ departure instead of singing each other into death?’”

Third day, same letter: “A couple of seconds ago I got your second cable. Playing that Schubert [on the piano], I’ve done some thinking. About the future: I should never have come back from Cairo. . . . We should return and make that tour. . . . I think I will mail this letter and save you more telegrams. Ahmed the Magnificent.”

Within the same time frame, he described how he returned home high the night before, having that afternoon told his parents he’d start studying

> and breezes of sympathy, gratitude, and familial love were still roaming through rooms and corridors. I went upstairs and decided, I don’t know why, to do something spectacular. Getting on the highest step, I let myself fall flat and straight on my back, found myself fourteen steps closer to the ground level, fresh and intact, only slightly disgusted with the animal screams which my mother, who had seen the whole thing happen, thought necessary to frighten the night and its silences with. She thinks I slipped, like so many illustrious forerunners (you being one, I believe). It was fun to fly on your own wings, but the next day I had visions of myself lying in a bed with a broken collar bone and that isn’t a part of my projects for the immediate future.

This one, he signed “Ahmed the Unique.”

But while they appeared transparent, Jan’s letters sometimes presented characters in him—as in a hall of mirrors. I had married "the poet," presuming the poet was "real."

Yet my mentor, Milton Klonsky, had told me, "Each of us has inside him a lunatic chained in the garret."

—2—

Letter from Hunter

In this interim I counted on returning to the MacDowell Colony, a working retreat for artists in Peterborough, New Hampshire, where I'd been a fellow the year before.

Meanwhile, a real champ, true friend, brother/sister for life while obviously more, Hunter wrote. I waited with baited breath and finally March 31, 1970 (I was married February 25), the letter came. From my earlier reports to him, I do not believe even the shrewdest detective could have deduced an imminent marriage. With great relief I pounced:

> Dear Margaret-Ann….
>
> Nothing weird on this end, but the strange and jangled pace of your recent mail left me wondering what to write, or where. First Belgium & marriage, then the Cairo Hilton, then back to Greenville for a while. It's hard to know what's happening. I assume you're married & of course I congratulate you and Jan. Is this the third life, or the fourth? What next? New York?
>
> Life here continues to boil toward some kind of heinous climax. My sporadic depression about [Jim] Silberman's book has jelled to a deep funk that never lets go. I brood about it almost constantly, then type for a while, then rip up the pages and brood some more. Meanwhile, the creditors are getting ugly & the tax man looms more dangerously each day. My affairs have become tangled; people

demand money from me almost constantly—vast amounts; I seem to owe about $25,000 at the moment, all overdue. Today the Harbour Detectives took my Diners Club card. Fortunately, I just used Diners as a reference to get a Carte Blanche card, so it hardly matters. To hell with them.

In the midst of all this I became a publisher. I'll send you come [sic] copies in a tube, but only when my mailing tubes come from Texas. The only tube outlet in Aspen refuses to sell us any, due to the savage things we publish. The Aspen Wallposter is the only newspaper in history to go heavily into the black with the first issue.* I was suddenly plunged into massive business dealings. Money surrounds me, but I can't use it. We were forced to incorporate to avoid libel suits; then we had to buy a press & thousands of mailing tubes & radio ads & subscription lists & rent a goddam office and get a phone and hire people for various fees & percentages and raise $60,000 for a lawsuit against various Boston bankers and local land-rapers....† and on top of all that, I seem to be running for Sheriff. I don't know if I told you about last fall's political campaign; we came within 6 votes of electing a freak-mayor....and the next few months should be extremely savage here.

The book-writing has come to a point where it either has to get done, or totally abandoned....and since I can't afford to abandon it, I have to write the bugger. For the first time in 2 years I'm beginning to see it as my book, instead of Silberman's—even though I used that

---

* These were seven well-laid-out wall posters, with (on one side) his artist friend Tom Benton's graphics; on the other, smart/wisdom/insult writings by Hunter or others that were political messages for his sheriff's campaign.

† Hunter often used dots in his letters. As in the earlier volume—*Keep This Quiet!*—in the case of Hunter's ... or ...., there is no space between the dots. In the rare instance where I omit something from his letter, I use the standard three dots with a space between each dot.

phrase, above. The moment I wrote it, I realized it was no longer valid, and therefore no longer an excuse.

It ends:

From the other side, let me know what kind of plans you have. I've given up anticipating or even guessing what you might do next. Every now and then, in the weird hours between work-time and dawn when I do my thinking, I find my head drifting somewhere around Cape Hatteras (is that it?) and wondering what goes on out there—and why a person might want to get off to a place like that. I still wonder. But then I wonder about a lot of things. Probably this time next year I'll be somewhere else & wondering whatever possessed me to spend all this time in a lost snow-cave like Woody Creek.

OK for now. I seem to be slipping. And I still have a lot of garbage to cope with tonight, before hunkering down to brood. If you get a chance, read my article on Jean-Claude Killy in the first issue of Scanlan's Monthly. I think you'd like it.

Ciao,
Hunter

Wistfully wondering about Cape Hatteras was an oblique reference to the Nixon Inaugural festivities one short year ago, in January 1969. Unsettled, disillusioned, out of sync in D.C., he'd wanted to warp fly to a sane sanctuary—the Outer Banks of North Carolina.

So he'd suddenly invited me to meet him at Hatteras. When the phone rang into the teacher's room at the Fred Astaire Studio in New York City, where I was briefly teaching, I considered it perhaps a crossroads in our relationship. Though I normally would have said yes and he knew it, and there was a long silence before I answered, at that particular moment I regretfully said no. For one thing, I had a brand-new boyfriend, which I didn't say.

It's years later that I discover I had in fact once been to the Outer Banks—because that's where the barrier island of Corolla is. As a child I'd been to camp there. And my stirring memory of that is a scene in which a counselor grabbed my diary and pretended to read it aloud. He made up the details, while I, red-faced at nine years old, hoped he wouldn't read it for real. Funnily, had I met Hunter at Hatteras, it would have brought to life the counselor's imaginary exploits he "read" to the kids back then.

—3—

Hunter at Milestones

Unknown to anyone at the time of Hunter's March 31 letter, his fortunes were about to take an upturn.

That past November, he successfully urged "hippie lawyer" Joe Edwards to run for Aspen mayor, an election Edwards narrowly lost.

Edwards remembers how Hunter got him to the film *The Battle of Algiers* at the Wheeler Opera House. After viewing the North Africans' bloody struggle for independence from the French in the late 1950s, they sat at the Hotel Jerome bar. Hunter reiterated "that we needed to organize all the young people, all the bartenders and ski bums, the kids working the ski lifts and in the restaurants and bars; that we had the numbers; that if we could just get them registered and get them interested and get them to participate, we'd have the political power to change the town."[1]

To encourage registration, Hunter promised that if Edwards won, he himself would run for sheriff! For three weeks he campaigned for Edwards practically without sleep in The Aspen Freak Power Uprising.

In the mayoral race he was finally juiced up. This was the narrow topic—the Grain of Sand—he'd desperately searched for as a much needed focus for his overdue second book. It was, at last, "that tight-focused chunk of absolute reality." (Letter to Silberman.[2])

Later that year he'd file to run for Pitkin County sheriff.

But in addition to politics, a further milestone loomed.

Scanlan's Monthly, in its first issue, had published "The Temptations of Jean-Claude Killy": Hunter's exposé of the celebrity-endorsements marketing tour of a twenty-six-year-old retired world skiing champ.

Now *Scanlan's* would assign Hunter to the Kentucky Derby, along with burly UK graphic artist Ralph Steadman. His drawing paraphernalia (lipstick and eyebrow pencil) in hand, Steadman was in the wings.

Hunter wrote me March 31. In Louisville the first Saturday in May, the two would have a historic meeting. Hunter was to picture Steadman as "some nerve-rattling geek all covered with matted hair and string-warts"!"[3]

If he could but look into a crystal ball, he would see that he was home free. The pumped-up energy of these two incursions will lead, in the great scheme of things, to the next big literary markers in his career.

Transatlantic mail was again normal. April 2: Jan announced he was "in a period that's full of roots out of which anything can grow." He'd told his family he wasn't going to take the exam. Then: "I don't know if I mentioned my plan to walk off, never to come back. I whispered it in your ear, once, long ago. I'm reconsidering it. . . . Imagine all it would involve: strong calves, clean lungs, a tan, no cigarettes, no alcohol and freedom. Passionate love-affairs along the roads. Why am I waiting?"

He ended: "I'm spoiling you with those daily letters. Ahmed the Superb."

This threat of galloping off into the sunset, plus the suicidal-tendency letters, panicked me in ways difficult to explain to my parents. I'd been trying to have it both ways: dote on Jan and conceal some of his worse traits, especially as they were partly absent in Morocco. But also I was quite aware that my complete focus on him, with no judgment or discrimination, was entirely unlike the Margaret they knew. Even unlike the me I knew, to some degree. If he snapped his finger, I jumped. If he made an outrageous statement, I thought he was just unusual enough to pull it off. Besides, the guy I'd met in Morocco was consumed by creativity.

April 6: "Thinking of, no, I'm not, I have decided to leave on that trip. . . . I need only four hundred dollars. . . . Imagine, I'll be seeing the pyramids along the Nile . . . seeing the market square (there isn't any such thing) in old Algiers and sending you photographs and souvenirs."

Abruptly he added: "Won't cut myself in the neck anymore, it's hell with the collar of my shirt opening and reopening the cuts all the time. If I feel tense again I'll stab myself in the nose."

Worse, he described playing a game with his friend Alain (Alain's idea):

> In French it's called roulette russe. . . . I used to wonder, reading about it (I think there's no great Russian writer who didn't use the theme somewhere) how one possibly can have the courage to do it. When you're drunk it becomes very easy and highly fascinating. . . . They are talking about Beethoven on the radio and about his suicidal tendencies (never knew he had any) when he realized he was becoming deaf. And to illustrate that they are playing the last part of the Moonlight sonata which was written then and is supposed to express them. There certainly is more of that in it than there's moonlight. . . .
>
> Will you be standing along the road somewhere? Stopped drinking. Really did. . . . [I]f I'm to go and live on twenty cents a day for the next months, I'll have to, anyway. Think I'll be leaving in something like two weeks, one month. Ahmed the Strong.

I knew that in Belgium he sometimes made cuts in his arm. I was horrified by the neck cuts (if that was true) and by the Russian roulette. It was not fascinating or thrilling to imagine the click, see whether the chamber fired. Combining that with the postal strikes, I was jumpy and not a radiant bride—busy cabling my new husband.

By luck I was accepted as a fellow by MacDowell Colony for artists in New Hampshire—for two months' residency—to continue the novel begun in 1965. It featured Robert (based on Milton Klonsky). And his hopeless pursuit of Patsy (later renamed Paula), the semiautobiographical woman who kept him at arm's length physically while adoring his gurulike wisdom and hipster Humphrey Bogart style.

In my three years at Random House, I had often gone out with Milton, in periods every night—sometimes correcting my authors' manuscripts at his rent-controlled West Eleventh Street apartment down the street from mine on Bleecker. He wanted a romantic relationship. I was captivated by his charisma and tried to make him a mentor while also jotting down his inimitable—an adjective often used about him—nuggets of wit and wisdom. I gave these to Robert in my "big book," titled at the time "The Erstwise Patsy, a Dialogue." I was not alone in treasuring his words as if he were my guru—but perhaps alone in warding off his attempts at deepening the romantic aspect.

In a subplot triangle earthy Anny (married to imaginationless Joseph) met the "Disturber" Ian—and had the socks blown off her world, though so far she had not been unfaithful.

I had no idea that the very physical Anny I'd dreamed up out of thin air and a mix of people bore any relationship at all to my inner struggles.

By mid-April, I was nestled away at MacDowell, which covers 450 acres of fields and woods. Like most Colonists, I isolated myself in a secluded studio cabin in the woods by day. I requested that the wicker basket dropped off wordlessly on my porch by pickup truck each lunchtime not contain mail. I read that at night. I loved spending off hours with Hannah Green (*The Dead of the House*) and meeting her husband, surrealist pop artist John (Jack) Wesley (who was painting erotic pastels of Dagwood and Blondie Bumstead).*

The first letter to arrive there from Jan said he'd had a psychiatrist convince his parents: "positively don't take the exams." Therefore, he no longer, when he drank, had trouble remembering the night before. He was applying for a scholarship to Cairo—as one option—and preparing to work on his novel "The Aziza Story."

* In 2008 Jack's painting *Plaque* (1967) brought $577,000 at a Christie's auction.

Letting me read the letter first, he wrote April 17 to the MacDowell admissions panel, requesting admittance May–June. Putting no effort into publicity, he was surprised when a prominent Belgian critic's recommendation said reviewers unanimously found his first book of poetry showed "a very passionate talent and a fantastic, sometimes enchanted imagination and transposition of words. . . he was one of the most important young poets in the Flanders. . . . And his wife must be considered one of the happiest women on earth."

He did sometimes try to avoid alarm. He described a note he didn't mail but woke to read, mentioning "the psychological documentation it threw on my drunk self":

> If that's the kind of thing I tell in my last degree of intoxication, I'd better stop drinking, being unable, once I start, to finish before reaching that degree. To give you a sample, the beginning and the end of the letter. Hark! "Walking down the nightly alley, hands crossed over my buttocks" and finishing "in spite of you there's nothing there but me and death."

He added that he'd been looking for his violin concerto in the attic—in a jumbled heap of music composition. He'd forgotten that he "touched everything, going from short pieces for the piano to a ballet and even to an opera." Then he found "two more cases . . . drawings . . . mixed with flying pages of music."

What this again underscored to me was the reality of his potential, outdone only by his perilous assault on it.

Ink Doodle (Freehand)

Greek Temple Sketches

Near the end of April, Jan realized that financially speaking, he couldn't come to MacDowell. I breathed a sigh of relief, as the rural, woodsy Colony was defined by quiet and isolation.

But he went on: "Am kind of picturesque. Have a wound on the back of my head, a brain concussion, a twisted arm . . . and bruises all over. The funny thing is I went to bed with all these things, never knowing I had them. And slept rather well too, till my mother came at seven to get the dog and started screaming in a very dramatic, though convincing way: this blood, all this blood, where does this blood come from?"

He was mulling over finding work in Brussels or Tienen. Some of his crazy letters, he attributed to the anti-alcohol pills he'd been prescribed, which he'd now stopped taking.

April 30, he says not to worry, his suicidal days are in the past: "If I were ever to do it again, it would have been last night. I got terribly drunk and got my suicidal tendencies under their purest form. I walked down 'the nightly alleys' with a razor blade in my pocket and poison and everything one usually uses when trying to exchange this world for a better one. I didn't do a thing."

He closes: "Ahmed who misses you too but who doesn't know what he could offer you right now (see, lack of inspiration). You'll have to tell me and maybe I'll tell Ahmed and maybe he will do it. Jan."

May 11, a short Belgian mail strike ended. He mailed three long letters in one. The first, he said, was "the balanced Jan speaking." It was of poetry and lively observations. He included freehand translations—either from his "Gospels" manuscript, modeled after *Thus Spake Zarathustra*, or the actual Nietzsche work. In one passage the protagonist decided to descend the mountain into the valley; "still, the shadow of none of the peaks had reached it." But as he went further "his heart became empty and slower and even faster lost its blood. Then he arrived at the bottom; how it asked, and begged, unanswered, laughed at. How he asked for love."

He returned to the top: "The air became colder and thinner, he breathed more freely, freed and to laugh became a closed mouth. There he became the one who said, I predicted you and why didn't you listen. The one to whom he answered, I wanted certainty among the certainties."

In another translated passage:

> How easy to break down the mountains, how difficult to build them up again. And how easy to be called: humble. How quickly one finds himself accused of pride. Beauty is lost by fright, ugliness can't find means enough to be excused. How many people have a fear of heights. For fear knows many caves in which to hide, beauty is a thing exposed to all looks and, in her nakedness, appreciated by but few compared to those who hide her or fear her or excuse her with averted eyes or stone her with the stone of the accuser. How many of these stones are necessary to build a new mountain.

He closed: "MISSING YOU" (triple underline).

Then a sudden alarming letter—drenched in whimsy: "Dear Margaret, Don't jump into a plane and dash off to Belgium. I'm in a worse mood than when you so bravely came to rescue me in Germany but then you should consider yourself as being the confidante kings and heroes have in classical tragedies. You are supposed to listen, to wring your hands at particularly pathetic moments, to say yes or no when there's one syllable missing to make a perfect alexandrine, but never to take part in the action."

He mentioned frequenting the "Alain-with-the-gun café," the Beaux Arts.

The letter breaks off. Surely my future was not to be the confidante of kings and heroes. Yet he described a second game of nerves—a variant of drag racing as in *Rebel without a Cause*, where he lay on the road. Alain revved up the car, barreling toward him, full throttle as if not to stop, while he, the other contender, lay still—to see who was chicken.

Even from MacDowell, I leapt into a plane—arriving in Tienen at the Beaux Arts Café. In a note at the time I described:

> walking through yellow sparkles under green trees—everything alive!—would he be there? would he be glad? Beige hat. Across the grass, past the archery, the sunlight. The café owner Josine says, "Jean-Marie, that's Margaret." "I know." (Not believing.) Till he looked up, a face at the window, and Alain and Jan both ran out. He was glad, almost his real self; yesterday had been, he said. Wrote it in a letter, a real-self letter. He called his parents. "Guess who's here." "I'm not worrying anymore," said his mother, and his father didn't bring up the subject he'd mentioned when Jan left home: "This drinking has got to stop."

No one could make you feel more welcome than Jan—rushing over, embracing, liltingly, manically glad, intuitively confident, all practical thoughts out the window. Himself the center of attention, happy as a child without restraint.

As I flew off, Hunter was beginning Gonzo Journalism with "The Kentucky Derby Is Decadent and Depraved." In his 1974 *Playboy* interview he recounted how it got into print: "I'd blown my mind, couldn't work. So finally I just started jerking pages out of my notebook and numbering them and sending them to the printer. I was sure it was the last article I was ever going to do for anybody." Instead, the *Scanlan's Monthly* cofounders, Warren Hinckle III and Sidney Zion, loved it.* Hunter said this breakthrough experience was like "falling down an elevator shaft and landing in a pool full of mermaids."[4]

In "Kentucky Derby," which William McKeen in *Outlaw Journalist* calls a "'process' piece—*getting the story* was the story"[5]—Hunter writes that he and Steadman "didn't give a hoot in hell what was happening on the track. We had come there to watch the *real* beasts perform. He and the newly arrived European stood in the press-box balcony the day before the race:

* Hinkle, a veteran political journalist, was later a *San Francisco Chronicle* columnist and winner of the Thomas Paine and H. L. Mencken awards. Sidney Zion was a New York journalist and author, winner of the Ben Hecht Journalism Award.

> I pointed to the huge grassy meadow enclosed by the track. "That whole thing," I said, "will be jammed with people; fifty thousand or so, and most of them staggering drunk. It's a fantastic scene—thousands of people fainting, crying, copulating, trampling each other and fighting with broken whiskey bottles. We'll have to spend some time out there, but it's hard to move around, too many bodies."
>
> "Is it safe out there? Will we *ever* come back?"
>
> "Sure," I said. "We'll just have to be careful not to step on anybody's stomach and start a fight." I shrugged. "Hell, this clubhouse scene right below us will be almost as bad as the infield."[6]

He had hit his stride—struck true comic mastery—found the voice of HST. In teaming up with Ralph Steadman, he'd found a fast-sketching, hard-hitting satirist who captured his wacky vision. Steadman, he said, had "a really fine, raw sense of horror."[7]

Had we zoomed off to the Outer Banks the year before, I would probably not, at least yet, have visited Belgium. Who knew what turn Hunter's life would have taken? Destiny, of course. It was destiny, to begin two "second lives" not together but apart.

Almost to the month, the formidable Steadman, ready for every Gonzo stunt that led to a story, stepped into full foreground. The Outer Banks—all it represented—subsided, slid under the surface, remained a "what if." I looked out the plane window. For the next thirty-one years I would spend most of my time outside America. Gonzo was beginning. Going in precisely the opposite direction, away from fame and everything publicly splashy smelling of successful author, I was about to discover a female's sheltered life in North Africa while my book dawdled, pushed forward in spurts in the States, battered at other times by a male's skepticism about all professional creative ventures by a female, at least a married female, in shock to me. I was going into challenge with my back against the wind.

—4—

Back to Morocco

Through my seatmate I sublet an apartment for Jan and me in Brussels while on the plane—by luck—not to live one minute with my mother-in-law.

Undelivered letters from Jan were forwarded. His secret wish: "To be with you somewhere carefree and love and write. And in the mania and depression periods (but would there be any) be wild. Tanned, salt on our skin, face hair."

He'd also written: "Don't think you were cheated because I suddenly decided I would have a job [in Brussels] and lead something rather close to a normal life. That's part of me. I've had those fancies before. It was your luck to marry me with such an uncomfortable period dawning. And only heaven knows what my next period is going to be. A breakdown or a trip to Indonesia. And what your part is going to be: nursing an ill brain or a second honeymoon under the stars."

But this was the home of Jan's "Belgian disease." One night he stole pills from his mother's medicine cabinet, took them, and went with me to the Beaux Arts café, where he lay his head contentedly on the table ("Popeye the drunken sailor man," an owner said). Because I alerted his mother, he wound up in the hospital—from which he escaped after I smuggled in a suit.

He "walk[ed] out with my hat over my eyes in a thoroughly bad movie style. I decided then I was ridiculous enough in Tienen eyes and that Margaret and I would emigrate to some place where I still could pretend."

I left my job as a legal secretary in Brussels, not even giving notice (that felt terrible). And Jan and I were on our way to the safety of Morocco—to the drumbeat of "You have courage . . . But not in ways that lead anywhere."

However, that warning subsided as we giddily began hitchhiking. Eight pieces of luggage in descending height were half hidden behind us—including a bubbletop hair dryer and heavy Underwood typewriter for me, a battered portable Olivetti for Jan. (In sharp contrast to his usual lone rucksack.)

After we crossed the border from Spain to Morocco, he bent to kiss the soil.

Then there was the ride to our new home, Larache, a town I liked.

Having given me many insights about his life in Larache with Aziza, his delicate, fragile doomed love—now dead—riding the rickety bus from Tangier (suitcases strapped to the top), Jan grew silent. He wondered if she had "rotted. That is, completely."

Larache (El Araich) is sixty-seven kilometers from Tangier, which was a favorite of the Beats in the '50s. In the Villa Muniria, William Burroughs wrote *Naked Lunch*—joined afterwards by Jack Kerouac and Allen Ginsberg. In World War II spies rendezvoused in Tangier, the real model for *Casablanca*.

Dotted with camels, donkeys, and date palms, Larache basked in a sensual simplicity. We rented a roomy house, where I would cook on old-fashioned lump charcoal—no refrigerator, no stove. We took turns fanning an accordion bellows to get the fire blazing. On top of the charcoal would sit a tagine (an earthenware dish) or an aluminum pot. Not many people had ovens or refrigerators; everyone had running water.

Lacking all the physical conveniences, one other thing was missing in Morocco, and that was Jan's suicidal tendencies. Could I say they vanished into thin air? Yes. True to my prediction, he was back at his writing desk, and whether he drank or not (he drank), never said a word about cutting himself or throwing himself over a cliff or whatever other devious destructive device he thought of when in Belgium.

Countryside Sketch

— 5 —

Hunter, Milton, Jan

Meanwhile, Hunter was embarking on projects that would cause our paths to cross sharply.

After the Kentucky Derby he and Steadman covered the America's Cup yacht race in Newport, Rhode Island, in September 1970—again for *Scanlan's*.

Journalist Ron Rosenbaum recalls being in a loft with Hunter when the "pipe dream" was hatched:

> The idea was to charter a motor yacht up in Newport where the Cup race was to be held, and to charge into the line of sailboats, flying a pirate flag and—this detail was added later—bearing on board a noisy, indeed noisome, band from the Lower East Side led by madman street rocker David Peel blaring out their best-known anthem "The Pope Smokes Dope." The idea—if it could be called an idea—was to bring some street chaos into the midst of the snooty choreography of the Cup race. It was Hunter's idea of how to "cover" an event.[8]

As Ralph told it in *The Joke's Over*, with a boat manned by a captain and a rock band, they entertained the coastline day and night for a week. But the wind was low, and the weather caused some cancellations. Hunter, taking a mysterious pill, was left unbothered by the delay, and to cure his seasickness, Ralph asked to try one.

A novice at drugs, he swallowed the "magic mushroom" psilocybin—not knowing what it was. Psilocybin was a natural hallucinogen, like peyote, prescribed by the old Yaqui Indian Juan Matus to the anthropologist Carlos Castaneda, in teaching him nonordinary states of reality.

It had also figured in psychedelic research at Harvard. Ram Dass later stated that when he received psilocybin at the hands of Timothy Leary on March 6, 1961, he experienced "the most significant single event of my life."[9] It "undercut the models I had of who I thought I was. . . . Fear in losing that familiar identity [brought me to] a place in myself where I just say 'I am,' not 'I am this or that.'" In wonder he felt that "in everything there is everything . . . in the spilled drop of Coca Cola is the entire universe."[10]

Steadman, however, went berserk for over forty hours.

During that time, loaded up with black and red spray paint, Hunter rowed them to the Australian challenger, the multimillion-dollar *Gretel II.* Ralph was supposed to write the graffiti "Fuck the Pope" on the yacht where the crew members couldn't see it. When the yachts sailed, the graffiti would be visible to the spectators. But the plot failed dramatically; Ralph and Hunter fled.*

Severely hallucinating, Ralph got on the plane to New York and wound up alone there, hyperventilating, barefooted, near death; he stumbled into the home of a friend, who called a doctor.

Hunter, in *his* version, said that Steadman did his best illustrations feeling anguished. Hunter added that he observed things *he* could slough off but thought, "this'll really give the bastard a jolt," so he deliberately put Steadman in tight spots—and that, it seemed, Ralph got into situations in order for Hunter to extricate him.[11]

Sometimes he tested the "edge" (just short of snapping) in which Ralph's best work unfolded. Not to mention his own. Assured that Ralph would be met in New York (he wasn't), Hunter did not fly there with him; he had to meet the deadline that day to file to run for sheriff of Pitkin County, Colorado.

As the Freak Power candidate, Hunter campaigned against "land-rapers": he wanted to ban Aspen's downtown auto traffic

---

* Psilocybin mimics the effect of the neurotransmitter serotonin. A Johns Hopkins University School of Medicine experiment published in the September 28, 2011 *Journal of Psychopharmacology* reported that—with the right dosage—it touched off intense transformative spiritual experiences.

("Chicago-style . . . in a town without stoplights") and "drive the real-estate goons completely out of the valley."* It was, he said, a "perhaps atavistic experiment with the idea of forcing change by voting."[12]

His sheriff's campaign drew nationwide coverage, such as by NBC; he lost after having, unfortunately, revealed his strategy for winning—in an October article: his first for *Rolling Stone.*

Thus mobilized, the anti-Freak Power turnout included, as Hunter later put it, people in wheelchairs, on stretchers, who still thought Eisenhower was president. Both parties would unite against him. Nevertheless, "In a town where no candidate for any public office had ever considered it necessary to pull more than 250 votes, a stone-bald and grossly radical Freak Power candidate for sheriff pulled 1,065 votes in 1970, yet lost by nearly 400 votes"—carrying Aspen but not the outlying areas.[13]

In Larache, I loved walking on unpaved roads among unpruned trees. But by local custom I could not go out alone except to shops—not to the beach, a bar, or movies. There was little to buy. Even furniture, such as a *catré* (sofa), we commissioned from a carpenter.

There was no English TV. Of course, no DVDs, no telephone, e-mail, texting, internet, computer. No interruption. Also, in Larache insofar as I saw, no bathtubs or home showers. (There were public showers and lovely, steamy Turkish bath-like *hamams*, where you filled buckets with hot or cold water and sat on the floor—moving from a warm to hot room—to scrub yourself or be scrubbed with an exfoliating stone. Men and women went separately.)

Bathrooms were typically squat toilets, little more than holes in the ground with foot rests to put your weight on. Beside the toilet

---

* In another description he promised to "*Ed:* Rip up the streets? *HST*: With jackhammers . . . and sod them . . . use all the asphalt to build a huge parking lot at the edge of town." He also "found [himself] . . . defending the use of mescaline by the sheriff," though promising not to take it "while *on duty*" (*Fear and Loathing: On the Campaign Trail*, 467). Ripping up the streets would be a blow to the developers who were transforming the former silver-mining town into a resort for the rich and famous. It now had a three-story condominium hotel at the base of Little Nell ski run in the heart of downtown.

hole was a low faucet and bucket for washing (no sink or toilet paper) and flushing.

Lack of stimulation, however, can prod the inner life. I needed to get this first book settled safely in stores. I came with baggage, as it were.

As before, we began our mornings with fresh-brewed coffee at a café terrace, where Jan read the newspaper *Le Monde* (Paris) and did a crossword. I sometimes bought the European edition of *Newsweek* or *Time*. To my shock, I saw a photo of Hunter during his sheriff's bid. Because the Republican candidate had a crew cut, Hunter stared out of the magazine pages, startlingly bald, with a quip about "my long-haired opponent."

Jan and I managed on $500 a month, thanks to his wealthy uncle.

A decade earlier, Jan had discovered that his poetical imagination opened if he smoked kif (cannabis). He had never smoked to paint or compose music. But here he daily rolled his kif or hash cigarettes, all lined up in a row, which he diligently smoked till ready to write. Cannabis use in Morocco is a centuries-old tradition. Fields of it grow in the remote Rif Mountains. There is nothing against cannabis by name in the Koran, though its use has often been, as now in 2012, technically illegal. In contrast, drinking alcohol as a Muslim was and is an enforced arrestable offense.

Jan did not get the kif precut. He got branches from a supplier and rolled the seeds down a plank, saving the leaves, which he cut into tiny bits, then added fresh tobacco leaves he cut as well. I quickly learned that for me a joint shut down my mind and opened my sensuality. So in the daytime I didn't indulge, though occasionally at night for obvious reasons. But Jan was dependent on it for his poetry. I suppose it opened up his unconscious, whereas I was so introverted that my unconscious was an extravert.

Our pet barnyard owl "Mokka" sat on his shoulder as he typed. We also had a chameleon, and a tiny secretive creature Jan called a wolf, which lived in a drawer.

For reading materials I'd go to the U.S. Embassy library in

Tangier. Once, riding there in the battered, bouncing bus (with live chickens on the top), I got lice—crawling on the back of my seat. No local remedy—orange powder, purple powder, hands in my hair crushing the eggs—could kill all of them.

Because of visa-extension problems at local police precincts, after four months we left Larache for Marrakech—approved to live in the *medina* (Old Town), which was rare for a Westerner. Our otherwise elegant house there had only an indoor well for water—which we hoisted up in a pail by rope. The well worked fine except during rain; then the water was brown.

Often embroiled in visa-extension issues with corrupt local officials, we made quick moves that first year.

Larache was fine. Likewise Marrakech. But closer to the Sahara Desert, coastal Essaouira on the Atlantic Ocean was one of the least conducive spots in which to start married life. Western hippies loved the town and settled on the beach, sunbathing nude to the delight and horror of the locals. Jimi Hendrix visited Essaouira and nearby Diabat in 1969 and is still beloved there. I saw his signature on a bar wall. Bob Marley is also a town hero. However, Essaouira was rife with male camaraderie. Unlike Larache, where Jan had taught French in a Moroccan school in the 1960s, here he knew no one and seemed to meet locals who kept women in a box. When the wife of one friend painted her toenails, which showed beneath her djellaba or kaftan (a loose-fitting, ankle-length robe), he had to be persuaded not to divorce her by verbal fiat—for being flirtatious.

Also, here unlike in Larache (colonized by the Spanish), there was no daily 5:00-p.m. stroll, or *paseo*, with bar hopping and tapas, which the whole town—myself included—enjoyed.

Jan often went to a friend's at night. No respectable women were allowed. Young prostitutes were. There was nothing wild or crazy going on with Jan, just drinking and singing. But I would be alone, to have a drinking party of one or be bored in another fashion. Knowing he would return relaxed, if I just sat and twiddled my thumbs (or read) I would get tense, resentful. If I drank a few glasses of wine, feeling I didn't have to obey some other society's rules, I'd relax. But I knew something was not right. Yet how to change it? Jan liked being indigenous. I enjoyed other cultures but felt there were rough adjustments, especially when he was out at an all-male party.

Essaouira Port: Portuguese Cannon

I immediately felt the stay in Morocco was temporary. I didn't know why, but it was "temporary," my intuition told me. Impossible that I would linger indefinitely in this lifestyle.

Therefore, I enjoyed the charm. What thrilled me: fantastic meals, mouthwatering salads of finely cut vegetables, exotic soups (orange-and-tomato purée, or bouillabaisse with brightly colored Mediterranean fish), prepared from a French cookbook that I wore out. I learned to make Coq au Vin, tripe tagines, couscous. I loved the relaxed, picturesque atmosphere, the long stretches of nature, the air of fun, music, and open markets, the exoticness, the many hours bantering or in serious talk.

Without window screens, I tried when writing to tune out (or choose the time of day, to avoid) radio music from the nestled-together houses.

One thing I didn't like—in Morocco only—was that, adapting the local custom, Jan threw his cigarette butts on the tile floor. I was supposed to pick them up. I recoiled: *is that what he thinks I'm worth?* I didn't mention it. It was a detail. I didn't have to dwell on it. However, it stung. This happy-go-lucky, sometimes thoughtful person had this dominating side that I identified by the butt lying snubbed out *on the floor.* But this feeling was offset by his charm. It didn't have to grow, like a split in a fabric. A barracuda in the relationship.

In March of '71, a well-known Flemish poet, Erik van Ruysbeek, reviewed Jan's work as poet of the decade in "Poetical Afternoon," a lecture at Ghent, Belgium. His article describes what I felt. Jan is called a Villon. François Villon was the very poet, obscure to Americans, who authored the epigraph to *Hell's Angels.* Why Villon? this poetical rebel lawbreaker who disappeared (like Rimbaud into Algeria) early in life?

> The first impression he leaves us is of an adventurer (he is that in real life), and of a rapscallion. In poetry he is rather like an outsider who, on a fine day, also wrote poetry plus a weird book, belonging to no known literary genre. The poems are called *Poems from the Pawnshop* (1966), an eloquent title, and the second work is what he himself names a "libretto for a baroque opera" and is called *Slow Night on the Meander* (1968).
>
> The image of the poet which comes to meet us from his poetry is complex. And it is not, in the first place, the image of a poet, it is the image of a man. His poems are a connected inner monologue, as a reaction to the many situations of an unbridled life. Unhewn, sometimes raw and rough, without fine manners, occasionally even in bad taste, but always deeply feeling and true, he makes for the reader and talks. Through his talking, a man arises in our imagination who,

to his own damage, has learnt a lot about human character, an idealist who has bruised himself at all the corners of the world, who has lived so much that he would be left without illusions if it weren't for the fact that the yearning for what didn't or cannot come true in itself hides the toughest illusion of all, if it weren't for the fact that an unquenchable vitality makes him start again and again.

Yes, stronger than these disillusions, one hears everywhere *con sordino*: an unrefined-in appetite for life, an urge to live, which flares up occasionally and allows him, after each crash, to determinedly get up. Mensaert is not a weakling who grieves and wails; rather, he is a lovable man with many weaknesses, which then, like Bredero, he simply confesses. That makes him a brother to us all and this is gratifying. Never does Jan Mensaert lose sight of the humor of the situation. He always remains lucid enough to see the relativity of all that happens and especially of all misfortunes. The result is a healthy scaffold humor and self-mockery, which are proof of his basically solid doses of philosophy of life and his love for life. This scaffold humor occasionally may grow into macabre mockery, eerie sensations, blind grimness, and then we approach sarcasm. Fruits of despair. But these usually are only moments.

Jan Mensaert is at his most lovable when he doesn't spirit away his human weaknesses but simply seems to tell us: what do you want: that's how I am. Thus, he never takes himself seriously and never becomes stately or pessimistic. Thus he usually shows the charm of a child. . . .

All this wouldn't be so much if it weren't for the way, the personal stamp, with which it marches over us.

I've called him an outsider. How did I dare! An outsider who, for instance, completely possesses the stream-of-consciousness technique . . . I repeat: a world marches over us, with the self-evident force of a river, carrying everything with it and shoving it along . . .

Meanwhile in New York City, Milton Klonsky was beginning to emerge from a writing desert. Having been highly praised for the publication of a prodigy poem, "The End Pocket," at the precocious age of twenty, he'd had a mostly dry period afterward. Then in 1968 he wrote "Mc^{2}Luhan's Message, *or*: Which Way Did the Second Coming Went?" for the *New American Review* magazine, followed by "Down in the Village: A Discourse on Hip; Or, Watch Out for the Cynosure" in 1971—contributing alongside Günter Grass, E. L. Doctorow, Gabriel García Márquez, and Jorge Luis Borges.

In eye-popping, witty language in "Down in the Village," he described the weekend invasion of the Village Hip scene by the 9-to-5-world squares, "people born with corners, but recently turned on and converted."[14] He traced *Where did they all come from?* backwards through Kierkegaard's concept of irony. Then backwards again "to the very source of irony among the Greeks of the fourth century BC." He said that when we do so, "peering at them reflectively as through the wrong end of a telescope until they dwindle in the mind, dwindle and diminish into minikins, diminkins . . . we also must do a double take, for there *we* are, as large as life!" This was because "the ironic style had social consequence for the Greeks similar to our own, resulting in a 'proto-Hip' movement throughout the ancient world." He placed Socrates' irony "under the old Hip word, 'down.'"[15] This inside a dazzling panoply of the Village menagerie.

Milton spoke in a clipped speech like Humphrey Bogart—even moved like him, chain smoked, and wore a trench coat but not in emulation. It was the way he was. Wiry, dark-haired (though silvering), of medium height and Russian Jewish ancestry, he was nineteen years older than I was.

Beat author Seymour Krim described his "fearlessness of intellect" and "fireworks-livid imagination." He found "nothing a hair's width false," though Klonsky's mind (Krim wrote in his four-times-anthologized essay "From *Two Teachers—Nuts, Two Human Beings!*") "seemed to contain the ENTIRE hip literary-intellectual university and closely grasped with an IQ that could stutter your butter too." Yet, at times, "he electrically bit out the language of the ballpark and streets."[16]

In meeting him, Krim had written:

> I got the downhome gooseflesh warning that I was on the way in for the most significant human and intellectual experience of my life up to then.
>
> I wasn't wrong.[17]

I felt the same.

I wrote no letters to him, however, from Morocco—all wrapped up in my life there.

In the summer of 1971, I returned to North Carolina for an extended stay at my parents,' diving into my basement to write with concentration again. This would be an annual occurrence, a deal I had with myself. En route, I made a one-night stopover in New York. (This too would become an annual occurrence.)

After checking into my midtown hotel room, filled with anticipation, I got off the Sheridan Square subway, walked up Bleecker onto West Eleventh and then up several flights of stairs and rang Milton's bell. (He had no advance notice.) In his smoky-gray corduroy pants and maroon sweater, he opened the door. After ushering me inside, he acknowledged how time moved back into position or never left, waiting for its development along *this* line: "Well, here we are again."

In only 1 of 365 days, I poured out what my psyche held poised for his circumspection—sparing no detail—relieved to hold nothing back. He was the only person I could talk openly to—who seemed "hip" enough yet blunt enough to impartially decipher some of the puzzles, even embarrassments. For he seemed deep in the core of my being, where "steady keel" was born and reaffirmed.

After listening intently while I summarized the last year, he said, "I've had those Siren calls before. You sink to the lowest common denominator."

So that was it, bleak but clear: I was sinking to the lowest common denominator, I thought—encouraged by the light bulb of understanding.

He strongly recommended I "look out for yourself."

As to Jan's suicidalness, he advised me to "have foresight, which isn't by the way foresight; it's *immediate sight.*" Otherwise"—he made a prediction—"imagine someday Jan's here, saying, 'I'm going to kill myself!' And *you're* saying *go ahead.*"

The calls of the voluptuous Sirens had so enticed Ulysses that he had himself tied to his ship mast with wax in his ears in order to resist.

In Essaouira—debating whether to move back to Belgium—Jan was living in the Hotel Central. He had many blush-worthy notes for his bride. July 19: "You missed a couple of good occasions when I was lying there in agony of sex, biting my pillow, tearing my sheets and moaning your name." After a rocky road he was into a novel: "the prologuli, antiprologuli and first chapter."

Last night: "All I had to do was to close my eyes and caress the sheet. Don't laugh, you were there as real as real can be."

However, my stomach soon flip-flopped: "Temptations of the flesh are gnawing with their sharpened teeth."

He consoled himself with my letters, which suggested to him "a series of happy discoveries ahead for my sober hours."

But—soon—he wrote that he "fell in love with a girl here (she left the day before yesterday having stayed only 48 hours) with an IQ of 149 which wasn't the reason. She looked like a Rubens maid servant of serious build and me being a true Flemish . . ."

Had there been a passionate forty-eight hours?! I pulled my hair, fretted. But anticipating this unpredictable "letter effect," I adopted a MacDowell-like routine—no mail till evening. I bargained with myself: while writing, keep an out-of-sight/out-of-mind mindset.

Jan inclined toward the opposite: out of sight, longing and yearning for this dearest of presences but not so much if in full sight. At least, I began to suspect this.

Few people would get this close up to a psychology as complex as Jan's, or at least this particular psychology, I thought. I adored when his letters missed me and I rather begrudged when they stirred me up emotionally if planting jealousies (with a tantalizing closing that left me gasping, wondering what happened next). So I did not wait for them with baited breath. They might be disruptive—might put a knife into my emotions. But I was committed to the marriage.

With his many dreams—that went in various directions—it was imperative I finish the fifteen-year-old book so as to freely join in. I had the return date open. Any Moroccan mischief, I was sure, would not be life-threatening. His energy was restlessly looking for a path, fuming, stalling, building toward that exit into "the work."

—6—

Hunter's Two Manuscripts

By August, I was still in North Carolina. Off in the Mountain West, things were at an auspicious point for Hunter. A few months before, a flag went up on what would become his signature and brand. In unbridled inspiration in a hotel room, he had written the genesis of a masterpiece, *Fear and Loathing in Las Vegas*, or rather, his alter ego Raoul Duke had.

As Rory Feehan puts it,

> Thompson's dissection of the dark side of the American Dream would catapult him to rock star status overnight and confirm his status as the infant terrible of the literary world. Through the pages of *Rolling Stone* he unleashed upon an unsuspecting American public what is undoubtedly his greatest artistic creation, not Gonzo Journalism as many would have you believe, but rather his compelling and brilliantly subversive literary persona—the Hunterfigure—as best exemplified through the guise of Raoul Duke.[18]

Now Hunter began searching for me—with two book manuscripts.

"The Battle of Aspen"—"The B/A"—had sprouted up from his *Rolling Stone* article "The Battle of Aspen: Freak Power in the Rockies"—published October 1, 1970, shortly before election day in his own sheriff's campaign. The article's subject was Joe Edwards' 1969 mayoral campaign. It invoked the principle of seizing political power ("Punish the Fatbacks / Make Sure that Today's Pig Is Tomorrow's Offal") by expanding the voting base. Hunter thought a book version could be a strategic—potentially important—presidential-election-year offering.

To his agent, Lynn Nesbit, Aug. 12, '71, he outlined what it would take for him to finish: another advance, a hard deadline—even an "ominous warning." Then, to induce "feverish concentration . . . people screaming at me on the long-distance telephone about *specifics.*"

To that end, he wanted to be assigned someone who would "prod me unmercifully, in the same way a copy editor named Margaret Harrell kept me locked to the daily grindstone on the Hell's Angels book."[19]

He thought he'd "try to locate Margaret," whom he'd last heard from "a year or so ago, and possibly she's back by now. If so, she's definitely the Missing Link."

That same day, he wrote me, proclaiming on the envelope: "Important" (in blue) and "Please Forward Immediately" (in red). The letter returned to him—with a big X, "Addressee unknown," and "Not box 390."

It took some time to reconstruct what happened next.

Eventually I realized I'd written Hunter. The letters crossed. Unable to establish contact normally, we managed nonetheless.

Now, firmly in possession of my address, he made a second attempt that winged across the continent inside an even more beautifully ornate 8 ½ x 11 envelope. In giant green-ink lettering he penned: **DELIVER THIS! THINK!!!** A red arrow curved to "M. A. Harrell (Mensaert), P.O. Box 159 (one-five-nine)"—all in red ink. He slipped both creations inside, the die now cast.

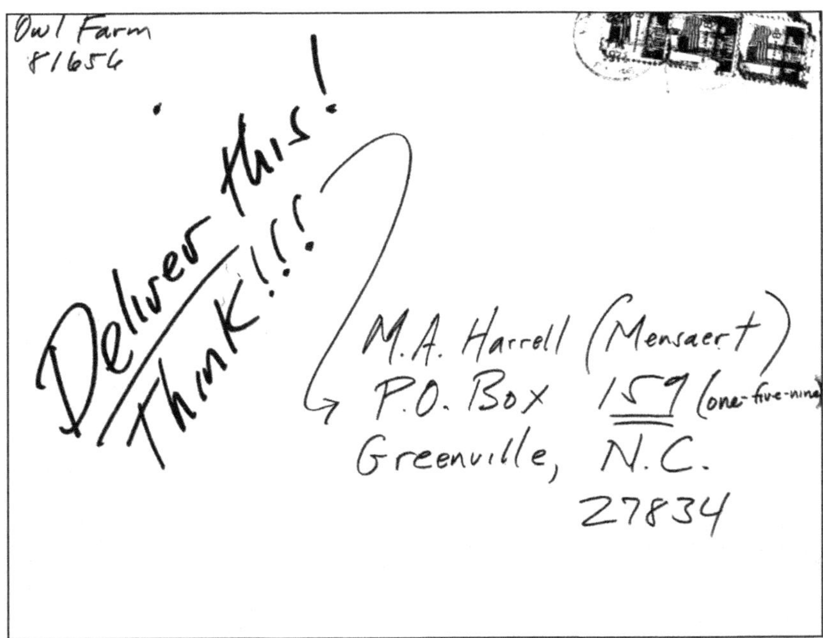

As Hunter mailed his first endeavor August 13, Jan probed deeply into his Byzantine convolutions: "I was shocked reading in your letter I was right being such a tyrant in sending you away. I never sent you away; you decided it was better to go and once you made up your mind I just helped you stick to the decision."

This led into his "real letter." It began: "Dear (stupid English language again) Margaret Ann Harrell and Mensaert, I love you. I know with such certainty that it's even more beautiful. OK. I want to see you as much as you want to see me (but I'm sure I want to see you more); I'm preaching patience to myself." He wanted what came next to be a fresh start: "No things which have to be done in the pocket. I'm going to love you so much. Not more than before."

He drew a comparison between the Acropolis and the Taj Mahal: "I told you the Greek thing was disappointing for a long time and still is because it didn't look any better than on a photograph and the Taj Mahal was a 100 times better than what was expected. Forget what I was heading for but I seem to remember you were in the Taj Mahal vein."

Then he lists the twenty-eight male characters in his novel in one column matched to females in another. His old friend Moulay had arrived, so he was eating regularly: "You made me see in Larache he was really harming me (he was) and I started wondering if it hadn't been like that before. But he's so different again":

> I love you (and judging after your reaction on that very innocent flirtation I should tell you more often).
>
> The next day. I went to see the doctor and the guy was very nice telling me I could drop dead tomorrow or could live till 45 when I'll be an ugly wreck. I had some trouble with my heart, when waking up. That's why I went. I don't think my heart made the doctor worry too much because the crisis was over and I was still alive but there was something else which he wouldn't say because he wasn't sure and that predicted cirrhosis is well on its way. The thing I didn't like was his advice not to have children. . . . The doctor expects a crisis soon and so do I, but there's only thirty dirhams left and that wouldn't be enough for half the things he prescribed. Am invited on a cruise on the fishing boat and may go tomorrow. If I had 100 dirhams in my pocket I'm sure I'd take the plane [to Belgium] this very Sunday. It's been a whole week without a letter from you. Blackmailing again?

This was offset by an Express letter:

> Forget the nonsense I wrote in my last letter. I guess the doctor scared me a bit, which is good for I knew it was all drinking and irregular eating but something had to make me react. So I stopped drinking. I really did and feel fine. . . . Guess that if my father could stop drinking (he was my age then) and even my brother I should be able to. The difference from <u>before</u> is that I want to live now. Next thing I'll stop smoking. . . . Geniuses do have complicated lives, don't they. You're one of the few stable things and my love

is too. Think we'll be seeing each other soon now. Certainly before your birthday. Love, Jan

Finally Hunter's double whammy sailed in. Though securely married, no matter the ups and downs, I still had feelings for Hunter. And the old me he brought to life. *He'd sought me out! Did he miss that fixture in his world?*

Having received my news 9/2, he handwrote that day in red ink on *Rolling Stone* stationary:

ROLLING STONE 9/2

Dear M.A.

— see enc. pack.
I had the wrong box no.
But my conclusion was that
you'd disappeared completely.
— But apparently
not. Your letter today was
hard to deal with. Very heavy
hash ~~footprints~~ all thru
it — no real information, only
flashes.
— Consider the
enc. packet + send word.
Vegas is about 3 days away
from the end — at least as
a 2-pt. piece shot for RS, but

625 Third Street, San Francisco, California 94107 . Telephone: (415) 362-4730

Ouch. My footprints were not from hash. The real information would have been about a rocky, odd, exotic marriage, not a manuscript I was editing or other staunch and stable conversation points.

He asked me to "Consider the enc. [returned letter] & send word. Vegas is about 3 days away from the end—at least as a 2-pt. piece shot for RS, but after that I'll probably make changes & additions for the book ms. (for R.H.)."

He went on:

> I'll be in NY around Sept 8–9–10, leaning on [Jim] Silberman—then down to Washington to set up hq. for the winter. I've agreed to start there (D.C.) on Nov 1.
>
> OK for now—send me a note that says something. I can't handle any more of this impressionistic gibberish. Love, H

Another *ouch.* (Steadman said, "He would insult you with such vitriol, but you'd think, 'The worse it gets, the more he loves me.'"[20])

In the inner letter Hunter gets directly to the point:

OWL FARM

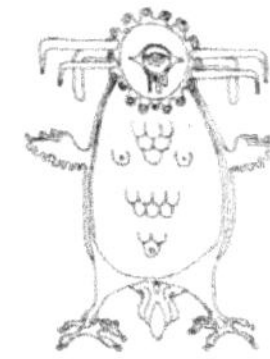

Aug 12, 71

Dear Margaret ....

Where are you? And why? I've lost track completely. My last definite word was from a water-closet in Algiers.

Anyway, I'm sending this on the odd chance that you might have bounced back to the US since I last heard anything. If so, I've been hassling Silberman severely to assign a "Margaret-type" copy editor to this goddamn book that I finally seem to be on the verge of getting together. But god only knows who he'll assign .... and it worries me, for all the obvious reasons.

The bastard has to be "finished" (*) by Nov 1, because that's my date for moving to Washington DC, to become the "Chief

He says: "The bastard has to be 'finished'* by Nov 1 [* -+ pub. by June '72], because that's my date for moving to Washington DC, to become the 'Chief Political Correspondent' for Rolling Stone—a contract job for one year: Nov '71 to Nov '72. The book is now titled 'The Battle of Aspen,' but the main thrust is toward the idea of translating our Aspen 'Freak Power' tactics into the national politics arena—so it will have to be out by the summer of '72."

Were I "loose and within hailing distance," he'd recommend me "pretty heavily for a job—beginning almost immediately, although the pressure won't get serious until around Sept 15 or maybe even Oct 1. That's when I'm going to need somebody who can <u>deal</u> with the book without having to waste 2 months 'getting to know me.'"

He recounts the now familiar story of the genesis of *Vegas*, the prior spring: "I went out from LA to Vegas to do a 'Quick caption' for Spts. Illustrated…but I got so involved with the place that the caption is now a book, incorporating what Silberman thought would be the final section of the 'big' book."*

To back up a step, in February for his second *Rolling Stone* piece—"Strange Rumblings in Aztlan"—he had gone to L.A. to investigate the suspicious circumstances surrounding the death of journalist Ruben Salazar. Salazar had been covering the National Chicano Moratorium March, which protested the disproportionately high percentage of Chicanos killed in the Vietnam War. When the sheriff's department broke up the rally at the end using tear gas, rioting ensued. Merely on the tip that an armed man was inside, police fired a tear gas bomb into the Silver Dollar Café in East L. A, striking the innocent Salazar.

Recruited by his pal Oscar Acosta to get to the bottom of what happened, Hunter hung out in the barrio. His report April 29, 1971, would expose a detailed police cover up but not necessarily an intentional killing.

In corralling Acosta away from East L.A. for private time—Chicanos did not like him hanging with a gringo—Hunter took him to the Polo Lounge. There, when the two were drinking Singapore Slings (according to the manuscript that developed), a call from New York put through to their table asked Hunter to work with a photographer to write captions of photos of the Mint 400, a 410-mile desert race. He set out to Las Vegas with Oscar, whom he rechristened in the manuscript his infamous sidekick, the Samoan attorney Dr. Gonzo.

---

* Jim was still waiting for his contracted manuscript.

So what I'm looking at, right now, is two books. Vegas is almost finished. It's called "Fear & Loathing in Vegas: A Savage Journey to the Heart of the American Dream"—by Raoul Duke,* Doctor of Gonzo Journalism.

If you hurry, you can deal with that one, too. I've promised to have it all finished by the end of August. Jim [Silberman] already has about 35,000 finished words, with maximum of 25,000 more to come. I'd prefer to keep it down to 50,000 or so, but I don't think I can. It's a boomer—a spontaneous outburst that almost wrote itself.

Let me know where you are & if there's any chance at all of tracking you down to help out on the Battle of Aspen. I'm not worried about Vegas, but the other one makes me nervous. I suspect I'll need a friend to make the bastard work & beat the deadline. Send Word at once, from anywhere. Even if you can't make it, I'd like to know where you are & what you're doing, thinking, feeling, etc. Ciao. H

* The name "Raoul Duke" had appeared in *Hell's Angels* in a short list of real outlaws like Frank Sinatra and Elizabeth Taylor, opposed to celluloid fakes (263). He used it once in *Scanlan's* as his penname. Now in "Fear and Loathing in Las Vegas" in *Rolling Stone*, Duke as his alter-ego narrator shielded Hunter the reporter from being the straightforward author of the drug story. Later he was the inspiration behind Uncle Duke in the *Doonesbury* comic strip.

— 7 —

Hunter: "The B/A"

It was another fork in the road. He was fired up—about to explode—with momentum.

A turning point—for him. But I was boxed in.

I couldn't just dial overseas from Morocco had there been a home phone, which there wasn't. In villages like Essaouira the air space didn't permit such international calls. You queued *at the post office*—for hours. If no one picked up when it was finally your turn, it was back to the end of the line! To join him was impractical—which had never stopped me. But with all my wits, I didn't see it.

For *Fear and Loathing: On the Campaign Trail* (as it turned out), in fifty-five consecutive hours Hunter's editor would have no food or sleep; some sections Hunter dictated; the editor snatched tapes out of the machine, to be bustled into a satchel for transcribing, then straightaway printed.[21] Notoriously, he got fueled in that instable moment of "time's up"—playing the red-hot insecurity boundary of all backs against the wall.

It boggles the mind to think what saying *yes* might have led to.

Furthermore, if I had accepted, Jan would have been jealous.

However, nothing if not persistent, Hunter took a shot in the dark. Things work out if "you go with your instincts," he famously wrote.[22]

I was tempted, that kind of instant *yes*—that adrenalin rush at the real possibility of being back in the groove together. That sheer, rising-up-out-of-nowhere unexpected solution by "changing the subject." Bohemianism satisfied a locked-in part of me. But what about outcomes, making plans, carrying them through?

Obviously I could not have comprehended the scale he was

embarking on, moving to D.C. in November '71 to inaugurate the *Rolling Stone* Political Affairs Desk.

What if "The Battle of Aspen" had been published *as a book—before* the '72 election—crossbreeding the Aspen strategy into the McGovern–Nixon race? Hunter saw the topic as—he wrote Jim Silberman—an "accidental framework" for a book that would "delve into politics far beyond Aspen," somewhat as the Hell's Angels provided his prior organizing center. He thought of flashing back to the 1968 Chicago riots. His experience in Aspen political battles would provide the "definitive framework" for the "nebulous 'American Dream' bullshit" he'd struggled to peg.[23]

Comparing tactics in two elections, one presumably the John Lindsay mayoral campaign, Hunter wrote Jim Silberman: "The NY vote was a triumph of a New Coalition, but the Aspen vote signaled the appearance of a *whole new electorate*."[24]

With the twenty-sixth U.S. Constitution amendment ratified in June 1971 (in an "old enough to fight, old enough to vote" victory), the registration age was down—since his sheriff's campaign—from twenty-one to eighteen.

He hoped to influence the 1972 presidential battle: help defeat the incumbent Richard Nixon, who was anathema to him.

But this was not to be. "The B/A" was scrapped.

Fear and Loathing: On the Campaign Trail '72 would cover the twelve months *after* Hunter moved to Washington: "a kind of high-speed cinematic reel-record of what the campaign was like *at the time.*"[25] Part of its brilliant underlying analysis was the premise that the McGovern campaign was wrong to revert to the old-style party politics after gaining the nomination. Hunter had considered the Aspen model "ready for export."[26]

He supported McGovern in '71—on an anti-Vietnam War platform. McGovern said sometimes the two were alone in a "little putt-putt airplane": they were "entirely different personalities, but we hit it off. He used to tell me I was an honest man. . . . He said, 'You're the best of the lousy lot.' But I always took it as a compliment."[27]

Possibly inevitably, "The B/A" would have been replaced by *Campaign Trail.* But it was the proverbial "now or never." Hunter mentioned the job casually, emphatically—an opportunity to give your eyeteeth for.

It was a critical juncture in even more ways. By this point Ralph Steadman, over in London, had changed residences.

Months after the America's Cup, as told cinematically in *The Joke's Over*, Hunter located Ralph at his new address—to ask him to illustrate *Vegas*.

Ralph later said that following the race, he spent six months in "nightmares and daymares, ugly flashbacks and palpitations, dream-scarred eyes behind pulsing flesh lids, trying to sleep, trying to forget."[28] Illustrating *Vegas* allowed him to vomit up demons incited by the psilocybin pill he took at the America's Cup. In view of that harsh reaction, he added, "I already knew the story."[29] When Raoul Duke described his terror at the registration desk of the Mint Hotel ("The woman's face was *changing*: swelling, pulsing . . . horrible green jowls and fangs jutting out, the face of a Moray Eel!"), to Ralph, the job of imagining the scene was a welcome relief.[30]

Hunter asked him to do the illustrations at the beginning of 1971. He was hard at work on this regurgitation at the time of my August/September letters from Hunter. Ralph would mail his drawings at the end of September. At which point the whole staff at *Rolling Stone* in San Francisco "flipped."[31]

He was firmly on board. And we know the rest. The peak of Hunter's career loomed. He really needed an answer. Bringing me in on the project suited us perfectly. I would have liked it (stealing a quote from the Jefferson Airplane).

Hunter called *Vegas,* "only half sarcastically, 'a vile epitaph for the Drug Culture of the Sixties.'"[32] He was compared to Kafka, Sartre, Camus. In *Rolling Stone,* P. J. O'Rourke asked him if it was difficult to write about drugs. Hunter: "Well, that's what *Vegas* is about . . .

the altered perceptions of the characters. To me, that's really the bedrock of the book—their responses to one another's questions. It's like in *The Three Stooges*: that story where they were out in the rowboat in a lake and it sprung a leak. And the boat was filling up with water. So they decided to bash a hole in the bottom of the boat to let the water out. Now that's drug reasoning."[33]

In another interview:

> **HST:** Do you think we were surprised [in *Fear and Loathing*] to find that the American Dream was a nightclub that had burned down five years earlier? That we were surprised to find when we tracked it down that it had been the old Psychiatrist's Club? Prior to that its name had been the American Dream. Do you think that we were surprised to find that? No. I went out there looking to reaffirm Horatio Alger. I knew what was happening. That's what the book is all about.[34]

In late September, I left North Carolina and returned to Morocco—arriving suddenly after all letters from Jan stopped.

To find out why, I phoned the Hotel Central. Someone said Jan had "gone to Paris." Letters of explanation wound their way across the ocean as I flew back. He was by then safe and sound in the Majestic Hotel "in the middle of inspiration." But earlier he couldn't mail anything, unable even to buy a stamp, having one day "opened [his] wallet and found it empty." A forwarded letter eventually reached me: "I've had two really rotten weeks trying to live on nothing. Don't ask me how I ran out of money. I don't know myself. . . . The very first morning of my discovery [that his wallet was empty] the Hottentot Venus from downstairs threw me out, slept a couple of nights on the beach, deeply regretting to have left my sleeping bag in Marrakech." After selling a few things, he

> got an invitation from some very vague Marrakchi acquaintance to stay with him, four friends, three prostitutes and three babies in a little room with a couple of mats on the floor. Which I accepted of course. Never saw so many bedbugs, I could have had a meal on them. Not shy, gaily crawling around in the open. Then the Marrakchis left and I was sent back to my beach and my fasting. . . . Picked up the cigarette buds [*sic*] in the street, went finally to the port where they throw tons and tons of the small sardines to the seagulls, had fights with the birds but usually managed to get my share. Couldn't write, of course. I realize that's what made me more unhappy than the rest.

Now in a "room, four floors high but with a view on everything in a circle of ten kilometers," he concluded:

> Man is a wonderful thing. I thought it was going to take me years to forget about those two weeks and the very first night I got money I was at the Chalet feeling happier than I would in heaven. It's been since Iran though that I felt that miserable. . . .
>
> I love you, yes. I couldn't see anything I more want to see than you, yes. I could wait a tiny little bit longer as long as I work, yes. We're going to be very happy soon, yes. Come the 23rd or 22d or 24th, yes. Only twelve more days, since this is the eleventh. [He drew a huge heart with four sets of doors with hearts.] Guess what's behind those little doors. Don't open them until you're in the plane.

And so I did return, with much accomplished on my "big novel." But with ragged places, question marks, and the sense of a *missing section*. Jan, for his part, said, "I *never saw a question after which I didn't put a period.* For me, every question is a suspicion. Every suspicion is a certitude."

— 8 —

Hole in My Manuscript

My book remained unfinished. The end was clear, but the book felt incomplete. Impervious to my tenacity, it led me on. As described earlier, the plot revolved around a couple hopelessly mismatched on the physical-attraction scale, but the female hero-worshiped the male for his mind and spirit. This closely paralleled my relationship with Milton, with his spicy, elegant, pithy statements thrown into the book like salt and pepper. The counterplot involved a couple sprung out of my imagination—where the female, Anny, was very sensual, happily but boringly married. And suddenly her world fell apart in a chance encounter one night with the iconoclastic Ian. The name "Ian," I took from a Scotsman in Paris, whom I met in 1965 about two weeks before synchronistically meeting Jan in Marrakech. I much later learned that "Jan" was "Ian" in Scottish.

This novel I titled "The Erstwise Patsy," but it eventually became, in publication thirty years after inception, the *Love in Transition* series, volumes 1 and 2.

Why couldn't I complete it? What was missing?

Jan had shocked me that in his repeated lists of the top ten writers, painters, musicians of all time he included no Americans—and only two females: Sappho and Emily Brontë.

His scale was of giants and he wanted to be in it.

Reading a section of my "big book," he enjoyed the counterplot (Ian and Anny).

He suggested revealingly that after Anny gave Ian her address, he obliterate any possibility of contacting her—by *burning* the paper.

(Later it would be glaringly clear that he associated "burning" with an infant trauma I had yet to find out about.)

In March '72 a letter arrived in Essaouira from a robust rabbi/comic novelist Herbert Tarr. I'd copy edited his 1968 best seller, *Heaven Help Us!* (that rose to number 10 on the *New York Times* list). He'd just finished *A Time for Loving*: "It's now reached the editing stage—and horror of horrors, there's no Margaret Ann around here at Random House. I'd very much like you to be the one to edit the book . . . It's in much better shape than HEAVEN HELP US! was when you saw it. Know why? Because I've put into it (or tried damn hard) everything I learned from working with you. So for one thing, I've pared it and pared it down to the bone."

I accepted gladly. But the only post-Random House work I did for Tarr was in Oostende, Belgium. Ergo, this dates that time.

Years began to pass in a topsy-turvy way. Intending to relocate in Belgium, Jan and I visited his parents. But becoming furious with them, he told me to pack *for India* in one hour. No discussion. He had an impulse. *We acted.* Drolly re-creating my 1965 impression that he couldn't live without music, I crammed stacks of classical LPs into his suitcase!

What would have happened had we arrived in India with few clothes and tons of LPs, I never found out. In the train station he said let's toss a coin: India, Oostende? India lost.

We rented an apartment in Oostende on the North Sea coast, being still financed (at $500 a month) by his rich uncle. This had been a hard-won concession so he could write. After four months, inevitably, it was back to Morocco—the ocean-front village in the South, Essaouira. More to my liking, and coming again soon, would be Larache.

Slide: Moroccan Souk

With Jan accompanying me to North Carolina to meet my parents that summer, we stopped overnight in New York. I phoned Milton, to arrange to join him alone briefly. But Jan heard the excitement in my voice and decided to come along. We met at the Lion's Head off Sheridan Square. Or maybe it was the 55 Bar. As a Belgian, Jan rarely drank hard alcohol and did not nurse a drink. Milton, unaware of this, had the bartender load up his stingers heftily, which Jan began to gulp. Then for no discernible reason but no doubt jealous, *mano a mano* Jan struck: "You're a hypocrite," he stabbed.

Milton (unflappable) replied, *"Do you know where 'hypocrite' comes from? To play a part on a stage."*

Expecting me to follow, Jan stomped out. Rapidly, we traversed thirty blocks to Times Square. Squinting into a sidewalk porno peep show machine, he gestured me to look. I was infuriated.

He was now ready to turn in. I wanted to cool off, feeling he had been churlish. Jan balked. I rebelled—this was *my city*—and sat around the corner from our midtown Pickwick Arms Hotel over a quiet drink, proving to myself I could. Only to get to the room to find the door bolted from inside. Jan too soundly asleep to wake up even as the desk clerk banged loudly on the door. So I was forced to rent a second room!!!

Inside, I phoned the familiar CH2-2067 for my once-a-year talk with Milton after all. In a glimpse he had nimbly fathomed Jan's psyche. Mentioning a candle lighted at both ends, he said, "He's burning alive." Contrarily, Milton, had been undaunted, cool, available.

Later Jan said privately, "I think I'm a genius. I begin to think I'm special. But geniuses aren't special people. Special people are would-be geniuses." He resolved the issue: "I think I'm a genius . . . of a special kind." I answered, "But geniuses are always of a special kind."

He went on, "I've said it so simply. In three words. And you don't understand. If you did, we'd be perfect. Why do you think I'm so extreme? Am I extreme with other people? I'm usually the contrary."*

---

* This paragraph and the preceding one were taken from my "little book," a novel eventually titled "A Lecture upon the Shadow."

With Jan in the United States with me, I made no attempt to contact Hunter, who was out covering the election.

In *Fear and Loathing: On the Campaign Trail '72* he brought me in obliquely—in between the lines—in the snake story.

As his Random House editor, Jim Silberman, recalled, "He'd come up to the offices on Madison Avenue when we were still in this mansion, and he'd sneak down the halls with this yachting fog horn attached to an air canister, which he'd blast, and we'd send out for the whiskey and he'd hang around and talk. He soon became one of those authors who are a celebrity in the building. When Hunter was around, people showed up to look at him. It was life as performance art."[35]

The snake stunt was one of the earliest—in January 1968, the last of my three years at R.H. In a Christmas visit to his in-laws in Florida, Hunter had acquired a pet blue indigo snake. He intended to take it to his Owl Farm ranch. But he lost the snake in Florida and flew to the Big Apple alone. Soon recovered, the blue indigo followed him to New York City in unaccompanied airline baggage.

I offered to keep it in a box in my R.H. office. That was supposedly safer than leaving it roaming alone with electricity sockets in his hotel room. Then at Hunter's instruction, against all my animal-loving instincts, I placed a brown pet-store mouse into its box for food. When the snake refused it, I yanked the mouse out, returned it to the store.

But afterwards, fearing the blue indigo might suffocate while I was out, I loosened the lid. This set in motion the fatal slaying.*

In the *Campaign Trail* version, after Hunter ensconced the snake in a sealed-tight cardboard box in his editor's [!] office—with a second occupant: a mouse—the latter valiantly gnawed a way to freedom.

Followed, of course, by the snake "through the same hole—and somewhere around dawn, when the night watchman went out to check the main door, he was confronted with a six-foot blue-black serpent slithering rapidly up the stairs, flicking its tongue at him and

* After the first volume of this memoir came out, Jim Silberman told me, "I was glad to see that your memory of the snake story matched mine."

hissing a warning that he was sure—according to his own account of the incident—was the last sound he would ever hear."

Hunter explained that "Most natives of Manhattan Island are terrified of all animals except cockroaches and poodles."

The night watchman was numb with fear, till, with the snake advancing, "some primal instinct shocked the man out of his trance and gave him the strength to attack the thing with the first weapon he could get his hands on—which he first described as a 'steel broom handle,' but which further investigation revealed to have been a metal tube jerked out of a nearby vacuum cleaner."

With snake and vacuum tube smashed, the watchman was discovered later in the day (by "a copy editor") beside the Random House Xerox machine in the basement in shock, "gripping the mangled tube," speechless.

The moral: "But the psychic scars remain, a dim memory of corporate guilt that is rarely mentioned except in times of stress or in arguments over money. Every time I start feeling a bit uneasy about running up huge bills on the Random House tab, I think about that snake—and then I call room service again."[36]

Jim added the long view: "When Hunter came in on Monday morning and found that his pet snake had been beaten to death, he was in a total rage. That snake story came up once a year for all the rest of the time that I knew Hunter. It had nothing to do with him being at all at fault for leaving a giant snake in a cardboard box in a midtown office building. It was this insane, crazed night watchman who had lost his head."[37]

—9—

Celebrity Endorsement of a Sort

Finally, my MacDowell Colony friend Hannah Green, who had studied with Vladimir Nabokov and taught creative writing at Columbia University and NYU—revered for her slender novel, *The Dead of the House*—gave her verdict on my "big book," titled "The Erstwise Patsy" (later "The Erstwise Paula" and finally *Love in Transition*)*: It had "a very powerful hypnotic effect . . . fascinating and often brilliant . . . The design of it is tremendous and I know you can bring it off."

She went on: It "really begins to take off" in New York. "But especially when Patsy meets Robert [Milton] it becomes very fascinating. He is a marvelous character. . . . It has that absorbing quality which is the real test of a good book." †

The novel opened with childhood vignettes based in my life. One was about a Man with a Slingblade, who—every spring—slashed through the undergrowth of the vacant, woodsy lot next door to slaughter the snakes when they woke out of hibernation. I compared the untouched woods with "a relaxed sprawling individuality." In contrast to the flattened, leveled-off, innocuous, safe woods after the spring bloodbath. I noted, "There are tall, strapping shoots of self to be climbed to the top of—and only then see in perspective."

---

* At MacDowell, Hannah and Tillie Olsen were considered among the top living U.S. female writers.

† Calling my book "a big work," Hannah recounted the final days preceding publication of her classic, *The Dead of the House*; then details of her marriage and a trip to Europe for the exhibition of her painter husband, John (Jack) Wesley.

Lending more support, in a cometlike incident, Andrew Lyndon III, a former lover of Tennessee Williams and Christopher Isherwood, descended upon Essaouira to visit his boyfriend Mustapha. Isherwood had met Andrew while visiting Andrew's friend Truman Capote on Nantucket.[38] Andrew was also a confidant of Malcolm Lowry (*Under the Volcano*), who, he said, at the end of his life consulted him on all his poetry.*

Anticipating my pleasure, Jan proudly introduced me to this writer and literary socialite.

Lending great support, day after day Andrew went patiently through my manuscript. At night if the electricity blew out, we sat at a large wooden table in our courtyard, surrounded by flowers and huge candles in brass holders.

We went over every in-doubt word. Immensely insightful, he said *yes* or *no* to cuts I'd tentatively bracketed. Also, he praised the book. What a relief. Confidently, he insisted on renaming Patsy, and we chose a two-syllable substitute, "Paula."

Something incubates—fraught with peril—perhaps threatened with never being completed. It might be thwarted by circumstances, go underground for a decade, as with Rainer Maria Rilke. Milestones along the way that remove the clutter—add validation—are incomparable.

* Correspondence with Andrew 1947–72 figures prominently in the papers of Truman Capote. And a chapter of *Conversations with Tennessee Williams* has Andrew in Key West, in Tennessee's apartment, throughout; it is a reprint of "Tennessee Williams Survives" from the *Atlantic Monthly*, November 1970.

— 10 —

On Jan

When I asked Jan to write a short autobiography, he composed a two-page account—entirely on childhood. In World War II he'd seen an admired female teacher and member of the Belgian Resistance dragged out of her home to her death; a woman run out of a barn, a rat clinging to her ear. He was three when his mother fled with the children to the countryside. Later, hiding under the table, he listened to tales of "a certain plague-ridden town in France, the smell of rotting corpses in a bombed factory, the long convoys of refugees under the gunfire of the enemy. And the hunger. . . . Nothing of this seems to have surprised me, certainly not frightened."

Then he described playing in a ditch filled with snow while there was fighting in the Ardennes. In a tunnel he'd dug with his older brother, he was "looking through a skylight," till his brother shouted, "Quick on your stomachs."

> I didn't obey, of course; I stood on tiptoes to have a look at what was obviously scaring him, and in the clear winter sky saw a big iron monster, tail ablaze, rapidly coming down on us, it seemed. I did duck then, and soon afterwards there was an explosion, the earth rocked, then there was a short silence, followed by what I now would term a heart-freezing scream. The roof of our tunnel had collapsed at the same time we heard the blast. We jumped up, shook off the snow and ran to a nearby group of houses from where the screaming came. My brother, ahead, suddenly stopped and held out his arms as if to protect us. A woman came running out

> of a door, holding the stump of her right arm with her left hand, then she stopped, looked in silent horror at the torn flesh and screamed again, even ghastlier than before.
>
> I understood so little then and later that, when I was twelve, I asked my mother how babies were born. Watch the animals, she said. I was taken aback. I understood instantly. But my last childhood myth had vanished. What I really had wanted to know was whether babies were found in cauliflowers or brought by the stork.

He wrote, "I was the fattest baby ever born [in 1937] and the skinniest child. My brother was punished for telling me (laughing at me, of course) when I was eight there was no such thing as Santa Claus. I really only wanted to believe in dreams. (I had read the Arabian Nights so often I knew them by heart.) And I really was only afraid of injustice."

The above was true. Jan told me he first thought of suicide at fourteen, when he got a bad grade. His uncle pounded on the teacher's desk and got his daughter's grade changed. Jan's lackadaisical, meek, kind father did nothing. Contemplating the unfairness, Jan stood in a window and thought, "why not jump?"

At times quite demonstrative, Jan would pump up the adrenalin with affection and twists of soft, fine-spoken imagination, which he meant. But often would not follow through. This situation began to baffle me. I hadn't thought it possible that a man of his incorrigible romanticism could react like this, and it wasn't clear cut; it was a tension of opposites, a seesaw, a maybe, *a yes and no.*

But two years in, the fact was that his "comas" did not suddenly vanish; he was both maddeningly attentive in passionate or playful buildups and underactive when it came down to it.

So though it was not of course a platonic relationship, he didn't chase me around the bed or, evidently, fantasize ways to get me there.

Our relationship had become (in that way) so trying that one night the frustration culminated. After preparing Coq au Vin and drinking too much with Jan and Moulay, who was living with us again, I blacked out. I didn't remember it but evidently I sat up by myself and with the spice mortar smashed every empty wine bottle into slivers of glass.

What did I pound to splinters that could never be reassembled?

Moulay played up the fact that I had only a partial memory. He scared me to death with joking accounts (snorting and laughing)—saying that I almost slept with him. Fortunately, a memory flash assured me he exaggerated. I felt mortified and fearful to be in the same house with him, watching myself to be sure the disturbing situation didn't arise again, which it didn't. But having to be guarded and suspicious in my own house really got to me.

Jan's reaction to Moulay's account was to throw a pan of spaghetti with bright red sauce onto the wall. He said, "The scales have fallen from my eyes." Jan would tell me much later that it wasn't Moulay's story he was reacting to but the confusion about me blacking out and continuing to function. It upset him, whereas even had Moulay's version been correct, which it wasn't, he said, "I'm a big boy I could have handled it." But that explanation came later.

Meanwhile, Moulay informed me that Jan would *never let him go*. But we soon moved to a new location without him.

Again, the reader may ask why I put up with this. I was still a new bride. There was a lot of magic in the exotic setting. A lot of magic in being married to an unpredictable poet. What did I know about a bohemian lifestyle? Maybe this was it. Walking to the open-air *souk* daily, selecting the fresh vegetables and meat, working on my writing, excitedly listening to Jan read his to me in the evening, and keeping up with his wild speculations about where our life was headed. For all I knew, this might wind up in heaven on earth for a writer. He was not suicidal here. His biggest problem was a much-abused stomach. I fed him vitamins and plied him with food.

— 11 —

Jan: "A Rembrandt in my yacht"

Because of the perennial visa problem, Jan and I temporarily relocated just over the Moroccan border in Ceuta in 1973. Ceuta faces the Rock of Gibraltar and is a Spanish enclave in North Africa. Here the suicidalness, absent in Morocco, flared.

Jan attributed it—charmingly—to dying of melancholia. Three musicians he named had died of melancholia, he said. I remember one was Felix Mendelssohn, who followed his sister Fanny to her death six months later.

Before, I had thought of Jan as not necessarily wanting to die. Just not calculating with that as a deterrent, a risk too great to buck. As a student, he told me, he intentionally got locked overnight in a morgue to learn to not fear death, of which he'd been mortally frightened. Another time, he said, he stole a skull to drink from.

In Ceuta, I began to mentally tape record his poignant conversation. Its lyrical originality fascinated me. He, on the other hand, said that when he was drunk that's *not me, I shouldn't* listen. This seemed unrealistic, he was so often at least borderline drunk. Nevertheless, I recorded some highlights.

I was very interested in "not me," turning it inward to such things as unlistened-to desires.

A few months later, when I put the conversations into a novel ("the little book") at MacDowell Colony, our names would be Knut Karel and Merry Lou—"Lou" from "Loup" (French: "wolf"—pronounced "Lou"); "Wolf": Jan's name for Mozart (based on "Wolferl," Mozart's nickname). "Lou" was also the first syllable of "light" (in

French). Milton, the Wise Advisor, I called Daniel. Memory being fallible, with these accounts as a reference, I reconstructed the scenes below.

Here I try to understand his penchant for suicide. The absurdity, the surrealism, of his comments, said in the most deadpan or sparkling way, always took me aback and piqued my interest. I was in a nail-biting suspense as to how to keep him alive.

In the Ceuta hotel room: "Oh, God," he said suddenly, "I'm turning into bitter almonds."

"Why?"

"That's the question," he answered—adding without blinking, "I've decided to die in a tuxedo because of the blood on a white shirt." He stopped. "I'm hesitating between a tuxedo and rags. Funny how the slightest thing goes wrong and I've got to kill myself. . . . Would you say I'm a compulsive suicide?"

"But why?"

"That's the simplest question you've asked me in a long time . . . Having so many possibilities. And turning into what I've become." He stopped again. "It's Greek tragedy, and Greek tragedy doesn't exist."

The next day his news was, "Do you know when you shoot yourself in the mouth your eyeballs come out? I'm a man of many possibilities. But only one solution. Because every possibility comes crashing down with broken wings to the solution."

The day after: "I've found a way. A masculine way. Shoot yourself in the liver."

"What would you have to have to make the circumstances right?"

"I'd have to have a Rembrandt in my yacht." He paused, "So I could throw darts in it."

This was not hypotheticals insofar as I was concerned. It was in the center of a now-hourly debate. The intensity of his gaze, the way he threw himself into these scenes as if they were really life or death, as if no world outside them existed, held me in its grim grip. Also, I felt some guilt, underscored by the fact that he would sometimes lash out at me, alternating with endearment.

"So it wasn't right," I began one day, after he whispered he didn't have—was born without—"a will to live—"

In my novel, borrowing Jan's words, Knut Karel answers:

> "It was basically very right. I think it comes from seeing all those people killed."
>
> "You mean dramatically?"
>
> "No. I mean casually."
>
> Nevertheless, said Merry Lou, Knut Karel turned everything upside down—
>
> He replied, "Well, why do flies walk on ceilings?"
>
> "But you don't have to be negative."
>
> "Yes, I do have to be negative. I get just as much out of being negative as some people get out of being positive, in my own way."
>
> #
>
> "It's got to happen every now and then—wasted lives," he said, then finished: "Oh, it happens often. But wasted talent—"[39]

That went straight to my heart. Could wasted talent be tolerated by the life force? Would it not outwit that statement?

Predictably, overriding Jan's objections, I phoned his uncle, who swept in to fly us to Belgium. I was to leave almost immediately for North Carolina—a trial separation (Jan's idea). But glued to the cliff-hanger, up-and-down hope of it all, I hadn't had enough.

I still believed. At least with reprieves and time-outs.

In New York, after I explained the dire details, Milton buffered me with his wisdom. In the next scene, which would go into the "little novel," we were in his rather bare West Eleventh Street brownstone, looking down on the tree-lined Greenwich Village street—twilight-strolling humanity below. The passage is in large part transcribed, as in a film undimmed with passing years.

I was devastated by the separation.

As always, I would excuse myself to go to the bathroom when my brain had recorded enough of Milton's precious words. I'd jot them down and return to the room.

Most of all, I could tell him anything; he would never proclaim me guilty but would be gimlet-eyed. After I filled him in, I ventured that I'd been "living *La Bohème*" in the twentieth century with Jan. He said no, well maybe *Tristan and Isolde* in a *La Bohème* setting but that every love story was *Tristan and Isolde*. "And if Jan died," he added, "you would be a bit relieved."

"That's a horrible feeling to admit," I said.

"No. Just as you'll be in some way relieved at your own death."

From my perch, seated on one of the large pillows on the floor in front of his low coffee table, I attributed the problems with Jan to "circumstance." He instantly objected, "No, there are only new colors in the same dome . . . You've taken a turn. You used to be <u>there</u>; now you're <u>there</u>."

He switched to a former girlfriend who'd been suicidal (beautiful blond jazz singer Beverly Kenney). At the time they lived together she performed in nightclubs till 4:30 a.m. She'd sweep into his apartment in an evening gown, and he'd be waiting or wake up. Living with her was the first time he doubted himself. And then he looked about and two years had passed.

"We're *all* committing suicide," he said. "*Not to work* was a kind of masochism. I became fascinated with it, wondering how long I could go on with it. And you know what? You can go *on and on and on*. I was always expecting something to stop it.

"You can't get away from yourself.

"Let me make a prediction. No"—he forestalled my objection. "It's good. I remember I made one before. He'll get over this spiritual crisis. You know that poem by [Henri] Michaux; he can't stay there [on a ledge]; no one will pay any attention."

He predicted, "It's this self [of Jan's] that's going to die. He'll have to trim his sails. And you know what? You'll both miss that old self." Meanwhile, he said, I was "passing through the temptations of St. Anthony—"*

He stopped suddenly, turned toward me swiftly: "Do I remind you of him? Did I prepare you for him? Is he in some way a fulfillment of what I should have been? He can go on twenty years"—abruptly changing key. "But you can't." His stubby fingers imitated a dagger at his breast.

"You'll be gone, and he'll be there"—his voice rose comically—"'I wish Margaret were here. I'm'"—theatrically—"'just about to—'

"Each of us has many personalities." But—he illustrated with Beverly—in her case they were all "a dimension away from reality. What's Jan's favorite fantasy?" he asked. I didn't know. "It's as impossible," he pointed out, "to have sex with someone like that as to sleep without dreaming. But you finally miss not being loved for yourself.

"Does he commune with you?"—meaning in bed. I said no. Good sex, though. My interest was very piqued by the question.

With this scene returned to "the little novel," the dialogue continues between Daniel/Milton and Merry Lou/me (Jan is Karel):

---

* After retreating to the Egyptian desert as a hermit St. Anthony experienced nightmarish trials. As *Time* magazine put it in Art: "Temptations of St. Anthony," in 1946, "Often he would glance up from his prayers [in the Arabian desert] to see Satan hovering before him in the gloom of his abandoned fort. And Satan was hard to recognize; usually he looked like the things Anthony missed most." Nevertheless, Anthony triumphed. From Italian fresco painters in the tenth century to Hieronymus Bosch to Dali and Cézanne, artists have delighted in depicting these scenes. *Time* went on: "If you take scholar Joseph Campbell's advice to view the cultures of the world with an 'unprejudiced eye,' you will see that all cultures reveal the same truths about the human experience. Christ's ascension provides the same spiritual symbolism as the Buddha's Enlightenment, St. Anthony's test was Siddhartha's test, and so on."

Merry Lou thought she knew the answer about Karel's favorite fantasy: "—that everything's awful and then we're fine and he loves me—"

"Lost and Found!" Daniel whooped. "That's a great one.

He went on: "But not to be too Freudian, Karel has been being your father. And you," he added, "are being your mother for him, and even more, the little girl's so little she can't even speak yet"—in the foreign language. He laughed.

"You're having," he said, "a love affair." He added, "You went toward him like into a harbor. Because you thought you'd found the outside equivalent of your own inner chaos. That now you could rest."

"How did you know?"

"I was with you then."

"Then I can't give him what he needs, can I?"

"You haven't helped him. Or hurt him. You've been a love for him. And a wife."

"Do you know many marriages that work?"

"No," he asserted emphatically. Then: "Yours. It's alive."

At the subway he left her. "I'll blink my eyes," she said, "and be in North Carolina."

"You know how time goes," he said.

"No! I don't know how time goes!"

"You'll blink your eyes and you'll be in North Carolina . . . and Belgium. And Paris. And New York. And let me tell you something. What you can always count on, given certain limits, such as that I don't get run over by a car, is my receptiveness."

He paused. Then: "But I expect some kind of reciprocity after all this time."

Milton and Beverly had broken up because "She had a fantasy, a nightclub owner in the Midwest. She went off again [on tour] and the affair became real," Milton explained. "I was turned on but in a bizarre way. The love affair was being invaded by life . . . and death at the same time."[40]

When I asked why several of his sui-generis friends killed themselves and he was never tempted, he replied, "I've got an amoeboid soul, my dear. I can absorb anything."

After a few seconds: "And I'm the perennial me."

My temptations of St. Anthony, he termed Dante-esque: "You know in Dante, the punishments were always *in excess of* the crime." Not only did you get what you wanted; "you got it forever."[41]

Years earlier while composing poetry, Milton had me write down lines. On half the sheet of paper he himself had written the following poem. He associated some of the stanzas—perhaps all of them—with Beverly:

A this-way, that-way frisky
and elusive little wind or whim or
will that wills itself,
visible or invisible, which
way it will, out of nothing but
air, out of nowhere arose one
clear November afternoon about
years ago and whirled diagonally
across the Square, crossed
back then paused, holding its breath,
lay low, feinted, lay
low again, stirred and
then twisted and hissed
around and around like an
S in the leaves, staining itself
with dust, and "Look!" it
appeared, whorl-shaped,
for the first time visible, and
blew into our eyes....

That less than nothingness,
without breath, without will
Phantom and symbol of
you, emerged and submerged,
stained with your memory:
how

— 12 —

Hunter Breaks Silence

Fear and Loathing: On the Campaign Trail '72 was out, adding to Hunter's fan base. In the *New York Times*, July 15, Tom Seligson praised its factual immediacy. He concluded that Thompson "lets us understand why the men we elect to the Presidency may have needle tracks on their integrity."[42]

At my parents' I cultivated the newsstand.

On August 2, *Rolling Stone* published "Memo from the Sports Desk & Rude Notes from a Decompression Chamber in Miami."

According to the "Editors' Note," Hunter's Scuba tanks mysteriously ran out of air in a dive off the coast of Mexico after an accidental brush with Henry Kissinger. He was for nearly three weeks unconscious in a decompression chamber in Miami. Waking, he watched the Watergate hearings on a TV brought into his confinement, communicating by notes, as he was unable to speak. With help from his alter ego Raoul Duke, he finished the article.

Denying that the break-in was business as usual in Washington, he affirmed that "they were all mean, hollow little bastards who couldn't dare turn their backs on each other." What nearly happened "was a takeover and total perversion of the American political process by a gang of cold-blooded fixers so incompetent that they couldn't even pull off a simple burglary."[43]

Never one to mince words, he wrote me one month later, September 5, 1973, in Greenville—the first time in two years. On *Rolling Stone* stationary ("Dr. Hunter S. Thompson: National Correspondent" at the top) in red ink.

> —OK, here's a note to confirm that you made contact—poked through the wall of smoke I've built between me & the world.
>
> —Send me a phone no. & I'll call some night. Things are very unsettled here—people's lives falling apart all around me. I'm beginning to feel guilty for surviving.
>
> —The reason I didn't answer your last letter has to do with the demented style & tone, as well as the lack of a return address.

Pure Hunter. I winced. But I was acutely aware he communicated only if he felt like it.

He went on: "And I couldn't take that gibberish about your husband 'deciding to die' very seriously either. Marrying a dope freak is risky business, at best. Sandy [his wife] can testify to that—but for the moment, at least, I seem to be coping with the world on a day-to-day basis."

I had never considered Jan a "dope freak." True, he smoked kif or hash daily in Morocco. In his odd case, it seemed like a coat or belt, a part of his technique to get under his own skin. Something his psychology latched onto as a creative tool. And there was no way to take it away, I felt. At least, in those days.

> Tomorrow, as always, is blank—except for a phone call today, indicating that I'm about to be subponaed (sp?) by the [Sam] Ervin Committee [which investigated the culpability of the President and his staff in the Watergate break-in of the Democratic National Committee headquarters (and cover up by the Nixon Administration)].
>
> But what the hell? Why not? Get <u>into</u> the story, right? OK / H

"Fear and Loathing at the Watergate: Mr. Nixon Has Cashed His Check" would come out at the end of the month (Hunter said

Watergate "has even now burned a hole into every American history textbook written from 1973 till infinity").

Without comment, he enclosed an August 27 letter from *Rolling Stone* publisher Jann Wenner to British Independent TV News correspondent Reginald Bosanquet, seeking full accreditation for Hunter and Ralph at Princess Anne's wedding to Mark Phillips.

This promising turn was counteracted immediately. In the same mailbag was a warm, genuine, touching note—from his wife! In it she revealed that "I feel over the years I know you." And "I'd like to be your friend." This was moving, but how could I correspond with both? Yet I felt honor bound to reply just once. I imagined the letter sliding into Hunter's box, his eyes popping.

That was the last letter from Owl Farm for years.

— 13 —

The Horizon

Though not meant that way, Sandy's note was a mortal blow. There was a part of me that hadn't asked for much—just one month a year of my time to be absolutely alone and write. And during that time take up contact again with Milton, perhaps with Hunter. Two guiding stars that were beacons in my constant firmament, who never left, however faraway they were. Now Hunter was gone. Not even the possibility of corresponding. He was off my map. There was a yawning hole there. The refuge demolished. What a deathblow to this side of me. Not romantically speaking, but in reaffirming who I was, who I *really* was. What I had done and could do, a little notch in time that moved forward "written in stone." Not that anyone knew. But that a thing had happened, had materialized, been experienced, and been kept alive and positive. I needed it. Now it was gone. It might not seem like a huge deal, but it felt that way. And it was. Bigger than I knew.

— 14 —

The Flea Essay: Chaos before Chaos-

Confused that Jan had insisted he had the right to die and that it was a test of my loyalty to let him (though I phoned his uncle anyway), I was glad to get Hunter's advice that Jan's view was warped.* Though to receive any word from Hunter was an intimacy, I felt roundly rebuffed on that score, and deservedly. I could lose all my friends by parroting back Jan's views, which normally I didn't. But Jan himself didn't disagree, once back in Belgium.

I could not imagine myself becoming an underachiever. It could not happen to me, I mused. I was alert to the warning signs deep in my core. Hadn't I looked at the signals as a mere child?

At seven, almost home from school—as I stood beside the woods next door, holding a booklet of poetry I'd written—suddenly I'd felt another mind inside mine. That mind knew it was a writer—a great one in fact, I heard it think. It could not fathom how it had done almost nothing at that late age. Mozart, it reminded itself, had composed at five. It vowed to catch up. That vow had been my drive throughout this lifetime, though it appeared inside a child who felt overtaken by another mind.

So I mused in the fabric of my being, not overly alarmed. But alarmed instance after instance with Jan, as if facing a grating dilemma. Not enough, however, to affect my hope to reconcile. This

* Ironically, Hunter argued at the end of his own life the same thing Jan had in Ceuta, though not for the same reasons. It's interesting, though, to see how he reacted when younger.

period, when practically assured of not returning to him, I found myself horny, my concentration weakened.

Letters from Andrew Lyndon III (back in Macon, Georgia) encouraged my application to MacDowell Colony.

By grace in November, I again went to that wintry wonderland in New Hampshire. En route, I made a stopover—where else?

I entered Milton's fifth-floor walk-up at a momentous moment.

When he opened the door, his look was almost disoriented. It was as if he'd just exited a Qumran cave after hiding the Dead Sea scrolls thousands of years ago. Or he were a Bedouin shepherd who, hunting for a lost sheep in 1947, stumbled upon jars in which some scrolls were hidden.

What had his face misted over? A manuscript he was working on: "Art & Life: A Menippean Paean to the Flea; or, Did Dostoevsky Kill Trotsky?"*

This Flea Essay plunged into the complex phenomenon of nonlinearity. Tracing the disconnected appearances of the flea through centuries, it implied an invisible order. Following a hidden trail, he pulled aside the underthicket to emerge with what appears to me to be an early encounter with the then-not-widely-known theory of chaos.

As Edward Lorenz in December '72 asked in a meteorological presentation (unpublished till decades later) if the flap of a butterfly's wing in Brazil might instigate a tornado in Texas, Milton was to ask—practically simultaneously—if a Dostoevsky plot *in Russia* was the prototype for the *murder of Leon Trotsky in Mexico.* If so, how? That is, assuming the process was unconscious.

---

* The title combines the idea of Menippean satire (a comical treatment of philosophical subjects as in some Shakespeare and *Alice's Adventures in Wonderland*) with paen: a joyous, fervent, gleeful song or hymn.

Was the book a pollinator? This was deep. Trails, tracks, coincidence had him in hot pursuit.

The essay opens with "the spectral presence of Robert Hooke, Curator of Experiments for the Royal Society, on that April day in 1663 (to begin this roundabout trip at the beginning)" getting the first close-up look at the flea. Hooke is "about to peer into what, at one time, might have been taken for a magic speculum but was, in fact, his own newly devised compound microscope."[44]

From here Klonsky skirts past such incidents as the insect's nonfatal appearance in Sir Isaac Newton's personal life—not biting him, which would have changed the course of science—and plunges toward the present.

Under Donne's banner that whoever would find the craggy hill atop which truth stands "about must, and about must goe," Klonsky hurdles forward to see poet William Blake as—among other things—perhaps anticipating the Heisenberg's Uncertainty Principle that underlies quantum theory: "'And Accident & Chance were found hidden in Length, Bredth & Highth.'" Or, he adds, "'For the Eye altering alters all.'"

Klonsky noted that Heisenberg said he got the idea of Uncertainty in talking with Einstein, who said casually that the theory determines what we can observe, which led Klonsky back to Blake: "'What is now proved was once only imagined.'"[45]

Finally, as for his own "participation mystique"—to penetrate reality—Klonsky rubs his hands together and gets to the heart of the plot: he recounts how, while reporting on *CLASSICS Illustrated*, he stared at a comic book *Crime and Punishment,* at which moment multitudes of coincidences bull's-eyed. Here, he realized, was the format of Trotsky's murder!

In Mexico, Spanish-born NKVD agent Jaime Ramón Mercader, a.k.a. Frank Jacson, seemed to have plucked the Trotsky murder plot out of thoughts in the air, wafting from the fictional killing by Dostoevsky's Raskolnikov. Besides a similar use of a dress rehearsal and a diversion, or pretext, to gain entry, the murderer hid the weapon—in both instances, an axe—in his coat pocket or kept his hand on it inside that pocket.

Klonsky's roving treatment of the relationship between art and life came to rest in the enigmatic question whether

MAN like a Flea shall
*jump from star to.** [46]

The essay pointed to an unformalized illustration of *interconnectedness,* a word he didn't use.

Lorenz's title ("Predictability: Does the Flap of a Butterfly's Wing in Brazil Set Off a Tornado in Texas?") closely parallels Milton's title, "Art & Life: A Menippean Paean to the Flea; or, Did Dostoevsky Kill Trotsky?" Yet in 1974, Lorenz's was unpublished and neither title creator had laid eyes on the other.

Lorenz focused on minute weather turbulence and calculations that, *if carried to different decimal points*, produce different events. Milton's initial condition was the flea's first observation, under Robert Hooke's microscope. How could—or did?—that, in some chaotic way, have to do with Newton's escaping the plague (carried by fleas) to research laws of motion for the *Principia*? he implied.

Newton ended dissatisfied; he had no mediator of gravity other than instantaneous "action at a distance" (which he rejected, but there it was).

Milton's jet-propulsion-speed discovery of unknown concomitants in "Art and Life"—its starburst—would stay with me. What was he saying—really???

I don't remember what we said at this meeting, so I can't reconstruct the conversation. One thing I remember he said, about my prospects with Jan: "You know, Aristotle didn't have that confusion about plot being something you can retrace your steps in. I think it goes back to the word *plot* being English. To Aristotle, *plot* meant beginning, middle, and end. But not reversible."

— 15 —

MacDowell, Belgium, Vietnam

Soon the hugely intense Tillie Olsen, known for "a slim output of raw, powerful works,"[47] arrived at MacDowell from MIT to work on *Yonnondio: From the Thirties* in Mansfield Studio. I was in the nearest studio to hers. Winters were cold, with just a few cabins winterized. So there were maybe only a dozen Colonists there. Tillie had put the novel aside for forty years.

Scott Turow notes how in 1971 as Tillie searched through old papers, the manuscript resurfaced: "typed and handwritten on greenish sheets, the paper so brittle with age that the edges flaked cleanly like chips of paint."[48] Eventually, it would be published, unfinished.

Silences—a nonfiction work based on the transcript of a Radcliffe talk—would come out in 1978. In it, Tillie describes unnatural gaps in authors' productivity, such as when—after the scandalized reception of his novel *Jude the Obscure*—Thomas Hardy quit writing novels. Tillie begins: "Literary history and the present are dark with silences; some the silences for years by our acknowledged great; some silences hidden; some the ceasing to publish after one work appears; some the never coming to book form at all."[49]

In our MacDowell cabins we enjoyed what Melville called the "silent, grass-growing mood in which a man ought to compose." Additionally, we had private quarters in another building, to sleep in (if not in our studio) and bathe.

Finding Kafka's *Diaries* outside my bedroom door (put there by Tillie), I avidly copied his lament: "Distractedness, weak memory, stupidity. Days passed in futility, powers wasted away in waiting. . . . Always this one principal anguish: If I had gone away in 1912 in full possession of all my powers, with a clear head. Not eaten by the strain of keeping down living forces!"[50]

However, even had he resigned his job, Kafka couldn't have lived just from writing, "if only, to begin with, because of *the slow maturing of my work* and its special character."[51]

I somehow sensed this as part of my battle—which had popped in as the knowing awareness at seven. I felt I'd escaped the Kafka fate. In fact, the shock of RFK's assassination in '68 had *catapulted me into the reality of sudden death*, sparking me to resign my job at Random House because if one could die at any moment, suddenly, better do what one thought the most important as soon as possible.

Meanwhile, in his very first letter to me at MacDowell—four months since we split up—Jan wrote, "I love you, I'm amputated without you." He said he'd "known it for a long time but refused to admit it." In December he added a condition to my coming back: "that you realize the time for follies is over and that we'll have to lead a regular life with job and Frigidaire and voting. Think it over."

The reader may feel, as I did, how ironic. But this practicality was in spurts a side of Jan, especially now, when he was riding around the countryside with his father, recuperating and getting his health back.

Over Christmas a letter from my mother understandably counseled not to go back to him, noting that I'd done my best and while "perhaps not perfect," I was a human being.

On New Year's day Andrew Lyndon III wrote. Hopping through topics such as the details of Malcolm Lowry's death, he described his renewed contact with former lover Tennessee Williams:

> I told him that as soon as possible I was either going to San Francisco and on to Mexico. Or: just on to Mexico. . . . Anyway, he said those/that were/was/is his plan, too. And why didn't we keep in touch. . . . [F]rom previous experience he'll get in touch when he's ready to. . . .

> How much longer will you be up there? And then?
>
> Doesn't Morocco seem a far and long-time away? . . . I hope the writing is up to your usual marvelous complexity!!

By then Jan's father had had a heart attack and he himself was in observation in a clinic. The gloomy atmosphere cut into the possibility of my returning. In fact, Jan said it ruled it out.

I worked not only on "The Erstwise Paula" but also pulled out my notes from live conversations in Ceuta and letters from Jan and used the most sparkling to create a character, Knut Karel, to go into a new novel I called "the little book," from which I've quoted earlier. And in this way helped heal the rift in my psyche and the relationship, lifting it into a semiautobiographical fictional frame, all the while I felt the relationship wasn't over. I wrote him that we'd been through so much it would be a waste to let all that growth go into another relationship instead of the one that inspired the growth. Nevertheless, in my MacDowell cabin as spring flowers bloomed, I debated the finality of our separation.

Milton had said, "Other men bring out your weakness. I bring out your strength," which, while not true in the case of Hunter, had up till now, it turned out, been true in the case of Jan.

In April, Milton sent me the *American Review* issue with his Flea essay.

Shortly after that arrived in Greenville, my mother called me to the phone. It was Jan asking me back. Neither she nor my father wanted me to go. In fact, my mother said, "He wants to keep you scared to death." But they knew it was my choice.

Jan called me back. He was working irregular shifts in cargo at Zaventem, the Brussels airport. In May he telegrammed he'd booked me a prepaid ticket. I arrived with a melted heart. As odd as it might seem, the fact that he sent the ticket—the first time he paid for my flight, depleting his shoestring salary—told me that he was taking the responsibility seriously, putting me first. I knew he'd carefully weighed the decision, going to and fro on it, and really wanted me there. Right away—I don't know how—he gave me a ring with two pearls.

But he quit work when I got a prized secretarial post at Euroclear in Brussels in September. A part of Morgan Guaranty Trust, it was a clearinghouse for international trades of securities. Among other things, I edited a stocks brochure!

In a bar Jan awaited my return "like a kid waiting for Christmas," he said. Seemingly unfazed by the caffeine, he drank up to seventeen cups of coffee a day. But the experimental medicine he was on that prohibited alcohol made him feel like he was on LSD. Written in Morocco, his *Merovingian Odes* came out.

To the extent he was trying to be "normal"—"no more follies . . . a job and frigidaire and voting"—I thought he was fooling himself.

He'd said—about himself in love—that to understand, "Did you zig and zag? Did you turn at least three corners?"

His love was "zing-zang-boom."

In April 1975, the Vietnam War would end. Hunter—I didn't know—was a *Rolling Stone* correspondent in Saigon when it fell.

In an interview later Hunter told William McKeen, "[Jann] Wenner folded Straight Arrow [the *Rolling Stone* book-publishing arm] at a time when they owed me $75,000. I was enraged to find that out. It had been an advance for *Shark Hunt.* I wrote a seriously vicious letter—finally saying all I was thinking as I was taking off for Saigon."

Wearing a Hawaiian shirt, bermudas, and basketball shoes, he disembarked with $30,000 taped to his body (*Newsweek*'s payroll and evacuation money for bureau chief Loren Jenkins). A sign at the Saigon airport warned that anyone with over $100 must confess or if caught be prosecuted.

In the McKeen interview Hunter went on: "I thought we'd all be executed. It was total curfew when we got off the plane so we were herded into this small room with all these men holding machine guns. There I was, with three hundred times the maximum money allowance. We got out and leapt on a motor scooter and told the kid to run like hell. I told *Newsweek*'s Loren [Jenkins] I wouldn't give him the money until he got me a suite in a hotel. Not an easy task, but he came through."

He also revealed: "While in Saigon, I found I'd been fired when Wenner flew into a rage upon receiving the letter." * Other correspondents received war-risk salaries and insurance! Hunter said, "Here I was in a war zone, and no health insurance."[52]

With a massive Hanoi offensive supposedly under way, it seemed to him "ominously clear," looking at the million-plus refugees fleeing *into* Saigon, "that Hanoi had never really launched any 'massive offensive' at all, but that the flower of the finely U.S. trained and heavily U.S. equipped South Vietnamese Army had simply panicked and run amok."[53]

In the rooftop restaurant of the Palace Hotel, Musak played "bye bye, Miss American Pie" ("singing this'll be the day that I die") while Hunter, picking at his Crab St. Jacques, "stared balefully out across the muddy Saigon River to where the earth was trembling and the rice paddies were exploding in long clean patterns like stitches down the sleeve of a shirt." Of the American journalists' fate, he anticipated, "We will be put in cages for a while, then set free."[54]

Just before Saigon fell, he left for Laos. From Hong Kong on May 1, he read in the *South China Morning News*: "Marines had used their M-16 rifle butts to smash the fingers of desperate South Vietnamese trying to climb over the barb-wire–topped wall into the American Embassy compound in Saigon yesterday, trying to get aboard the Air America helicopters evacuating the last of the journalists, businessmen, U.S. Embassy staffers and other American refugees out to

---

* At a March 2005 memorial in Aspen, Jann Wenner insisted that despite Hunter's contention, the truth was that *Rolling Stone* did not cancel his health insurance (reported by Jeff Kass, rockymountainnews.com)

waiting aircraft carriers, just off the Vietnam coast."[55]

Back in Woody Creek, in August 1975, with a *Rolling Stone* anthology still possibly in the works (published eventually in 1979 by Summit Books as *The Great Shark Hunt: Strange Tales from a Strange Time,* Gonzo Papers 1), Hunter writes Jann Wenner, the *Rolling Stone* and Straight Arrow Books publisher: "I think you know me well enough to know I'm going to brood & bitch over every comma & column breaker all the way to the press." He predicts:

> some poor, unsuspecting woman, unknown to either of us right now, is going to have her hair turn cotton-white on this one . . . and now that I think on it, the only person I know who could naturally handle a nightmare like this is a girl who used to work for Random House who did all the editing on *Hell's Angels*; her name is Margaret Harrell, and Silberman could probably find her if necessary. As a matter of fact, she's the only editor I can think of right now that I could work with on a book like this in total confidence . . . she married a Flemish poet a few years back & went off to Morocco, but her forwarding address is Margaret Harrell c/o Harrell Family, Greenville, North Carolina. . . . I once recommended her to Alan,* but that one went by the boards like all the others.[56]

If a letter was sent to me by Jann Wenner, it didn't arrive.

Meanwhile, in New York, Milton Klonsky continued to enjoy his cult reputation. A 2012 remark on the web states, "I mourn the day 'hipster' stopped having its Milton Klonsky/Norman Mailer-era connotations."[57]

Milton's anthology *Speaking Pictures: A Gallery of Pictorial Poetry from the Sixteenth Century to the Present* was published by Harmony Books. In the Introduction, he explained that he'd compiled examples of an obscure five-hundred-year-old tradition "that, from the start,

* Rinzler, VP/Associate Publisher of *Rolling Stone* and president of its book division

has been cast inevitably under the spell of Hermes." He was talking about "the genre of the picture-poem and/or poem-picture," which had originated in Renaissance Italy mainly as "a misconception of Egyptian hieroglyphs."[58] I received an e-mail in 2012 from avant-garde artist/author Richard Kostelaneetz, suggesting that someone write up Milton's "extraordinary contributions to the understanding of visual literature."

Milton had struck gold with his publisher, Bruce Harris—the founder of Harmony Books, a division of Crown. Harris was soon to release such classics as Ram Dass's *Be Here Now.* He recently reminisced in an e-mail: "[Milton] seemed my image of the West Village intellectual, supporting himself by his wits and nourishing himself on the exciting life of the mind. He seemed much older than me (though I guess it was no more than fifteen years but that was a lifetime then). I remember him speaking to me at long liquid mideastern lunches about Auden. I had dropped out of the NYU English MA program and lunching with Milton was like going back to school."

This relationship was to lead, next, to *William Blake: The Seer and His Visions.*

"We both loved Blake," Harris went on reminiscing. "And it was pretty easy for him to convince me to do a Blake book."

In packed days, I worked at Euro-clear and housekept our Leuven apartment (a floor of the building)—half an hour by train from Brussels. Jan's antiques—grand piano included—covered hardwoods frolicked over by our German Shepherd. We saw Bergman's *The Magic Flute* eight times.

The relationship was hurly-burly: "I bet you can't wait to come home tomorrow. It'll be either cutting my throat or poetry."

Christmas '75, I received an autographed copy of *Speaking Pictures.* By then or soon afterwards since my return, Jan had attempted suicide twice: once it was up an elevator trap; the second time in a woods. He took pills and was found twenty-four hours later but survived.

— 16 —

Milton: Vampire and the Blood Donnee

On my next yearly visit—when I popped into his apartment unannounced in 1976, after not seeing him since November 1974—Milton peered at me at the door as I stood there in a short head kerchief I'd taken to wearing in Morocco. He called me "a little wraith almost" and invited me in. Milton, like always, tried to make sense of the situation. As he had a date this particular evening, he phoned his girlfriend—a beautiful young woman whose best friend, a Brit, had by a fluke gotten eye cancer from her dog—to invite me to her party. Both women were there—about to fly to London for the Brit to have the eye removed.

Seeing Milton sitting alone at the party, I went over and we continued talking. Covering all the bases of what it was like to live with a self-destructive person, however *sui generis*, he said, "He's the vampire and you're the blood donee." He recommended, "Get out before the horror comes."

"How?"

"By an act of cruelty. And if after all you've done to me I can forgive you, I think you can forgive yourself.

"She thinks I'm normal"—he turned momentarily to the woman he was currently seeing. He laughed. "I'm giving her advice on how to be normal."

Then back to me: "Get out of the childhood stage. Don't expect life to push you out of childhood. It will anyway."

Milton said about that sort of self-destructiveness there's nothing you can do. He illustrated with an example from jazz singer Beverly Kenney, his former girlfriend. Once post-breakup she phoned, having taken the deadly Seconal, and he arrived too late.*

He added, "I think we all 'enact' our lives"—as if speaking from a prewritten screen play. The words rolled spontaneously, emotionally off his Mediterranean-looking lips.

"What happened to you?"—suddenly. "I think ever since I've known you you've had him out there as someone you could drown yourself in . . .

"Either"—he counseled, no one in hearing distance but me—"exalt him or leave."

Penetrating: "Give him something to rise to. Don't sink with him. *Or* sink with him and then kill yourself.

"*But don't be a bystander while this man commits suicide.*"

He went on: "If he's looking for profundity, tell him to look somewhere else. . . . Death comes. Life is something we're all *sentenced to.*"

He walked me home, to return to the party immediately. He said sometimes it added spice for a girlfriend to feel a tinge of jealousy. So

---

* Famous with jazz buffs in Japan, where her music is regularly reissued, Beverly opens journalist Bill Reed's book *A Fine Romance: My Lifelong Affair with Jazz Singing and Singers*. In it he mentions "a dazzling, legendary fifties Greenwich Village professional intellectual, Milton Klonsky. A kind of Beat Generation guru" (12). In the mid-1950s, *DownBeat,* echoed by other music/showbiz publications, praised Kenney as "a new voice of unmistakable jazz quality," predicting that voice would take "its place beside those of Sarah Vaughan, Billie Holiday, and Ella Fitzgerald" (11). Decades after she toured with the Dorsey Brothers and Decca released *Beverly Kenney Sings for Johnny Smith,* fifty years after her suicide in 1960 at twenty-eight, her remastered CDs sell on Amazon.com. She can be watched live with Hugh Hefner—Ellis Larkins on piano and celeste, and Joe Benjamin on bass—at http://people-vs-drchilledair.blogspot.com/2012/02/beverly-kenney-on-hugh-hefner-playboy.html. A handbill for Jack Kerouac's only nightclub performance places him—during the Christmas holidays 1957—at the Village Vanguard, along with the great trombonist J. J. Johnson (with his Quartet), jazz singer Beverly Kenney, and the Ellis Larkins duo.

he had no qualms walking out with me; he expected a robust reception when he got back.

I left with these words ringing in my ears: "*The world expects certain things of poets: that they . . . decorate the world, that they commit suicide . . . BUT— POETS EXPECT OTHER THINGS OF POETS.*"[59]

— 17 —

India to Essaouira

In September 1976 my parents offered to finance Jan and my studies for a teachers' education degree in my hometown university, East Carolina. In January we shipped our antiques, acquired in a period when Jan was an antique dealer before we married, and traveled to North Carolina from Leuven, Belgium, via a detour to India—in my case partly to postpone the move. I was habituated to large or exotic locations.

Before his first test, Jan was hospitalized because (being a European, not used to quizzes, in fact, fearing them) he put himself in peril—and put off taking the test—by becoming dehydrated. In the infirmary they saw the scars. Did not think: hero! He told me half jokingly he would commit suicide by boring a screwdriver into his head.

Based on Jan's growing list of wonderful reviews, which he carefully translated (my mother drove him to Chapel Hill for interviews), he transferred to UNC for a PhD in French in the fall. This was more his level. That he would study French in the United States—his father's mother tongue was French—might seem far-fetched. But his supervising professor, the distinguished Edouard Morot-Sir, hailed from France.

At UNC, Jan knew how to write original ideas only—not footnote. But in November he took what (as I looked at the bottle) appeared to be an aspirin overdose. I persuaded him to have his stomach pumped—to be bright for a test.

The hospital official assured me they would not keep him against his will: "This is America," he said. It was a trick.

In fact, they locked him up in the psych ward overnight for "his own protection" to be sure he didn't commit suicide. Afterwards, heavily medicated, Jan, in his absurdly unrealistic approach to such things, signed the admissions paper they put in front of him and then we had no idea how to get him out.

When I was present at a psych-evaluation, he refused stone-faced to answer questions. A very hostile interviewee, he indifferently did a crossword, encouraging me to follow suit. I had not mastered the art of remaining aloof, warding off privacy invasion. Jan later likened his forced incarceration, with mandatory drugging (as they expected alcohol withdrawal), to Russia's detention of artists and scientists. In his case, having admitted him as a possible "danger to himself" (because of the unknown number of Aspirin and history of suicide), possibly with an idea of avoiding a lawsuit. Suicide had been a common-law crime in North Carolina and was only recently removed from the criminal books.

The drugging created disorientation to the point where I saw him start to put spaghetti onto the upside-down plate in front of him. He even had a brief catatonic episode—sat in a pose, unmoving for some time, disconnected from reality, as if he had ever been connected to it in normal terms.

Several days passed before I learned the release procedures—which could have gotten him out earlier.

It was an understatement to say my attempt to get him in good condition for the test backfired.

Further, his wounds were deep. Very far behind in his courses, in North Carolina on a student visa, he left—the plan was—to wait in Morocco for three months while I filed the petition for his work visa (best done by me from the States), then return here and get a job. I stayed on in my apartment, finishing the semester. He went to Belgium, filed visa papers at the U.S. Embassy, and was off to Essaouira.

However, before leaving North Carolina, he took down two of his best paintings, shipped from Belgium, and slit them. One, *The Dying Bull*, was giant lavender-and-gray blocks of a deconstructed Picasso-esque bull. What in him was devalued, ruined?

Further, he never spoke about the incident. Didn't twirl it into one of his adventure tales about which we laughed till the tears ran rivers. It recalled that infancy trauma *I did not yet know about*, in which he'd had burning cigarettes put to his mouth when he cried.

The hospital next threatened that if I didn't pay, they would confiscate the European antiques we'd shipped; I refused adamantly (having resisted his being kept overnight and stressed that our insurance did not cover that service). They backed down.

No sooner was Jan gone than my father was diagnosed with cancer and operated on immediately without a good prognosis. I stayed in my apartment in Carrboro, North Carolina, just outside Chapel Hill. Going to the hospital and keeping in touch closely.

Jan had left in November. In Essaouira he lived initially with Moulay's friends "at what is called a Moroccan hotel, floors of cells around a central courtyard; the cells are about 6x6 feet, contain 2 tiny beds along the walls, a little table in the middle and 3 nails. Finding M. here has saved me from one worry. I've never been out in the street starving when he was around . . . It's the same old thing: cards for food & other expenditures, wine, kif, tagines." By the end of the letter, he had moved into the Hotel Central.

Also in November, *William Blake: The Seer and His Visions*, by Milton, arrived in my mail. In the Introduction, "W. B.[4]: or, The Seer Seen by His Own Vision," was his account of an event he'd described to me ten years earlier. He'd returned from Fire Island beach, near Manhattan. At Fire Island he'd tripped on LSD for the first and only time. Among the dunes he alternated between hot and cold. He felt himself "twisting and turning, as if on a spit," and, as Blake put it, "melting apparent surfaces away." He fled to the cold ocean, then sprawled on the beach and began reciting: "To see the world in a grain of sand." Wait. Something was terribly wrong. He tried again: "a world." To see *a* world.[60] He wrote:

> The "blue Mundane Shell" (as Blake imagined it) of the sky—a "hard coating of matter that separates us from Eter-

> nity"—cracked open for me at that moment, and I perceived the sun with acid clarity as *a* star, one of billions, so many that the grains of sand I then held in my palm would comprise only a handful; and in that split second the shell of my own time-hardened and encrusted ego, of which the material universe, as Blake thought, was merely the sensual reflection, also cracked, and something within me but not quite me—the Ka, or Atman, or Pneuma, or whatever—that had been brooding coiled up in itself, stirred awake.

Enrolled at UNC for a PhD I didn't want, I nevertheless had fascinating courses: Latin, Middle English, Romantic poets.

Invited by Milton to New York with a freelance job offer, I went. Despite his sparse income, he paid the $100 ticket.

Sitting me down, he showed me the illustrations for his next book, *Blake's Dante: The Complete Illustrations to the Divine Comedy.* He asked to hire me to write a detailed description—for publication—under each watercolor, sketch, or engraving. I said yes, dumbfounded. Such a task required prodigious intelligence. *Did he really think I could do it?*

In fact, I had no idea how to match the artwork to the passages. One had to call up at will much of Dante! How would I have identified, for instance, *Beatrice and Dante in Gemini amid the Spheres of Flame* (*Paradiso* XXIV: 1–18), then within that identified Revelation 19:19—in pre-Google, pre-Search Inside days? Milton was indeed in sacred *terra.*

His Introduction opened: "During his last years, from 1821 to midsummer of 1827, Blake lived in near poverty and obscurity with his wife Catherine at 3 Fountain Court, Strand, a house kept by her brother in-law, where they rented two small and sparsely furnished rooms on the first floor. . . . but of course, the real Blake, the visionary Blake, lived elsewhere, in what he referred to as the 'Divine Imagination,' and that was expansive enough for him to contain even Dante's Heaven and Hell."[61]

Taking me uptown to Harmony Books, Milton laughingly revealed that they considered him the "resident genius" there. Introducing me to his publisher, Bruce Harris,* he said, "Get used to her, you'll be seeing a lot of her." To me, he suggested that I get paid a hefty $1,000.

But it did not go well. We sat on cushions around his low table. There was the usual dinner—the rare steak he prepared (I was not yet a vegetarian), brushed with garlic. He made a move, running his hand up my leg. I rebuffed him. We had a fight. He became angry, not violent, but explained that he was between relationships himself and thought I was over my husband and we could finally get together. Wishful thinking.

I stayed on the little sofa that night. However, cool to the end, he said before retiring into his bedroom, "When we wake up, let's be as civilized as possible."

Unfailingly, my fictional Milton, Robert, got new lines. I don't remember which, but a sample might be "'I think I live in floating time,' he said, when she rang the bell, climbing the steps, as familiar as ever, the air the same, the ambiance, the feeling between them. 'I think I live in floating time.'"[62]

Getting a nonstudent visa, even when married to a U.S. citizen, was proving a nightmare. I began to wonder whether—with the black mark of mental institutionalization (however short)—Jan had lost all chance to return here to work. This was not to mention the Belgian arm of his psychiatric history.

By January he'd begun a play, though having no typewriter. Eaten a sweetbreads tagine made by Moulay. Was "perfectly happy but could be happier still" with me there. ("It is me love you too much.") Would like to return to the States. "Not really, I guess—while I wrote

---

* Later president of sales and marketing, Random House; publisher, COO, Workman Publishing

that down (my liking to come) the nerves around my stomach went pinch, pinch."

In April, the Atlanta Field Office of the U.S. Citizenship and Immigration Services said his visa went through; he could collect it in Belgium. But by then he'd started *Cap d'Antibes*; he couldn't possibly leave ("Oh, I do get lyrical when I talk about that book! It's going to be my best one by far").

He'd found a stray puppy, "barely two weeks old and as thin as a nail," in the middle of the street. He was boiling water to give her a bath. "She's got a big head and bulging eyes but that's from undernourishment. . . . Like a Biafra baby, with crooked legs. That's because she's so thin. She'll be a beauty someday."

Pent-up poetry was churning out. He would eventually realize that the morbid nature of *Cap d'Antibes* reflected his belated understanding that his brother's recent death was a suicide. This letter concludes with four poems. And "a really short one. Hark." I liked the almost tongue-twister compactness of the sounds when read aloud:

Als een kaars [later "ster"], *puur en koud*
in de nacht, zwart en rood
van de bommen die branden in Dresden

Like a candle [later "star"], pure and cold
in the night, black and red
of the bombs that are burning in Dresden

Then a final poem: "After this death became like a friend: after the despair of wishes. After this death came to live within me: after the mists of being. I've received her: no bride better than that. I've loved her: no heart was so wide or a sea so wild. There are little boats sinking on the sea when she's like that. When she's like that gulls are screaming everywhere. Then it's winter around Cap d'Antibes. When she's like that she is like me. No heart so wide that could do everything: it was my heart then. . . ."

He was using many formats: chamber poems, a Xmas carol, a lullaby. "Oh yes. The Ch. Poems (almost Ch. Pots) . . . The C. P.'s are or should be 4 long poems but each in a different form." And one that's "composed of an elegy, a shanty, a Xmas carol and a lullaby and tells some kind of story, which is a detail. . . . It's amazing how those things write themselves."

He would "end that Rilke poem (starker Stern) . . . you that sinking down the solar line / overtake such infinite arising / by the purity of your decline."

— 18 —

Death of My Father

I stayed in North Carolina longer. My beloved father was bedridden, dying of cancer. I moved into my parents' home. During the surgery, he'd lost his sense of direction. Watching him fight the disease—his mind wandering, weakened in the operation—I saw him come toward me after a daily walk, using his cane. But as he reached me, suddenly his wit was back and would stay so. It was *himself again that spoke.* Fully present.

I flew briefly to Morocco, only to immediately get a telegram to return—as I'd requested—"if you ever want to see your father alive again." What scrambling, a turmoil inside, begging for an emergency plane seat.

July 1978: my father, J. Henry Harrell, was leaving Earth. I am exceptionally glad I was there those last weeks, including even holding the pan to his mouth for the death rattle.

That last night, he had missed his pain medicine. After he got to the hospital my mother realized that to take it would make him unconscious for good. Unspokenly, he wanted to wait. He prolonged the delay till everyone was there; that included my eight-months-pregnant youngest sister, who was driven two hours. He was still alert when she entered and said, "Hello, Pops." I heard him answer, "Hello, Sweetheart." With everyone there, my mother offered the pain potion.

He looked around the room one by one; his eyes rested on each, eye to eye, *in* the eye. He circled the room. Then he started again, eye to eye, all round the circle. He was giving us his love, his blessing, his hopes, his memory, everything he could offer now and forever. Then she administered the medicine. He went under the painkiller. I asked if he could hear us from the coma to squeeze our hand. With the left he squeezed back, listening, unable to speak, knowing he was dying, knowing he was leaving.

Then there was the funeral and at last I had my aunt feel the lump in my left breast. I'd detected it a week before but said nothing. I was rushed to the hospital, after which my mother almost collapsed.

Had the lump been found malignant in the operation, they'd have removed my breast without waking me.

From my account of my father's death—written a few days afterwards—I drew lessons: "He was always a man of strong will. He willed himself not to die with himself but to go, instead, into his example."

Arriving at the hospital, he had to relearn to breathe, and he began saying aloud to himself as he breathed in, out, "That's right," as if, it seemed to me, it were his soul there in person talking to the dying body. As if some wise counselor were his only presence. And the next time he breathed, he said "O. K." And the next, "Mm-hmmm," the sound rising, intoned, going up; it worked. Afterwards, I saw an ethereal, not death-pallid look.

He appointed my mother executrix.

I drew other lessons: "Sunday. A wax figure at the funeral home, perfectly resembling him except for the tight mouth. And yet the only feeling of his presence was in the freckles on his forehead, a stray wisp of hair, a bump on his nose, and one hand that bent and felt alive.

"Maybe he stayed in the hand just for us to feel."

At the graveyard everybody else left when digging started, but I stayed till the last shovelful.

On a legal pad inside his black notebook, which I confiscated, I copied from Jung's *Psychology and Religion:* "Although our mind cannot grasp its own form of existence, owing to the lack of the

Archimedean point outside, it nevertheless exists. Psyche is existent, it is even existence itself."

Shortly after the funeral, one final time, I saw the parapsychology pioneer J. B. Rhine—whom I'd formed a bond with through interviewing him while at Duke University. He was recuperating at home. His staff was flabbergasted that he okayed my visit. After a marvelous reunion he startled me with the ringing counsel: "Don't be driftwood. YOU ARE A WINNER. BE ONE."

— 19 —

Jan, Hunter, Milton

I finally returned to Morocco in early August, and as clearly indicated in my "little book"—refreshing my memory—Jan was ambivalent. Why? In particular, after my father's burial July 9, I had exploratory surgery on suspicion of breast cancer—a false alarm—then stayed on briefly to help my mother settle in and to recover myself. All told, excepting my one enjoyable but curtailed trip back, he'd been alone November–August. I'd forgotten this. In fictionalizing our reunion in "the little book," I wrote:

> How he loved her— He remembered it so clearly. He went to the Casablanca airport, flung out his hand as if waving a hat or handkerchief, and then (how will I be able to keep my hands off her? he'd been thinking), his lips stiffened.
>
> (Sat in his unearth arithmetic, knowing that the longer she stayed away: one^2 . . . three^9 . . .)

I wrote and rewrote the scene, putting the stuck moment into fantasy contexts. But it wouldn't budge. Under that blight, I finished the book about Jan and me, intending to show it to Milton my next trip. I finished it in a dreary, hopeless fashion. It was a novel, though, except that a lot of the conversation was exact. But after this point it became wild fantasy, which, I now think, was pushing away the growing reality of a big problem.

I gave up on the attempts to take down Jan's words and ended with the pair by letting them disappear into the air, unfinished, "dead and buried." But as to the facts, we were still married, and things were, in a sense, going to look up.

More from my novelistic rendition of the story that now seemed irresolvable. I was predicting a future that would not turn out nicely. The story was not over, but this did not bode well:

> He had always known she was too good to be true.
> She had always known he was too bad to be true.

#

So they went to live in the little house with the perfect circumstances, with bird calls for cock crows, with sea air, with an African sky with everything their hearts could want. Lived there, side by side, a perfect pair, a pair at last: Dead and Buried.

And then time raped him (let's keep him for observation, here in this institution). It killed her father. And then for the first time, time decided to tell what it had meant.

#

> Why were they together?
> God only knows, she thought.
> God only knew, he said.

#

"Do you think—" Daniel had said once when she came dripping wet into his apartment, uttered it in a stentorian tone. "*Which* do you think"—hand up in a theatrical gesture—"is stronger?" He looked at her wet head and drooping body. "Spirit or matter?" It was 9:30 p.m. She'd phoned hours ago. Said she'd be right over. He said he'd make dinner. She lingered to talk at another male friend's in New York City, then took the subway. The rain poured down. Dinner was endangered. Daniel, like commanding the elements not to spoil their one evening together, used the full force of his powerful voice to draw her out. Which was stronger in her world? He didn't have to say which was stronger in his. Was a downpour, her hair plastered on her cheeks, going to dampen her mood? Her late arrival going to make him testy? He controlled his irateness, his disappointment. Didn't scold her for dallying en route after phoning that she'd be right over. Spirit could do this. Matter often couldn't. Which was stronger? His emphatic words left no room for question.

The matter gravitated the parts together. Persisted.

Karel and Merry Lou wasted time, turned a deaf ear.

#

Some things take time— No one believed it.

Days passed. Karel was sure tomorrow they'd wake up and find a new day.

They *would* get together.

But?

It would take forever.

#

When their story died, there were no daffodils put on its tomb. No one followed it to the grave. No one even watched the casket lowered. No one heard the gravediggers making jokes. No one cried.

No?

Life did all of that. The very ground was soft there, crumbled. No need of a spade. The leaves shook on their branches and fell to cover the spot.

Generosity, Karel once said, is spontaneous.

There was no arena the slave was put in. He had to fight no lion. He had no life of his own, which life prepared him for by giving him no will of his own and by making him impetuous. She wasn't spontaneous. She would have held on forever in imagination. But no matter, he was generous. So one day he opened his mouth, and—

The story deliberated. But Knut Karel and Merry Lou were pulled further. No escape now. Into "you know the story."

#

Once there were two children born in a land where everything was whales. The sea was a whale. Xxxx was. One of his parents, one of hers. And finally when they married, they both were: two whales.

He learned the danger at his father's knee. She learned the details at her mother's. His father did not say: do not be like me. Did not say: watch out for whales, or even look, your mother—your real mother—is—

One day this young boy, now a young man, met a fairy princess. they married, and— He couldn't believe it. Was it possible?

It was not possible.

Around and around, over and over (paralyzed on the same point). Glued to the spot. He met her at the airport, and— His—! She was his—!

#

"You know the story" liked all crazy kids. It wanted to eat them up. Was their enemy.

So it gave him her and gave her him, and if it was a marriage made in heaven, sometimes heaven has something other than happiness in store for her marriages. They walked into it with open eyes: the end of the fairytale. Or rather, it was the fairytale that walked in, that saw them walk in, that could do nothing to prevent it because "you know the story" was the end of the fairytale.

At some point the novelist took over, and everything became speculation. What is going on with the characters? The marriage appears to be in some kind of rigor mortis. But who thinks so? I ran out of answers and wound up writing a story that will be explained psychologically—despite the flights of symbolism—when I get to the Jung Institute a few years later. Not before. Looks like I fell into the shock of feeling eaten up. But I decided it was mutual. That was fair. Putting these feelings aside, though, beyond the end of this semiautobiographical "little book," Jan and I did go on and things looked up again. He would soon be writing a novel. That was enough to turn things positive between us. His delight spilled over.

Where was the man who climbed mountains? He was still there. And he was about to climb some. I have to add that Jan was such a complex person that I've cherry picked what to quote or remember from him. Borrowing his words about his art gifts, "I had *him* coming at me from all sides." That is, good, bad, sublime, ridiculous, loving, hating, stabbing, cynical, lilting, praising.

On the Hunter front, about this time, in 1979, *The Great Shark Hunt* went to press at Summit Books, an independent imprint at Simon & Schuster. Wondering how Hunter got his new publisher—did he just leave Random House with his editor, Jim Silberman?—I learned the answer in 2006. Over the phone Jim told me that when he left R.H. in 1976, Hunter (under contract) remained behind. But though articles for *The Great Shark Hunt* existed, no book was "lashed together." So R.H. let Hunter go.

At which point his agent called Jim, later heralded as "one of the country's most distinguished publishers."[63] Soon Hunter was under Jim's imprint. And the stopped-up faucet for *The Great Shark Hunt* poured forth. I still wonder had *Rolling Stone* written me when Hunter asked the founder to, four years earlier in August 1975, would things have sailed along on that book? Except that—I'm forgetting—I would probably again have declined to jump on board. But who knows?

In reminiscing on his life for the Author's Note, 12/23/77, Hunter had picked up the language of numbered lifetimes we started using in the '60s. Looking out from the Random House office, he wrote that he'd better jump "straight off this fucking terrace and into the [Rockefeller] fountain, 28 stories below and at least 200 yards out in the air and across Fifth Avenue." Because—reflecting on his career and adventures—"Nobody could follow that act. Not even me." If he survived,

> everything from now on will be A New Life, a different thing, a gig that ends tonight and starts tomorrow morning.
>
> So if I decide to leap for The Fountain when I finish this memo, I want to make one thing perfectly clear—I would genuinely love to make that leap, and if I don't I will always consider it a mistake and a failed opportunity, one of the very few serious mistakes of my First Life that is now ending. [Signed] HST #1.

If the death of HST #1 in his Author's Note was symbolical, the death of Milton—gearing up in 1981 for a *live* performance—was not.

In his rapid reemergence from years of a writing block, Milton had successfully edited one hefty book after another, though his poems and his novel, "White Designs"—for which he'd been paid an advance from a major publisher—didn't come. His friend the author Seymour Krim had written that Klonsky often chanted Blake: "O why was I born with a different face? Why was I not born like the rest of my race."[64]

Milton told me: "The Greeks didn't go to the theatre to be surprised the way we do. They *knew what was going to happen. That's fate,* the predetermination. And then, *knowing your fate you choose it.*" He often quoted the Jewish *Sayings of the Fathers*: "It is not *given* you to complete the task, neither is it *allowed* you to leave off."

With haggard but burning eyes he once exclaimed to me, "*I was always expecting something to STOP IT* [his writing block]. But it can go on and on and on." As with Columbus, no land in sight—expectant moment after expectant moment. In all these ways, encouraging me to seize the day, as a true mentor who prepares and shows the path; as a literary father and Example, passing his knowledge, as we all must, not only to me but carefully fashioning exactly the seeds meant just for me, very precise, customizing any statement, and paradoxically all the while being universal.

He advised me, "*When the time comes to finish, JUST FINISH.*

"*It's not going to be easier tomorrow.*"

I remember seeing him for the last time. It was 1980. First—if such a thing were possible—it almost didn't happen.

In my brief stopover in New York, I started walking my mini-dachshund in midtown Manhattan on a sunny afternoon, past the cafés and stores forbidden to pets. Thirty blocks later I was in the Village. My feet continued to 287 West Eleventh Street, just off West Fourth: Milton's door.

Nearly vanished on a subway, he had a single precious hour left. He spent part of it instructing Snoep (I didn't know he liked dogs) not to lick behind his knees, which Snoep did with a passion. And his tiny mouth tickled. I knew. Milton seemed to relish being accosted by this ten-pounder. He treated him like a sentient creature who could benefit from his instruction, while the clock ticked on.

He'd reevaluated our relationship (of fifteen years), deciding it must have been on his side only, he said; I wanted to reassure him *no*, but something came up, stopped me while I watched my mouth not contradicting.

He told me, squeezed into that lone hour, that he now knew how to finish his long-stuck novel—by working on *only one* chapter at a time! He was expecting victory *after nearly forty years*. I believed him. I did tentatively bring up the thought that he was a genius.

He smiled knowingly: "I've been told I have ***some*** of that." Milton, I saw, broke genius into quantities.

At a given moment he suddenly looked over tellingly, and as if daring rebuke, he said, "*I think after death comes muck.*" *Not Milton!*

Descending into the Fourteenth Street subway for Grand Central Terminal, he insisted that the guard admit my mini-dachshund. Otherwise, the daunting, impossible possibility would have been that we said good-bye then and there.

At the Terminal, momentarily I was delayed in the voluminous Main Concourse. He had to trot off ahead. I finally began to run; the guard in a corridor of the largest train station in the world assured me it was too late, I could never catch up. *I run. I have to. I mustn't let him leave without a good-bye—feeling it's so important—racing to where he's waiting, gone underground; demolishing the odds, beating the clock, not knowing consciously it is the last time.*

But as I stood on the platform, breathless, there with him against all human predictions by watch-tick counting—there because time would have it no other way and ourselves—he says his final words, looking at me directly like always, after kissing me lightly, *projecting the words* like an actor across the stage of the future, "You *cure* yourself . . . And I'll *cure* myself."

Always the master of departures, of rolling things into significance, cryptic but complete. It spoke volumes. Cure of what? Take how long? *And then what?*

Then he left, and the rest of my life came next.

I myself have been accused of speaking this same way—of going straight to a point to start speaking from and not indicate *where* it is or *how* we got there, *what came before*. But in his case, I always knew *how*: in his vibration.

From here on out, he would be taking the lead *after* death—initially prove to me he was still around, in all sorts of ways I will get to.

He'd agreed to critique the just-quoted-from "little book" about Jan and me—tentatively titled "Whistling Glass"—in which he played Daniel. (Hannah Green had told him he was in my other, "big book." His reaction, she said, was "pride and outrage.")

He wrote back that he read the manuscript through "at one sitting with roller-coaster elation at the way the narration zipped and curved around on itself. I had always suspected you could write with such an Ariel spirit but until now I had had to take it on faith, so this is the 'substance of things hoped for'" (Heb. 11:1: "Now faith is the substance of things hoped for, the evidence of things not seen").

He dubbed Daniel's—a.k.a. his—observation-post apartment a "Greenwich Village eyrie."

Regarding the style: "As a 'commodity' to be packed and sold, I think it might stand a better chance on the market if smells, sights, sounds, feels—all the sensual materiality of time and place—were present for the minor characters. Karel and Merry Lou can then reexist and merge and re-emerge in their own spiritual (or mental) ambience."

Milton paraphrased John Donne: "Love is a constant, or full-growing light / And his first moment after noon is night"—in "A Lecture upon the Shadow."

"So how about that for a title: A Lecture upon the Shadow?"*

He had never not come through for me. I was swept away. About us, he predicted, "I'm sure there'll *be other cross-connections and epiphanies and transformations* in the time to come." It was July 1980.

Now a cancer the size of an orange began to grow from his lung, pressing on his heart. He didn't see a doctor.

Fortifying my meager Moroccan library, in North Carolina I'd bought Carl Jung's *Man and His Symbols*. How important this book was to be just ahead.

The psychiatrist threw down the gauntlet: without exception, to know oneself, one *must* pay attention to dreams. Baldly stated: A human being "never perceives anything fully or comprehends anything completely." We can compensate, as with binoculars. But "at some point [a person] reaches the edge of certainty."

Even in perception, he wrote, the things one senses are translated. "Within the mind they become psychic events, whose ultimate nature is unknowable."[65]

* It's actually "short moment," but I like "first moment," as well.

Historically, it was *dreams* that "first enabled psychologists to investigate the unconscious aspect of conscious psychic events."[66]

Intending to record and study my dreams, I bought a four-volume set of symbol-interpretation books in French in Morocco. Suddenly I had a whole new means of stimulation. This was important, in that reading matter could only be bought at the local newsstand, in French, Spanish, and Arabic. My inner life needed this outlet.

Miraculously, dreams poured in. And assisted me in my writing. In fact, the dreams began to act out the characters' problems. I was excited to wake each morning.

Jung noted that *death* was "a theme of numerous fairytales and myths of the type 'Open Sesame': the closed door opens at the magic words and a strange creature reveals the hidden path."

I copied that text without knowing of Milton's plight. An even more significant statement for me was in *Man and His Symbols,* where Jung stated: *the "unknown approach of death casts an adumbratio, an anticipatory shadow*."[67]

I was *reading* about this advance apparition as it illustrated itself in tandem, barreling toward Milton in New York City.

I would soon be deep-set in the covert clues from this forecasting phantom about to strike him down mercilessly, with no objective news of the situation reaching me before or after.

Once in his apartment in my presence Milton wrote:

> And each moon-weird shadow cast its own
> shado*wier* shadow

— 20 —

"The Suicide Mozart"

With a publisher for *Cap d'Antibes* in Belgium, Jan worked feverishly in Larache, Morocco, on "The Suicide Mozart." This novel was in his view his soul's message. At the end of each day, he translated to me.

It begins with the crippling effects on (quasi-autobiographical) Little Fiss of extreme lack of family support for his artistic ambitions (even intrigues against them)—in anti-parallel to Little Mozart. When (in the chapter "Fiss Maak Muziek") Little Fiss on his own plays the piano, his worried parents remove it in his sleep *and substitute a drum.* Little Fiss finds out. Then goes peacefully to bed that night, pulls the covers over his head, and makes the sound of bomber pilots.

By contrast, Little Mozart's father praised his music. For instance—though "The Suicide Mozart" doesn't bring this up—take the account of Johann Andreas Schachtner, a trumpet player at the Salzburg Court. One day when Little Wolfgang was between four and five, Leopold surprisingly comes upon him, plume in hand. He asks, "What are you doing?"

"Writing a concerto for the piano."

Seizing the paper, Leopold spies "a jumble of notes amidst ink splotches. . . . Looking closer, very moved, [he] declares, 'Do you see, Schachtner, how everything is composed in a precise and regular manner? But it is useless because the piece is so difficult that no one can execute it.'"

Wolfgang explains, "And that's why it's a concerto! They have only to practice till they can. Look, this is how it will sound."[68] Another time, Schachtner said, Little Mozart returned from Vienna with a tiny violin he'd been given. His father's friend Wenzl visited, bringing sheet music. Little Mozart, who had never had a violin lesson, pled until his father let him try second violin; tears rolled down Leopold's face as he heard the boy play.

Not so with another instrument. Regarding the sensibility of his ear, it was such that, said Schachtner, "till he was about ten the sound of the trumpet made him afraid, especially in solo. When one slipped a trumpet into his hands, it was as if someone put a pistol to his heart. His father wished to deliver him from this phobia and asked me, despite the child's objection, to play the trumpet in his presence. But, my God, I would rather not have been there. Scarcely had the child heard the thundering sound than he turned pale and almost fainted."[69]

Underneath the miniature Anti-Mozart world, this parallel lies wordlessly. Little Fiss (*"fils"* in French is pronounced *fis* and means "son") is not able to accept the whisking away of his piano and substitution of drum.

In "Ballad of Little Me" in "The Suicide Mozart," Jan described in variations how when very small the semiautobiographical Fiss engrossed himself in his puppet theater, creating "magical unusual scenes, / in which no one saw an ugly thing / and everyone spoke the truth, / then Little Me could forget his lesson." Page 119 (with a guitar):

> When Little Me was a toddler
> strommeti-strom, strommeti-strom
> his Papa gave him a puppet theatre
> *pingele, dondele, bangelem tong!*
> and Mam made puppet clothes
> He played then all by himself
> *strommeti-strom, strommeti-strom*
> even for hours and hours, and no one
> *vliem! vloem! vlam! vlom!*
> was as happy as he was with his imagination
> *dingele, pingele, bimbam en bom*

Doodles: “The Suicide Mozart” folder

One day when Little Me was more rough
strommeti-strom, strommeti-strom
he took his favorite doll
dirreli-dom, strimmeti-strom
and broke her leg, the shavings bleeding
That time Little Me took also
broeme! broeme! brame! brom!
his puppet theatre and kicked it
STRRROMMM!
And went away to search for his truth.
rommele, grommele, potverdie-dom.

By page 121: "Now Reality has killed it all." More precisely, he said, it was premeditated murder.

In writing "The Suicide Mozart," Jan reexamined an infant trauma incurred from a babysitter, who sometimes struck him. And when he cried, she might put a burning cigarette to his lips. Having now devoured *Man and His Symbols*, he realized how much she'd damaged a portion of his psyche: his anima (a man's inner feminine, or muse/inspirer, his soul, who connects into collectively unconscious content).*

A second short circuit in Jan's biography was his failure of a final university exam he thought he'd passed, a fluke that pushed him out of a teaching career.

But in "The Suicide Mozart" the protagonist encounters a different sort of final exam—on the soul level. After death Fiss finds himself on the star Vegafünf, where Lord Buddha and other highly evolved beings, muses, gods, goddesses live. They wait there for their Replacements (Plaatsvervangers) on Earth. To speed up the process in his case, Wolf (Mozart) had tampered in the life of Fiss. It being

---

* Puanani Harvey, a distinguished Jungian analyst, examined this topic in a paper for Museum "het Toreke." She pointed out what happens when an anima is wounded—how the anima archetype differs from the mother archetype, and Jan's relationship to the two. Psychologist James Hillman puts this experience into the "child in danger" motif, which is part of the hero myth if the child survives.

forbidden to break a person's will, Mozart had made him drink and taken away his genius.

Now through a tunnel as if out of a dream, Fiss steps into the Greek Agora at Vegafünf—for his Entrance Exam. Wolf quizzes his protégé: *just how much has he suffered?*

Mozart probes: "And you don't love anybody anymore? No, that question was not necessary. You have lost your faith in love a long time ago." The dialogue continues:

> "I no longer believe in anything," Fiss said defiantly.
> "But you do hope?"
> "Nothing, nothing!"
> "That's wonderful! [Mozart congratulated Fiss.] That's marvelous! Yes, it is. Look how much place there is left now for hope, faith, and love. Here they are, the three of them, waiting impatiently to face daylight. . . . God gave them to you, so that you would recognize Him in time and he has never taken back his presents. So they are still in you. Let me see. May I? Oh yes. . . . It is surprising how well they survived."

Looking into Fiss's heart more deeply than permitted, Wolf creates a whirlpool, with Fiss's thoughts spinning like a dizzy cork: he is changing back the suicidal Mozart to his positive spinning state, united with him.

The above text sits on top of a famous passage from St. Paul, without mentioning it. Thus, "The Suicide Mozart" ended in reaffirming, after death, the survival of all that had been thought lost forever—specifically, hope, faith, and love were still in Fiss's heart. And in his death as the Anti-Mozart, he is turned back by Mozart into Mozart.

He has come full circle from the night when as a little boy he thanked his parents ("'Oh!' Fiss said, thrilled. 'A drum! A real drum! Thank you, Mama! Thank you!'"). Then in his bedroom, in a section called "The Parasite," his father tells him that not everyone can be a genius and that geniuses are considered parasites while alive—that everyone is given love, intelligence, and will power from God but not genius—says good night and leaves. "Fiss is in the cockpit of a fighter bomber. He sees a town. Is it marketday? Or carnival? What a lot of people. Vrmmm! Vrmmm! Tsjiow-tsjiow. The bombs. They are falling!! *Bang, Fiss.* Bang. They are all *destroyed,* Fiss!!!"[70]

In the last paragraph of the book the author says it is dedicated to Replacements. "To let them know what happens after death. And why they live. And so, finally, if they have more severe pain than usual, they can know why they are agonizing. Because they are expected on Vegafünf. (The rest is misleading.)"

But this period turned up something else. Flying into Morocco, I sat beside a female who told me how—after eleven years of marriage—her husband admitted he was gay.

I would not say Jan made the revelation in this exact fashion. But he did, in 1980, tell me to sit down: "I have something to say that I don't think you're going to like." He then explained that all his legendary tragic girlfriends—Pong the reformed prostitute in Bangkok, Aziza in "The Aziza Story"—were males! Before marrying me but not after, he'd been gay. Moulay, who had sometimes lived with us, had been his boyfriend when I met him.

I couldn't breathe. I felt duped. *How could something I lived with daily as a fact of life be so distorted?* Continually falsified! To what lengths he must have gone.

That he'd hidden being gay, I could possibly have forgiven. But the misinformation was tightly threaded, right into minute-by-minute situations. I felt relief on the sexual front. But horror about this web of deception when I imagined its blow-by-blow play-out in not one lie but hundreds, every minute being a chance to come clean not taken. No wonder Moulay had said, "He'll never let me go"—never mind that they were no longer sexual partners.

Jan told me he'd been lured into his first sexual experience while reading Proust on a beach at seventeen but that in his case being gay was an accident. It stopped at marriage. He'd believed it honest to marry (remember the numerous canceled proposals!).

However, the reason he now revealed the truth was that he'd become attracted to the handsome earthy/mystical sidekick Moroccan in his twenties who provided him with kif.

The truth was out. There was an explanation to how this romantically inclined man, so chock full of life, did not have a passionately uncontrollable physical desire for me. Why he had often tried to make me jealous in letters, mentioning tempting nearby females.

Since my last trip to North Carolina we now owned Jung's autobiography, *Dreams, Memories, Reflections.* In writing "The Suicide Mozart," Jan had used it, along with *Man and His Symbols*, to help him work through his psychology. His anima explained that *it was she* who felt it when the villainous babysitter pressed the cigarette toward his lips if he cried while his mother taught school; thus, *she* sustained the trauma—till his mother fired the sitter. (This, his mother later confirmed to me.) After that, his anima admitted, she (he) was "suspicious of women."

So added to the other psychological traits—his suicidalness, his alcoholism (in developed countries), his genius—Jan was really a novice in loving females! With his typical unorthodox confidence, he had assumed past experience was no predictor. Thus, no need to mention what he'd given up.

To further complicate matters, it turned out that the handsome kif supplier, young Abdou, was fascinated with me. Abdou was now always in the house. In a climactic incident he stole the manuscript of my "big book" and threatened—unless I slept with him—to burn it.

I felt a wave of panic at the *loss of my only copy* but a sliver-sharp clarity that if I gave in to the blackmail, the book would be lost in another way. No matter that the written-on pieces of paper survived.

The decision was wrenched from my core, pulled out of my reserves: who was I, at the bottom of everything? When I refused, he returned it.

Jan, however, did not believe that Abdou could have been capable of this treachery.

This was another blow to the marriage.

I realized that it was resoundingly true the crux of his behavior issues were rooted in discouraged artistic drive, including demonstrations time and again by his mother that everything—even washing the dishes—was a worthier activity than taking a moment out for the boy's creations. Prior to that, the cigarette trauma. For a psyche that sensitive—not for everyone. But this one could flip to Anti-Mozart. Whatever portion was needed to create that chemistry, his dosage sufficed. Too late to change it.

But as his psyche wrestled with this new twist my dreams shed light on my inner life. Such a journey into the psyche will inevitably pay off, in particular when the material it first thrusts up has to do with the death of Milton Klonsky, revealing it in disguise before the fact—making me write the (thought-to-be-imaginary) death into my novel but never dare really speculate: Suppose it is real. Where? How?

So Jan used to be gay. *Relief rolled over me.* I'd known something I couldn't put my finger on.

I also felt a reason to stay had been lifted. If my heart said leave, my duty would not have to bend over backwards to assert: "But you haven't that right. He can't live without you. Suppose he kills himself. Could you live with yourself?"

I had been toying with this question, agonizing. Yet this new development began to tip the balance.

I could never turn myself into a male. I thought he was kidding himself that he could snap his finger and choose his sexuality.

I had forgotten, I have to admit, the lovely times when early in marriage he seemed sincerely to be trying to know me deeply. So I felt relief. *He can't help it.* I felt: *There's no hope.* I felt: *I have the right to choose not to want this type of relationship, not even to give it a try.* I felt I could try forever or longer than I had to give, and probably it wouldn't work.

As if to assist me (in this line of thinking), Jan marched head first into his temptation. Being his oddly strong willed self, he determined to eradicate the attraction by confronting it before it could reroot. Shut up in his writing room, he made alluring homoerotic drawings after I was in bed, then burned them. The next morning I would see black curled-up ashes in the toilet. For some reason, the sight of the few floating burned ashes particularly stung. I found it revolting, I have to say. But oblivious to that, he was confident this project would work, he said. However, something else was marching in a trumpet sound, an Easter *Messiah* concert, into my hearing. The Death of Milton.

As fate would have it, I went to Gibraltar in June 1981 for a minor medical concern; therefore, for financial reasons, did not go to the United States that year. Therefore, did know Milton's health was deteriorating.

In August 1981 in a matter of ten days Jan wrote a cycle of some of his best poetry. He translated it into English, giving me what became, for some poems, the only surviving copy.

One, that begins, "The road signs show Mecca as usual / and which to choose is the question," says:

> Listen to the grasses growing while you watch them,
> no one can cut them down fast enough,
> till a pop teaches us nirvana has been reached
> till a whole fusillade shows that nothing
> that leads away from one's own celebrations
> is spellbinding forever, whatever one may wish.

On 8/VIII/1981 another poem reads: "step to where the universe pushes you /. . . / or then go to where light found its origin, / the straightest line that ever existed between the clouds."

An ocean away Milton was beginning to cough, weaken, still with no suspicion he was dying.

In Larache as I walked through the streets it seemed to me that nature portended something.* The landscape sometimes seemed to be in a strange suspension. It seemed to have a secret it would not reveal but only hint at, as if to say, *Keep watching. Something is happening.* I noticed the peculiarity, as if nature were dilated, beckoning to get my attention. Something palpable was in the atmosphere, as if trees were pulsing, stretching, qualitatively different, involved—but with what?—something that related to me, important to me, that it was whispering all around. I had no idea it was as if counting the weeks, days, hours remaining in his life.

* In Shamanic lore, the death of someone else can lead us into initiation. It is the same in the Bible. Elisha, because he was personally present, received the gift of Elijah.

— 21 —

Death of Milton

The tiny town of Blankenberge, Belgium, was right on the North Sea. In off season, September 1981, Jan and I and our mini-dachshund Snoep sublet an apartment there in a high rise overlooking the windy, wave-pounded piers. Jan was again attempting not to drink—the only way he could live in Belgium.

While Milton lay in St. Vincent Hospital in the Village—in the public ward—November 8–9, I fell asleep seeing dots of light in the water. In sleep I asked "if it's this floor my father's on." I'm told it's one floor down. From my notes: "My father acts as if there's been an accident and we're all afraid now of paddling." That same night I recorded a similar dream: "Is it my father [who] says he's—we're all—still not comfortable rowing downstream to the other house? On the phone I ask him if he's going home? I say, 'Don't go till I get there. I'm not afraid.'" (Not afraid of what?)

Dreams often revert to an analogy, perhaps a parallel situation; here, the metaphor "father." Going home and rowing to another house would be good metaphors for death.

Daily, as I walked past the Fire Tower café a beer sign teetered on the wire—"falling, leaning, braced by a rope," I wrote at the time. Hanging by a thread. It got into my imagination: "A sign is about to fall from the sky? . . The sign of the LIGHTHOUSE is about to fall? Leaning, precarious." The news was being "acted out" in my world, could I but read. And I could but not with my normal mind.

Meanwhile, an American, Dr. Batten, offered me a ticket to North

Carolina if I would deliver him some Nootropil® (piracetam), a then-non-FDA-approved Belgian medicine for stroke victims. It was legal to hand-carry but not to mail it. I would have stopped in New York. As much as I sensed something was wrong, I felt I was imagining it. On November 14, I wrote to decline, saying I could not fix a date. In fact, Jan was awaiting word from a publisher about "The Suicide Mozart." On November 16, by Express letter, I said I could "come to Greenville almost immediately." We'd just received word there was a final round of work needed on Jan's novel (he agreed), which probably necessitated a return to Morocco. My going to America first—on a free ticket—made sense. But by then I'd already located a stewardess to deliver the medicine—at no charge. Not surprisingly, the doctor chose her. Fatefully, I missed the opportunity. I find a copy of the Express letter in my dream notes. Too late. The wheels of fate were already turning another way.

On TV, I watched the Manhattan Project scientists, led by J. Robert Oppenheimer, build the atom bomb. No connection there except that Milton was in Manhattan. My imagination, however, thought otherwise. As the dreams zeroed in, a dramatic turn took place in my fictional Milton, Robert. November 17–18:

> Paula went off
> But the bomb it did not
>
> For it would be Robert the bomb who went off. And what would happen when he really did GO OFF? That would be all it took, like the end of the world that day when it came—the explosion and pain, Well, he was a bomb, wasn't he? AND THEN ONE DAY HE WOULD—
>
> GO OFF.

The last week of his life the dream intensity was relentless: November 26–27, "my father" had a heart attack or was "getting weak in the head." Amidst the confusion I was frantic—"in a huff, incensed, emotional, and said how could they not see he was dying?" (In fact, unknown to me, in exploratory surgery Milton had a stroke;

it paralyzed him on one side, though *till two days* before his death—that is, till November 27—he was expected to survive.

Contrary to expectation, they would tell him that day his death was imminent. In the dream, I insisted he was dying. No one paid attention, as if I were invisible, which an out-of-body observer would—obviously—be.*

I confirmed the facts with Anatole in 1990. He described a noisy nonprivate room. Puerto Rican music.

The Introduction to Milton's *Selected Writings* later called it "a poet's ending: ironical, whimsical, and agonizing."[71]

Back in 1981, needless to say, I did not yet believe that dreams, large on their scale, could "prophesy"—*cross over* into life—that a physical event might announce itself so dramatically in my sleep.

But wasn't this what Jung meant by the *shadow of the approach of death?*

November 29. My notes that day begin with a blast: "Day of Destiny: the Black Knight, all in silver, returned. It was Yullie SEAS. YULLIE SEAS! Yullie Seas! And I was waiting on the quai." This was word play on "Ulysses" ("jullie" is "you" in Dutch). What was I describing?

November 29. A windy Blankenberge afternoon. Walking my

* That same night I dreamed that Don (from my hometown Wilkerson funeral home) telephoned Jan and I saw a big orange that I commented on profusely. Milton, I would learn, had "a cancer the size of an orange" weighing on his heart. As if referencing my choice of staying with Jan rather than taking the trip, the dream revealed that Jan had a black eye; after the call, referring to it, he (mysteriously) said "I'm sorry, literally." The night before that, November 25–26, a very important Big Dream showed a transformation preceded by a terrible crisis: a giant monkey, almost a guerrilla, hurried menacingly from the underbrush and twirled me around repeatedly, then flung me to the ground. From above, I looked down at my lifeless body. Little Snoep turned me onto my back, then lay on my chest in the form of a cross. For a long time I looked dead. Finally, he got up. In the next scene I walked in the forest, where animals wandered freely, but I was safe. I thought the animals stood for emotions and instincts. This stream of unconscious images came in intuitively night after night. Steadily pouring in, recorded, examined, never ever in my conscious self taken literally.

dog all alone on the street, I came upon a numinous parade. The marchers brandished signs: NEPTUNE'S CHILDREN and NEPTUNE'S TRUMPETERS. "The band," I wrote, "rounded the corner, approaching me, playing something triumphant."

I went into a grocery store, out again, and "the band returned, coming straight to the corner where [my dog and I] stood, and I saw it was a procession for a beautiful silver little man, somewhat as one holds up a chalice in church. The silver man was the one I've seen, but not silver, rust-colored, etc., in dreams." The "triumphant band," I wrote, was "Trumpeting in the ending. Trumpeting the ending out of this. How can we? We can't. Neptune's Band can." I concluded with "Pen-elope. The Waiting Pen."

In the late 1960s Milton had addressed a post card from Greece to "Penelope"—signed "Ulysses"—mailed to me. On the front, tied to the bottom of a ram, was Ulysses fleeing the Cyclops's cave. Having blinded the giant, one-eyed, man-eating Cyclops, Polyphemus, in this way without detection he escaped. (Visually, the image raised the specter of male/female sexuality brilliantly.)

To which Milton penned, "*This is one way out. But what do you do about the Inner Eye?*"

Inexplicably, watching alone with Snoep as the parade turned back from *the end of the block*, I felt I was witnessing a spectacular triumph that sent chills down my legs, goosebumps down my arms. I had no idea what the situation might relate to.

In many reported cases a person's consciousness at death was experienced multiple places. Any numinous event seems fraught with meaning. The parade commanded my attention. At the end of the *block*, the Trumpeters of Neptune and Sons and Daughters of Neptune reversed course. They turned around and the whole band headed toward me.

So the incomprehensible had happened. He had died—he let me know—though I knew nothing whatsoever.

I asked Jan what special day it was, that there was this parade. He answered quite seriously, serious or not, it was the day Muhammad was told to write.

Jan couldn't stop drinking. He could not live in Belgium. We returned to Morocco.

On Christmas Day, I jotted, "I just learned, minutes ago, our street is named Rue de Damas" (Road to Damascus).

— 22 —

Ciao D Hunter

From the Rue de Damas in Larache, I secretly set up a poste restante (general post office) address, and—though I "knew" intuitively Milton was dead—wrote to ask him to use it. (We'd never corresponded before.)

In the now-constant dream undercurrent, December 13–14, I was "upstairs" in his apartment, cleaning it. Appearing overhead in a rectangle, he told me, *Now come up there, tell me good-bye. Go up into the eyrie— A passage. A key passage. I tell you good-bye with it.*

Here—here—I've FILLED IN THE BLANK.

Besides the word play on "Blank" in "berg" (mountain), this brought back his observation, "*You* see all the *un*ordinary things. But not the ordinary things—what any other woman would see in an instant. And the **ordinary** thing is— You fill in the blank."

I needed Milton to be alive. I sensed he was dead. But discarded the idea. What? This indomitable person, someone death would not dare approach (though unconsciously—or rather, unadmittedly—I knew my inner sense reported correctly). By all the laws of the universe I counted on, Milton could not be dead. But my rules were broken.

However, I had only my inner suspicion (half denied, half believed).

In the months before I got confirmation, Jan would write "Amanda" (the companion novel to "The Suicide Mozart"). He debated whether Amanda was me. I insisted that she was only inside him.

January 12, 1982, six weeks after Milton's death,* I had an important dream—in which I was driving toward a mysterious Vita

---

* November 29, 1981

Pass. Someday, the dream said, *an event in my life* would take place there. But I didn't know whether to welcome it or guard against it. Upon waking, I diligently used "active imagination," or free association, to find the answer.

Using this Jungian technique, the longer I couldn't decipher the dream, *if it still held energy,* the more it revealed. That first day I typed twenty-eight pages. Soon more, adding a cover: "Prologue, OR Premonition."

I brought in the term *Chow de Hunter, w*hich—in an earlier dream—had materialized in red ink on my palm. Every time the ink faded, then vanished, it miraculously re-emerged on my hand, as if unerasable. By 1982 the term had taken other forms, such as *Ciao.*

Though this was before I learned of Milton's death, the advice I gave myself, in attempting to interpret the January 12 dream, is mind-bending to me today because of its current relevance. For instance, that I should DECANT *(de-can't)*—outpour—in the time of "You say hello, I say good-bye" (which I think is now).

I plowed on, trying to find out what my unconscious was saying. I was fishing for specifics in this "natural amplification" process Jung used in working with dreams.

Like a blindfolded driver—with no idea who "he" was—I knew: "he wasn't dead."

For when they said caps off to him
he did a recap.

About my unknown future: "All the traffic in your life met there"; all the driving lanes would converge at this place, called alternately a mysterious number, "381," or the Vita Pass.

There everything would jell. And a funny phrase, of interest to me now, kept reappearing:

For you, my dear, have been chosen to be—
the Chow de Hunter.

Active Imagination, like this, lets through whatever comes up from the unconscious, in order to get to the aha moments.*

A few lines further on, I mention a Nuova Pass†:

Where the star blows up
. . . and what kind of Nuova would be on a superhighway?
A supernova‡
Supper.
It was Supper.
It was: On the Menu—?
The CIAO D HUNTER.

A few months later, learning of Milton's death, I would think this material related to that. Much later, in 2006 or so, I would think, *Well, the convergence of paths. That's now, isn't it?* This was energizing.

So while Jan was trying to get "the couple" together, I take from this that my own future path was protesting strongly against it.

---

* It uses "unconscious regulators" that, Jung said, helped him discover "an impersonal collective unconscious" (*The Basic Writings of C. G. Jung, 74–75*).

† I must have been thinking of Dante's *La Vita Nuova.*

‡ I now associate the "supernova" explosion in this trancelike material with Hunter's ashes shot out of a cannon on a towering launcher in 2005. At least, that's one way of looking at it.

— 23 —

A Delicacy

Unable to unite the couple in "Amanda" despite alternate endings, Jan wrote his best poetry instead. A translated sample is footnoted below.*

He had finished. Written a major message in "The Suicide Mozart" and his late poems. I was proud to have been part of it, but it taxed me to the limit.

---

* The suspicion I have is sensational
Sensational is the suspicion I have but keep to myself
fearing to go to the asylum where so many others, shone on
by the same moon, went to rust the rest of their years
for they thought they were a piece of God.

There they thought, throwing themselves on their bars,
with rolled up eyes, full of foam and looking like a beast
and indeed, screaming screams that
ever were those of a distant kinship, according to the doctors,
that they were a pure piece of God.

No one doubts it: madness is a disease like another,
in extreme cases nothing can be done
and it goes its way wherever that may lead to.
In most cases to death although one sometimes has the impression
to be a pure piece of God.

But death is a lot better, a lot easier,
a lot sweeter it is there even if it be without a God or
destination, even if it's rotten it is not mad and everything
has to be preferred to the idea of being a pure piece of God.

Well, that having been said—and a lot has to be added still
confirming my opinion, adding to its
exactness and proving, alas, that nothing resists its tragic—
a suspicion remains which I won't name.

Returning to North Carolina in July '82, I made the Greenwich Village phone call to Milton apprehensively. I learned—as I "knew"—he was "dead." Listening, I felt the floor drop out of my world.

Milton's obituary was in the *New York Times Sunday Book Review,* March 7, 1982. In it, his short autobiography, "A Writer's Education," sketchily revealed his history.

What I most appreciated—as his prodigy poem "The End Pocket" was not in it—was his position against grand, blanket statements: "It is not, as I had so long believed, in a Platonic transcendence of phenomena, rising on tiers of forms to the Good, the True, the Beautiful, that I have found my own truth and my way as a writer, but in the reverse, a descension into the unique and irreducible thisness of things and events, the 'haecceities' (as Duns Scotus called them) and what Blake referred to as the 'minute particulars.' These are so often overlooked because they are beneath our notice and, though all around us, are seen through like air without being seen themselves."

He concluded, "Even the games I played as a kid were never that Euclidean, as I now realize, for there was always a thrown-away cigarette butt, a wad of gum, a loose brick or a bump in the sidewalk that could deflect the ball in any direction."[72]

Unsure whether to return to Morocco, I consulted an open-minded Methodist minister, who told me if you go back, give it at least six weeks. And don't think that your choices are to stay with Jan or nothing.

Six weeks after I went back, we had a trial separation. I left for Barcelona.

This is the source of the following Big Dream that shone a flashlight into the coming years:

The Park Güell Fountain Dream

SCENE: *High up on a plateau with Milton, who's alive but in a hole, I'm sweeping up spilled milk. I associate the location with*

Antoni Gaudi's Park Güell (Barcelona). To my side I see huge stairs leading downward. I know the steps are usually filled with water in the dream reality. No water runs over them; they seem to be for recycling. Seeing Milton's head poking up from the hole, I try to pull him out but lose balance. I'm determined to stay on the plateau, till my legs get tangled in my clothes. Looking at the clifflike plunge to the level below, I realize one false move could send me crashing onto the concrete. After sweeping all the spilt milk onto the stairway, I come down.

SCENE CHANGE: *On ground level, a magical little woman hands me a horrid thing looking like a shriveled chicken; it was abandoned on a wall frequented by wild animals, she said, but is unhurt; if I hold it under a fountain, it will become "a delicacy." I will only have to pay 30 francs.*

SCENE CHANGE: *As I hold it under a fountain black gook pours out. And more. I watch the "monster" transform into a little fish.*

Soon after this, I moved to Madrid and worked as an au pair for three young Spanish girls.

— 24 —

La Maison du Diable

Perhaps the reader will think that I'd so wised up by now that I'd never return to Morocco. Why would I? However, after a restorative four months in Madrid, I felt up to anything. I remembered Jan's charm and opted for one last try at the marriage. Then I bought a countertop oven for Jan, imagining him happily concocting masterchef foods, and took the train/ferry/bus back to Larache.

In my fantasy he would greet me with open arms and whisk me away to a serious attempt to reunite. But I arrived at the bus station, pulled my suitcase through the few streets to our home, and instead of closeting me off jealously with his mighty beam of pleasure, Jan, in the house with his two closest Moroccan male friends, was preparing a meat fondue. Everyone was very warm and friendly to me. But soon, in a final narcissistic blow, the act that made it clear the marriage was on its deathbed, he proclaimed a hunger strike.

As if commanding me to give him up, all the while he copiously insisted I stay, he said he would eat nothing until I burned my only copy of "The Erstwise Paula." As a side demand, he insisted we have a child.

This radicalness, he said, was to convince my animus—his rival—that I was a female and should act like one. The absurdity, the outrageousness, the insistence on making unreality real, trying to convince me of a cartoon version of myself, impressed me, as his imagination always came up with something I could not have dreamed up except in a book. On the other hand, he had gone too far this time. I wasn't going to back down. He thought—or appeared to think—I would.

He started starving in earnest to impress upon me to burn the manuscript. I could now (later) step outside and see this showdown on other levels. But I didn't have that ability then. And no matter how brightly one saw on different levels, the fact was the fact. All the while, his friends got nervous. If they did not report this hunger strike to the police and he died, they would be implicated—no small thing in their penal system. They drew on their Moroccan psychology: *I should have a big bonfire and pretend to comply.*

During his hunger strike I became ill. I could not swallow, my throat was so painful. The doctor explained that my immune system had broken down, making normally harmless throat bacteria cause ulcers. Jan also, by now, had decided he was a prophet. Having dubbed me the "wife of a genius," he took it a further step. He had a scheme to move to Sidi R'bat—nearby—which, one legend said, was the site of Jonah's being vomited by the whale. I told him no one would believe him. But he piled it on. He banished me from the room when our (male) friends came. At this point, I had really seen the writing on the wall.

These demands spelled the end of the marriage. It became crystal clear to me it was doomed.

Was not my sense of responsibility grossly exaggerated? Would I be guilty if I left—calling his bluff—*and he promptly killed himself?*

In the village the house was now named La Maison du Diable (The Devil's House)—because of Jan's physical endurance, not succumbing to drink and kif, persisting day after day to use these intoxicants to induce his poetry and now novels. As mentioned before, he smoked kif every day to write, then read me the passages aloud. And yes, he was very functional in that state. Rather like an ultra-imaginative imp. Except when, as here, his imagination took him to such extremes all my attempts to live with him faded into a sheer wall of impossibility. I would not cede to his demands. He would not withdraw them. It was a Last Stand of Custer.

I dreamed: "*he came with a purpose, the mission of Divine Sin.*" Who?

Also, I dreamed of one who before birth looked golden; some commented on how astonished people would be—on Earth—to know his real form. Further—this later and for sure about Jan—I dreamed: "in his *physical* self, *wounded beyond despair.*"

I replayed the past: Hadn't I whitewashed the most objectionable details, such as—he'd told me—he made Pong, a Thai prostitute, stop working while he lived with her (of course, I now knew she was a he). But learning Pong was secretly seeing her sugar daddy again, he went to where her savings were hidden, stole them, and left. To punish her, he said.

To steal a hard-won prostitution nest egg that also supported Pong's sister, I'd felt luridly reprehensible.

I'd thought that last touch made up. Suppose I hadn't granted him the reality he tried, sometimes, to show me. If so, what a breadth of contradiction.

If I could lump these statements together, they show a dimension where, one day, I would see this whole story: why the attraction, the magnetism, how, at this moment, on that level if not this, he drove me away in charity, *in knowledge that otherwise for me time was running out. Never mind about him.*

One more detail: Since learning of Milton's death I'd begun to see or imagine his energy in something like a standing wave that occasionally rippled over someone's face as I talked with that person. It seemed the spirit presence was coming into other people. Especially Abdou. At least—not used to afterdeath encounters—my novice self thought so.

The whole situation caused me to do the most incredible thing. I wanted to repay Milton for not having slept with him "all the way." Abdou seemed to be holding his energy. So I had the wild idea I could reach the spirit of Milton through hooking up just once with Abdou. Immediately when it was done, I was completely horrified, for I realized it had not been Milton in any guise. There wasn't the slightest sensation of anything otherworldly, "Milton-esque," or nonphysical about it. What there had been before vanished. Jan, of course, did not know. And anyway, the marriage was on its last legs.

I was standing in the living room as Jan sat. On the wall hung a picture of a saintlike girl. He and Abdou mentioned how my heart was like that. I was astonished.

As Jan beamed up at me I put my hand softly on his head without any indication I was leaving; then I literally escaped. Forever.

I stole off to the bus station—my suitcases already there with the help of another of Jan's friends. A dream had shown my car pass through a green traffic light just in time, before it changed. Immediately, behind me, came a loud explosion.

Later Jan would tell a reporter for his hometown newspaper in Belgium that I left him on a bed of typhus. The town believed it. I would have to overcome this obstacle in steering the museum retrospective of his life away from casting me as villain. His letters to me would prove the timeline, the duplicities. Those too he'd given me, my defense in his own words. And of such was my strength to be forged. For if anyone had to learn to be strong and would almost go down learning, he would be the best possible Teacher. Never mind that the teacher, in this case, would be living his shadow, or, as he put it, antiself.

I left with no regrets, glad to have grown so much but glad never to have to put myself through these escapades again, not ever. Yet somewhere above it all he shone through, not the incidents but the entity, the soul, the one who sparkled and defied life to tie him down, who engaged in these sparing matches that challenged me to be stronger, more myself.

Tired of a *vicarious everything*, I left Morocco definitively at forty-three. I felt this was the last instant I could get out.

I felt I'd stuck my head in the lion's mouth. I could not imagine it, staying and "going down with him." I learned much while being, it turned out, something of an apprentice. Well, all apprentices made their break. Mine came now; there was no more marriage to save. Even, one of his friends had told me, "Face it. He's gay. You might make love once a month. That's it."

Still, I was glad to have lived the heady ideas. If only there was still time, I who had been "late" at seven.*

Milton, however, had told me, "You would have learned a lot *in any case.*"

---

* See page 76.

I discovered in writing this book that—his wife Sandy having separated from him—Hunter had at first boarded up his house in mourning, then gotten embroiled in drawn-out divorce proceedings. Not only was I entering Life #3 (in the old language),* so was he. By April 23, 1982, threatened with losing Owl Farm, he'd written Ralph Steadman "the joke's over" and was living with an important person in his life, TV producer Laila Nabulsi. Not that he and I had physical contact. That day was long past. But it would come back in a splash in the '90s.

---

* First referenced in a letter, page xxi.

PART TWO

— 25 —

Under a Fountain Future

> One talks it round and in doing so deprives it of its bite, by no means does one want to forget it; one forgets it in order to remember. . . . Forgetting is the shears with which one clips away what one cannot use
>
> —Kierkegaard

> I dreamed repeatedly that I died and remembered there was something I forgot to say
>
> —Kierkegaard (paraphrase)

Much has happened since. But before going farther, I had to change my consciousness. Well, it was foretold in the Barcelona dream of transformation under the fountain*—a Jungian blueprint if ever there was one. People were to come back in. But the next four years were a time of change.

A famous novelist—perhaps John Galsworthy—used to draw a line across the page in finishing one book, to start another just under it. A line was drawn in my life. It was a new start on the other side.

Our ego, Jung wrote, may experience being tossed "like a shuttlecock between the inner and outer demands"; that is, "standing between them, as between hammer and anvil."[73] He added, "We can understand at once the fear that the child and the primitive have of

---

* As discussed on page 129

the great unknown. We have the same childish fear of our inner side . . . One cannot even talk about the unconscious before many educated people without being accused of mysticism."[74]

Nevertheless, precipitated by Milton's death, I was to have an initiation into this unconscious, just as Jung dived down into it to bring back up the seeds of his later work. This Confrontation with the Unconscious, as he called it (or the Self), can be—was in my case—a rebirth. Nothing is afterwards the same. It is an initiation, a shock, a conversion.

What happened next would therefore cut my life in half. The person familiar to the reader so far in the book would, in a sense, disappear under new growth.

To go back to Hunter. In a BBC documentary in 1978, he said he'd used the character "Duke" as his mouthpiece but then became "an appendage" to Duke; that form was exhausted: "I have no choice. I have to solve this problem. I suppose that my plans are to figure out some new identity. Kill off one life and start another."[75]

Milton had balanced a pole of my life.

The other pole, I identified with Jan (Dionysus)—revelry, disinhibition—though Milton, rightly said to think of *him* as "a gangster poet."

This sense of being off balance if Milton was not there—that with him gone, I had no heart to go out on those oppositely extreme limbs with Jan—strikes me now as analogous to the physics entanglement theory. In a quantum system if particle A is observed to spin clockwise, then B—even at the far ends of the universe—will have to turn counter-clockwise.

It was as if *somehow*, in my private world, they performed a quantum balancing act.

So Milton—somehow—had allowed me to feel safe diving into his counterpole because somehow, present in my mind, he existed and would silently balance it.

Reaching at the only straw I had, I was following Milton in those hints I seemed to be picking up in dreams and even in the flutterings of his energy over faces around me sometimes. Baby seeds. Leading where? Calling where? Giving me something to wake up to.

This is deep. Something to think about. But for the moment, I was making another discovery. One so profound that it came all by itself.

There was no doubt about death. It was an irreversible fact. But it was not my factual thinking self who had the information first. What I thought was happening to my character was taking place in "real life." In a matter this important to me, I couldn't tell the difference! Did I want to go on the rest of my life this blind?

Milton had confided he was "an airplant, not rooted in anything. Certainly not in Earth." And that he used sexuality to *tie him* to the Earth.

I could see that he was my *tie to Earth.*

He had "given soul," Seymour Krim said, "*to his barest utterance.*"

If he were gone, reality itself would be eclipsed, and not momentarily.

A suspicion pounced upon me that *I did not believe such a mind could die.* I held onto the question whether this mind that had advised me so deeply could disintegrate. Could that much organized, experienced wisdom crumble into dust? I began to realize I did not believe it.

I picked back up his statement, "Some of us have more whites about the eyeballs. I was a *crazy kid*. . . . You know what I was crazed *by? Immortality.* . . . And *he's* still around. I can talk to *that kid* anytime I want to."

What might have been nebulous questions for years, if once they become convictions, can be stated as the most natural of things. The optic nerve, he'd explained intently after reading a book on vision, *begins* in an extension of the cells of the brain. The book also stated, as he remembered it, that visible light was *the exact range of light used in photosynthesis.*

"Blake was right," he'd told me, "though I don't know how the hell he knew. Conception *IS* perception. 'I don't see *with*, I see *thru*' the eye.' We're *tracked in*. We see what we **can** see."

About him and me: "Each of us has a self the other owns. Don't think me entirely monomaniacal. But I've missed *that* self."

Now **I** missed my self *he* "owned"; I could not survive if that "self" died also, with him.

I had to find out what I believed. There was no time to wait. No one to stand in any more for this part of me. Even keeping him on the pages of a book would not do. He was dead there too.

In the *New York Times* obituary Milton's close friend Anatole Broyard, senior *Times* book reviewer, made a comparison with Kafka. He wrote, "It seems to me that one approaches people through their compromises, but Klonsky was either unable or unwilling to compromise. . . . As a poor man . . . he knew that being himself was his only luxury."[76]

Anatole recounted how, "reduced by a stroke to single words or broken phrases," Milton said in a final farewell to him: "no transition" and "debauchery."

To me, one *had* to understand dying words. The deathbed fragment meant something. What? Even Anatole didn't know. He wondered whether Milton meant death debauched us all. The key, I interpreted, was a transition that, he'd stipulated, needed to take place—*in the same way, walking through the unconscious, he discovered his own version of the chaos theory by following "the flea."*

Whatever it meant, it was the most important thing to say at such a moment, the one thing not to forget.

Without a "transition" in the consciousness of the Earth—or individuals—would something about to occur send the Earth dynamics into debauchery? Something about which there was no warning or expectation, because there hadn't needed to be? I was clinging to remembered moments, phrases of his, trying to find a sense of direction if any direction for me there was at all.

My "big book" culminated in Milton's death. His postcard from Greece signed "Ulysses" squared us off. Ulysses' epochal voyage, his archetypal mission, was to *return home.*[*] Taking "no transition . . . debauchery" into its collective meaning, there was a level, in all the levels, in which it brought me my "big book" title, *Love in Transition: Voyage of Ulysses—Letters to Penelope.*

When Milton had told me I saw all the *un*ordinary things but not the ordinary things, in illustration he'd noted how "the astronauts almost crashed on the moon because one instruction was left out." He probably meant that while Buzz Aldrin and Neil Armstrong were in the lunar landing module, Eagle, the yellow alarm light went on repeatedly because of a data overload in the erasable memory; the docking radar had been left on. According to Milton, realizing the potential for this error in the planning stages, someone in Mission Control had offered to remind the crew while in flight but had been told no, "that was so obvious they'd remember."

What reminder did Earth psychology need? What little, obvious fact? What was uninserted? Needed deletion? Was in reserve?

I stared hard at the question. It was almost more than my brain could handle. But I seemed to be facing a dead end that would open if I said the magic words: "what transition?"

"And the ordinary thing is—" he had finished: "You fill in the blank. That all this scurrying is **not** to **do IT.**"

Jan was convinced that now that he'd weighed the importance of his gay tendencies, we simply had to work them through. However, it was the height of lunacy.

---

[*] *Archetype* means a pattern of events. It requires both an image and an emotion: "One can speak of an archetype only when these two aspects are simultaneous . . . by being charged with emotion, the image gains numinosity (or psychic energy" (*Man and His Symbols*, 87). Jung describes it as "a symbolical formula, which always begins to function whenever there are no conscious ideas present, or when such as are present are impossible upon intrinsic or extrinsic grounds" (*The Basic Writings of C. G. Jung*, 220). He calls archetypes "dynamic factors that manifest themselves in impulses, just as spontaneously as the instincts" (*Man and His Symbols*, 65–66). Examples are the Mother, the Wise Old Man, the Hero, the Divine Child.

That energy of love had gone elsewhere. Toward all those parts of me I'd been repressing.

I was an explorer, an artist. I'd written about Milton's passing (in *Love in Transition*)—given that fate to the fictional Robert—when it was real, physical, life. Similarly, I'd explored my emotions, finding their cul-de-sac in the little book about myself (as Merry Lou/Pouf) and Jan. I couldn't repress if finding out a part of me was stuffed away, calling itself Not Me and Pouf. But to Jan it was destiny and drama and in a sense "all about him." "Him" was "us."

He felt sure he understood what the unit of *us* needed—but Milton's passing created what others might call, but I didn't, loss of soul. I called it loss of Milton, loss of a vibration I couldn't live without, loss of wisdom and, as I put it, "the Highest Truth." How could I still be here?

I couldn't live without it—as if, if he provided it personally for me, then it existed and functioned as if through me. It was physically located in him. But that was a detail. I could not live without Milton. He had to be alive on the Earth and wasn't. Jan, on the other hand, literally believed this bond between him and me was undying, true love; if there was anything to work out, it would be together.

I thought that Herculean. I'd watched my heart shutting in alarm and lack of hope that it would be heard *by me*. No matter. That choice, when push came to shove, had already been tested and preconditioned. I chose myself and the Highest Truth, wherever it now was. If I had to find it in myself, so be it. It was *as if* I knew humanity holds God, or "You are God," as the Hindu teachers say. I did not reach the thought. The logic stayed in my intuition, which went into my writing. I just followed my deepest heart feelings—the heart, where my sense of self resides. My heart knew better and it was no longer involved in this level of love. It was involved in a survival mode, of its sense of self, the question which all mystics ask and answer, Who am I? on a gut level.

— 26 —

Flower Delivery from "Milt"

Blake died, living at Fountain Court. Hunter thought of ending Life #1 by jumping into the Rockefeller Fountain. I dreamed that to keep going, I had to be held under a fountain. My mother was born in Fountain.

Back in North Carolina, I lived briefly with my mother. Then in the summer enrolled in basic classes in modern and choreography at the American Dance Festival at Duke University in Durham, bicycling in 100-degree weather to the unair-conditioned studio.

While there, instead of searching through ads in a newspaper, I got the name of psychologist Robert Van de Castle from the back cover of a dream book. By letter I volunteered to work in his lucid dream lab in the UVA Medical School in Charlottesville, Virginia. Across the street from Duke, at the J. B. Rhine Foundation for Research into the Nature of Man, I noticed an announcement about the Parapsychological Association Convention at Fairleigh Dickinson University, New Jersey, to be held in August. I signed up to attend the convention. To my surprise, Van de Castle also attended and we met there in person.

One morning during the convention I unexpectedly woke in an altered state, and noticing me this way, a beautiful young parapsychologist with long dark hair falling over her back called over to me as I crossed the campus, "You're deep in meditation, aren't you?"

When I asked her in the bathroom afterwards what she meant, she said she had seen a being of white light over my head.

She added, "I don't think it was a discarnate. If so, it was someone very high." Normally she wouldn't have spoken, she said, but it was such a surprising sight at a place like this. She was a scientific researcher at an Ivy League university, so she kept most such observations to herself. But, she said, she had been able to see energy lines since she was a child. "Discarnate." Again the unfamiliar language. But it supported my daily diet indicating Milton might be alive.

I rode back down South from New Jersey in Bob Van de Castle's car, along with the author of a Scandinavian best seller about there being no death. She was a medical doctor who had joined a meditation group and after a year, she said, begun to be woken at night by entities who wanted her to channel. She rode to Virginia with us in order to meet with Elisabeth Kübler-Ross. It was all very interesting.

Van de Castle had offered me the job of putting his "definitive bibliography on dreams" into a computer that his staff would teach me to operate. I would pay my bills with the $1,000-a-month trust income my father had left me, intending it as a supplement.

Charlottesville, a small woodsy town in the foothills of the Blue Ridge Mountains, was abloom with sensational fall colors, including bright red leaves on the oak trees.

Here, Mexican therapist Graciela Damewood and her husband David had just opened the body/mind/spirit center Openway, "the open way to the positive feminine matrix through identification with earth." Van de Castle—dubbed the King of the Dreamers and the Prince of Percipients for his telepathic dream work in the Maimonides Medical Center Dream Research Lab—introduced me.*

Browsing at the popular Quest Bookstore, I bought *The Unobstructed Universe: An Unparalleled Detailed Report of Life after Death*—billed as a "definitive and corroborated picture of life after death."

The author, Stewart Edward White, a writer and conservationist whose credentials included being a friend of Theodore Roosevelt, had recently lost his wife, Betty. He noted that in a relationship people

---

* In that groundbreaking research, beginning in 1964, equipment was hooked up to participants. A test area was telepathy (target material, viewed by one person, that appeared in dreams of a subject). The work was led by pioneering psychiatrist Montague Ullman and humanistic psychologist Stan Krippner, Lab Director.

want "that rare inner feeling of companionship," which he'd had with her. Desolate one evening after her death, he felt "that companionship . . . but a hundred, a thousand times stronger." He began to experience "a merry sense of Betty—out of a clear sky—apropos of nothing. . . . I just called to her, and instantly she was there, and with a voltage that swept me right out of myself."[77]

Five months after Betty's death he visited a couple, Darby and Joan (pen names of the authors of *Our Unseen Guest*) in New York. Soon, Joan irritated herself—while running errands—by taking a crosstown bus to a remote department store she'd not been to for years; further baffling, she insisted on being shown a camphorwood chest of a *particular shade of red* not in the showroom. Adamant to the point where "they must have thought me crazy!" she found it in the reserve. She bought the chest, which she didn't want or need. "I can't *imagine* what got into me!" she said.[78]

Stewart had not received verbal messages from his wife on his own, but now Joan began to channel her. In this way, Betty provided Stewart with dozens of intimate authentications—known only to him.

Betty explained that *she* was the reason Joan bought the chest; it was for Joan's sister, Millicent. Betty had had Joan insist it be red—with *birds on it*—because as children she and Millicent watched birds. Wanting corroboration, White visited Millicent, who gasped, "Did you notice what *kind* of birds they are—painted on the chest? They are *swallows*!" She excitedly explained that it was swallows she and Betty "used to watch build nests. That's why we climbed the trees—to get level with the eaves!"[79]

Betty described to Joan "the unobstructed universe." With hairs on my arms practically standing on end, I incredulously read on. This was better than any grief therapist. On completely unfamiliar ground, I learned of the theory that different planes of reality *occupied the same space*, passing through each other. Only perceptual barriers separated the dimensions. In death one goes to an "unobstructed universe" that is all around us. With receptivity, we in the obstructed universe could make contact with the unobstructed.

White had shown his ideas to some physicists, who—the manner of his getting the information aside—found them important.*

Intrigued, I thought, *If Betty could send a gift that identified her, so could Milton.* I went to sleep with that dare—eager for this foray. But to make oneself a dare that Milton could maneuver a gift into physical reality is all well and good. To have it fulfilled is something else again.

I had rented half a condo and was to move in the next day with Barbara Kraft, who typed papers for NASA scientists and frequented Openway. As I was arriving, flowers were delivered—from, the card said, *her old NASA boss, Milt!* Congratulating her on her divorce!

This intense moment was further intensified by my having just visited (arranged by Dr. Van de Castle) the office of Dr. Ian Stevenson, whose life work was in reincarnation; he was the Chester Carlson Professor of Psychiatry and director of the Division of Personality Studies at UVA. Though tempted to speak up about Milton and the afterlife, I'd felt an inner warning to keep silent before this very serious man. What an intense moment when the flowers—mums, as if in confirmation—were suddenly delivered. I'd known nothing about Barbara's Milt. Imagine that they came straight from NASA. Like straight from outer space, where the rest of my life seemed to be originating now.

It turned out that Charlottesville was a haven for scientific investigation of the esoteric East. At the Openway center, I joined a group that had a "hyperventilated breathing" (Holotropic Breathwork) workshop one full day a month.

Holotropic Breathwork was devised to induce nonordinary states *without drugs* by psychotherapist Christina Grof and Freudian-trained

---

* Later I read the Nobel Prize physicist Wolfgang Pauli's reference to this material (in an unpublished essay, "Modern Examples of Background Physics," *Atom and Archetype*, 188). Betty's information, he attributed to the anima and "background physics" in the unconscious. More relevant to me at the time was that White thought the information came literally from Betty in an accessible "unobstructed universe" that intersected ours.

psychiatrist Stanislav Grof. In his first LSD trip Stan Grof had his brain waves monitored, in a pharmacological study in his medical school. To his great surprise, he shot out of his body and became "a disembodied consciousness of cosmic universal dimensions. I witnessed things that I would describe today as pulsars, quasars, the Big Bang, and expanding galaxies."[80] Grof reported that he had a mystical sense of "my consciousness becoming everything there was." And he "became the physical universe somehow."[81] No longer an atheist, he turned into a pioneer in consciousness exploration who believes that human beings are "fields of consciousness without limits, transcending time, space, matter, and linear causality."[82*]

Grof notes that every group in history except for the Western industrial civilization has had tremendous respect for nonordinary states and worked on developing safe ways to reach them.

In a nonordinary state there is a measurable shift in the electrical current in the brain. The normal waking brainwave in an adult—unlike small children and animals—is beta, 12–30 cycles per second,[†] or c.p.s., predominantly left brain. Lowering that moves into meditative alpha. Lower still is theta. Anything significantly different from the everyday, normal beta is considered an "altered state."

Soon Graciella's teacher Hector Kuri-Cano, a smiling, dark-haired profound Mexican psychotherapist of Lebanese extraction, arrived to conduct a workshop. After becoming a therapist, Dr. Kuri had studied with psychoanalyst Erich Fromm, Stanley Keleman (a leader in body psychotherapy and humanistic psychology), and psychiatrist

---

* Author of *Beyond the Brain: Birth, Death, and Transcendence in Psychotherapy* and other books, Stanislav Grof has been Chief of Psychiatric Research at the Maryland Psychiatric Research Center and Assistant Professor of Psychiatry at Johns Hopkins University School of Medicine.

† The electrical activity of the brain is measured through an EEG (electroencephalogram). The frequency is "the rate at which a signal is changing or vibrating. EEG frequency is measured in cycles per second. Typical frequency ranges are Theta: 4–7, Alpha: 8–12, SMR or Low Beta: 12–15, Beta: 15–20, and High Beta: 20–30," Biofeedback Glossary, The Association for Applied Psychophysiology and Biofeedback, Inc., http://www.aapb.org/i4a/pages/index.cfm?pageid=3462.

Alexander Lowen (Bioenergetics founder). Once, on a plane with a very serious illness, he didn't disembark in New York City but just kept going, to India. There and in the Middle East he studied with gurus and other masters, curing himself of the illness. Afterwards, in Mexico, he developed Energetic Metatherapy.

In the evening, before the Openway workshop began, he led a sunset meditation.

All my attempts to induce esoteric experiences as described in books—in my room in Madrid, Spain—had brought zero results: no crystal ball suddenly gave me trances or flights out of body. But a few hours after the meditation, my subtle sight awakened: I saw little circles in the air, round empty outlines. Then I dreamed the sun set on the *New York "Times"* building, turning it a solid gold; above it appeared a cloud that became a personified head, which transformed into cartoons.

The next day, I saw the small circles outdoors in the sky, plus less-than-split-second flying bits of sparkle, some in sheets. Hector said this was *prana*.* (Later I heard P. M. H. Atwater call the sheets "thought forms.")

Hector said that viewing stars on my eyelids in a single incident at twenty-four in New York City, I was seeing prana.

I did not learn till 2012 that he rose daily at 4:00 a.m. to meditate, followed by Tai Chi, before seeing clients.[83] And that he admitted to someone who experienced him while asleep, "I work with many of my clients in dreams." He added, "Most times they don't know."[84] Hmmm. I wondered, had he played some role in my sunset-meditation dream?

Once he asked me to close my eyes, tell him what I saw. Blocks of color, I said: gold, red, purple. He said those were his soul picture. I'd never before experienced someone transmitting into my mind. I was impressed. He asked me to train with him in Mexico, and I happily decided to consider it.

---

* The glossary in *Shakti: An Introduction to Kundalini Maha Yoga* by Dhyanyogi-ji defines prana: "Energy. The 'raw material' of Shakti" (149).

Meanwhile, besides typing a comprehensive bibliography for the UVA dream lab, I took ballet and jazz. I settled into a lifestyle of primarily female Openway friends.

I read Jan's letters selectively, avoiding the tiny-script, handwritten ones; I couldn't bring them into focus, as if they were scribble. He had in part been like my temptation, or secret vice, a mistake—though, as Milton had said about his own mistakes, "In some ways they weren't mistakes." No, but if you lean far out on a ledge, holding onto a rope or tied to a rope, you can no longer do this if there's no rope strong enough to secure you from a fall. I was fearful that he would just appear and upset everything. Turning my back on the old life, I was in this sense truly the child of the Rue de Damas.

At first, I kept my location undisclosed. Firmly behind the idea, my mother forwarded my mail. At his insistence, I sold his/our fine European antiques in a lump sum, which he hoped to invest in a Moroccan café. But much of the $10,000 wired him from the sale was confiscated by corrupt Moroccan bankers. At this point his plane began a nosedive, not entirely unpremeditatedly.

— 27 —

Al Miner: "Your own soul is guiding you into . . ."

In Charlottesville I woke late, read in bed a few hours, studied my dreams, and worked on my books; many evenings I spent at the dream lab or took a jazz or ballet class; on weekends I attended Openway seminars. And I sometimes had a therapy session with Graciella. Early on, among a voluminous number of dreams, one consisted entirely of a headline: DEATH SET FOR '83. Whose? It was the unknown newspaper's *lead* story.

The answer came without warning: my mother's.

In this admittedly feeble way, the dream was creating preparedness, or using the occasion to again assert some authority of my intuition. The idea of LEAD story, I later traced to her name, "Rosa LEE." Also, in hindsight, to the way she took the lead the last time we met.

1983, November—my mother died. A few months before, unforgettably, I was with her the last time. On impulse I asked, "*Mother, did you want me?*" Taken aback, she earnestly told me a story. *Had she not, this information would have gone with her to the grave!*

I was a medical miracle. With uterus damage from nephritis, she could not bear children. One day my parents learned of an experimental program at Duke University Hospital. For the first appointment my father took the wheel. He then taught her to drive, and, she explained, while he worked she thereafter drove to Durham for the treatments. One day the doctors said to go home, conceive, and if she could hold the child five months, the pregnancy would take. On that incredible note, my mother and I left the cafeteria.

She had insisted her own mechanic check out the used car we had just purchased, the first car I'd ever owned. He repaired the horn.

Satisfied that everything was perfect, she *led* in my car, me following in her old Cadillac to the edge of town; then we exchanged cars. That was the last time I saw her. From Virginia, I phoned, after which—I heard at her funeral—she called all her friends to say, "She made it!"

The weekend of November 12 my Charlottesville roommate was away. I unplugged the phone Saturday and that night watched Season 1, *The Yellow Rose*, Episode 6, "The Breaking Trail." It was during the program that I seem to have experienced, in parallel, my mother's death. I had known how deeply I loved her, how great the tie, but not that it was deep enough to allow the incident below, which to me was as profound as a miracle, wrought out of a desperate situation, a parting without saying good-bye.

A preview highlight flashed across the screen as the program started. At this point my mother was alive. A runaway car driven by Colleen Champion (Cybill Shepherd) sped dangerously without brakes around curves while Chance McKenzie (Sam Elliott) tried to stop it. The half hour came. The previewed scene reappeared with the theme song, "There's a yellow rose of Texas that I am gorna see. *Nobody else could miss her, not half as much as me.*"

"*Miss her.*" I felt my eyes well up—tears gushing. Why was I doubling over with sadness deep in my gut? It was only TV.

About *that* moment, a speeding patrolman's brakes locked as he rounded a curve on a highway and flew into the island, colliding with my mother's car. Watching a similar scene, I was gripped with grief. The song said her name: "Now you talk about your Clementine . . . and dear old Rosa Lee." But then something else happened.

Lyrics I'd never heard seemed especially brought in: "You saved my pride from dyin'." The song answered, "I saved your soul from hell." My mother, Rosa Lee, who protected me as I grew up—for instance, at twelve forbidding me to play kissing games (Spin the Bottle)—had dreamed during my marriage that she was driving me in a car. As we tried to get away from Jan he chased us.

In that stopped or correlated time, in the lyrics, it seemed we were rehashing and resolving, agreeing—in those instants as she left—through the simple expediency of a song and the phenomenon that arranged for it to background the event *at a distance*. I never experienced, in all the years since, anything so synchronistically precise and meaningful as this remote dialogue, which must have been with my mother as somehow she turned her thoughts to me in some overhead connecting place as the car struck and cut her artery, and she used the occasion of the nearly exact time and approximate scene.

Unbelievably, I watched the suspenseful highway chase that Chance tried to stop—successfully.

Not so, on that road on the edge of Greenville, where the brakeless patrol car slammed into the one where my mother was a passenger, as, correspondingly, on TV the driver found herself brakeless, helpless around dangerous curves. Desperation and death produce amazing ways to say good-bye.

It was as if I were actually there talking to her as my conscious mind interacted with the TV screen, as if time moved in sync almost to the minute. I do not know if forces of chance tried to stop my mother's accident, but it occurred as the dream predicted—in fact, had said it was "set" to. Set by whom?

In the condo basement I spread out my folders of dream records and manuscripts on a roomy feast of shelves and tried to finish *Love in Transition.*

Every night I asked my unconscious to give me a dream about a specific topic—ranging over a large number of types of questions. I also wrote down words to dream on—taken from the French symbol books from Morocco and runes. I woke intermittently to ask a new question, processing what I'd never processed.

Abruptly, by being aware of Milton's death, months while it was approaching, and *doing nothing about it except write it into my character,* had I smashed my thinking self's control over reality? And now it was neck and neck with my intuition?

Taking this huge risk (for a novelist) of changing my relationship to intuitive information, I forced the issue. Went at it as with a punching bag. I would have it out. Did my fiction-writing self quite literally in some cases know more of the *facts* of reality than my thinking self, who accepted outer boxes? Were the *fictional* details I imagined often a sort of translation? Else, how did *I kill off my character* exactly when the real-life model was dying?

Writing was "heuristic," Milton had said, "your umbilical cord to the other world." Was it truth pouring in with advance knowledge, because, perhaps, it was "tracked in" differently—less biased, less Hamletian, even less "local" in its sources??? I wondered.

Taking a break, I went to a dream seminar at Edgar Cayce's Association for Research and Enlightenment (A. R. E.) at Virginia Beach. Learning there of an internationally esteemed psychic in Florida, Al Miner, I ordered my second reading ever (the first having been shortly before and not helpful). The reading was by long distance in my absence. Considered the successor to Edgar Cayce (the "sleeping prophet") and rated number one in A.R.E.'s psychic accuracy tests, Al Miner, channel for Lama Sing, confirmed—in the mailed cassette in December that shook me to the core—that indeed I was in contact with Milton.

But he went much further. He mentioned "a cycle beyond the Earth"—saying that not only the Earth but "major soul groupings as are involved with the Earth are also in a transitional phase" (whatever that meant). Milton, he said, was from a soul grouping that was *coordinating its "transition" with the transition of the Earth* and I was in that grouping.

He went on: Milton and I had a conductor, a channel, between us, "which cannot be disrupted" by the loss of a physical body, for the tie was far deeper, at the emotive and spiritual levels. He said it was a "time of very beautiful opportunity."

I was flabbergasted, to put it mildly. I knew nothing about soul groupings, guides, coordinated transitions. Moreover, what did it mean that I was in a soul grouping in transition? It was shock wave after shock wave.

In speaking to my strengths and weaknesses, he mentioned past lives. I'd hardly thought about reincarnation, though Jan had a valued book in our apartment that quoted the many famous people who believed in it. Was reincarnation a reality? Maybe. My whole belief system was shattered anyway

Without being asked, Lama Sing identified two incarnations of mine: He said that in one, which I interpreted to be male, as an ancient Egyptian in a library I was very curious about other cultures. But being strong-willed, holding powerful convictions, I had few "close emotional bonds"; didn't make room for them.

Lama Sing plucked out a second—very different—lifetime from my energy: *a gypsylike female* who belonged to a "carefree, roving people, loving, kind, warm"—aggressive in taking what they needed though not intending harm, living around what is now the French–Swiss border. She reveled in relationships but endured *sudden losses*. This "renting" of the emotional self, he said, coincided with the ancient Egyptian's inclinations, creating a tendency to protect the emotions. Yet, he said, I wanted to "share a close bond" this lifetime and should enter it "with a complete aspect of self, not seeking from a relationship as such that which is missing in self."

So according to him, I had a male-female dichotomy, represented in two distinct past lifetimes, through which I was sorting out a balance. I could identify with this combination. In fact, it sounded a lot like me. The picture stimulated me. So that was me, in a larger portrait. Maybe.

Soon afterwards I found a tiny gold/red/blue metal mask of an ancient Egyptian male, which appeared—out of nowhere—in a box of my writing papers as I dug into it to bring out chapters to redo. I saved it.

Instantly, from a writer's point of view, I saw the storyline, the dramatic pitting of two such individuals as the intellectual, armchair-traveling Egyptian and the (nomadic flamenco dancing?) gypsy—that captured my current psychology. It felt right. I would say, the two had not yet met as a single person, as it were—that is, in me. Not yet—looking into the mirror—seen their combined reflection.

Compounding the wound, I saw, had been recent repetitions of the *sudden-loss syndrome*. Had that spur, in the deep recesses of my unconscious, made me resign from Random House the morning after Robert Kennedy's death? At this point, it didn't matter as much whether the reincarnation angle was literally true as that it was the means to see into my psychology further.

Lama Sing inserted an odd statement that if I could integrate what I needed to, "you build the opportunity to become a Living Example, a Living Christ." Al Miner was a teacher of "the inner Christ." Doubtless, this is what he meant. Still, the words leapt out at me, a goal, a new way to see myself in the very long run. Was this part of my future? Of everyone's? Of mine in a particular way requiring specific hurdles?

He concurred that I was correct to leave Jan. In fact, I had overstayed by a few years. In leaving, I had "broken a karmic bond," *though he had not.*

As Miner framed it, he should draw on his own strength, to survive (or not). I was relieved.

But trying to integrate something of this magnitude made my nervous system shaky. On the one hand, I felt completely vulnerable, but on the other I exulted in my newfound freedom. Part of me felt right at home, blending in with the Openway lifestyle and friends, taking ballet and jazz. Another part felt like to make a wrong move might send everything tumbling down. In Madrid I had regained my confidence in a brief four months. All my natural positiveness returned. The same was true here. But I knew how easy it would be to stumble and weaken.

I had to digest this. I was practically jelly inside.

Keeping the pendulum from swinging too far in one direction, I had an odd dream. As usual, I asked my unconscious to focus on something in particular. This night, it was—for no reason that I remember—to dream about Jesus in a way that *touches me now.* In the dream Jan and I were in a beach cottage, and he knew how to make a gadget work: push the lever forward. But which way was that? I didn't know. In pushing it forward, he *touched* my cheek with his. I had no idea why the dream showed me this, except that it was the kind of cosmic irony that kept me on my toes—a tendency I appreciated, liking to leave the door to final explanations open.

In late January 1984, I drove to D.C. and parked at the airport—to take the shuttle to my first annual MacDowell Colony party in New York City. I was later barely able to find my car in the gazillions of lots. Dream preparation had given me the clue that there was "a right way and a wrong way. Don't do something out of the top of your head." Nevertheless, I did.

I was hyperintensely emotionally charged, returning to the streets Milton had walked, entering the Corner Bistro we first met in. Though it had been a very long time since such a situation happened, I suddenly found myself out of my body in the classic instance of looking down on it. I was above my physical self with a spirit woman, who—on later reflection—was perhaps my soul. I'd left my body in public to fend for itself!

The next thing I knew was a sensation of swimming up from underwater. Landing in my body in a taxi, I saw another passenger—an actual physical male—beside me. I was returning to the hotel without my pocketbook—with no memory beyond when the spirit woman took me out of my body, no knowledge of where I went in spirit with her or physically with him. Staggeringly awkward, such a moment.

But someone from the restaurant had returned my pocketbook back to the hotel. This incident was highly disturbing and perplexing. I attributed the cause to the intensity surrounding my visit. But I could not explain anything else.

Yet in New York nineteen years before, I had had "the Little Dot" vision (which felt like a real experience) of me flying out of body accompanied by a determined "dot of energy." I had the sensation both times of returning to my body—becoming aware of my physical surroundings again—by swimming to the surface.

What was I carrying buried inside that a higher form of me watched over? What a strange kind of structure if I could be yanked out of awareness of my physical surroundings. I remembered this experience of her only in a quick snapshot, smiling down blissfully on my body below, myself at her side. She had no doubts, and I no second thoughts about leaving with her.

In this experience, which incidentally was the last time it was ever to occur—probably due to the consciousness work I was entering upon—I'd been shown that *no control had been lost.* Thankfully, I could ask Bob Van de Castle for a psychologist's analysis. Listening carefully, he produced the term *autonomous complex*. This somewhat reassured me. Wasn't there a limit to how dangerous a complex could be? It required attention if a part of myself could act contrary to what I consciously wished. Yet because of the fact that no control had been lost—after all, I landed in a taxi and my pocketbook even got returned—I interpreted it to be not that dangerous. Van de Castle stayed on the psychological level, which was all I wanted.

But now things had come to a head. To integrate the parts of me I was unaware of felt like a commandment. So someone "up there," who was an aspect of myself, understanding the complexity of whatever components and forces composed me, watched that this unintegrated aspect—in its infrequent appearances—did not go to such an extreme as to ruin my life. Yet this combination of sensibilities must have been there for some reason, those components I was conscious of and those depths whose structure I had been completely unconscious of. How? Why? I was motivated to find out.

I remembered Al Miner had further added about the present, *"Your own soul is guiding you into this position."*

He said I needed to allow myself whatever changes were trying to happen; that is, love myself enough without inflating or deflating. Seen from that perspective, this was inspiring. But it told me nothing more about where I was going and whether I'd make it. For I didn't take it for granted I would. I was putting one foot ahead of the other. Basically, I thought I needed to let my soul through without barring the way by doubt of self-worth or her reality.

That was quite an order because my days in Morocco still peered over my shoulder. In an overnight Al Miner workshop I had attended in December, when he made a visit to North Carolina, I dreamed I'd built a beautiful Viking ship of matches. Jan was tearing it down. That "Jan" character, I took to be an inner masculine part of me, hypercritical of whatever voyage I was about to set out on.

— 28 —

Mariah: "A consciousness is coming toward you"

What did it mean, to be held under a fountain? Though I didn't know it, Zurich was nicknamed the "city of fountains," a moniker it earned from its 1200 or so drinking fountains! With cobblestone streets and tram lines overlooked by the Alps, the city is the intellectual capital of Switzerland.

According to my Barcelona "big dream," if I came down from a plateau where after death Milton was in a black hole, and if—once on the lower level—I held a small, misshapen animal-like creature under a fountain, tons of dark gook would come out and it/I would be transformed into a little fish. The neglected "monster" needed cleansing. It needed to be held under a fountain.

If, by contrast, I tried to communicate from up on the plateau, I might take a precipitous tumble onto the "concrete." That is, be grossly misunderstood. It was time to integrate an outcast part of me.

Let me quickly add that up to this point my values had been governed, to a significant degree, by an Old World picture of the artist as a nonconformist fighter, a do-or-die, often poverty-stricken Voice for the future, a "visionary," a committed piece of energy out of the unconscious that had no thought but to Speak for Dear Life. A dedicated artist giving to the masses of the future with little recompense but the art, the Truth, found in dark and unknown places after mighty inner battles and pilgrimages—swords wielded into the unconscious. In other words, a pioneer, who might break a law or win against overwhelming odds. Who was heroic and might die unsung yet get discovered just afterwards.

I knew the examples: Bizet, who died with *Carmen* booed; or Emily Brontë, who died with her creations, Heathcliff and Cathy in *Wuthering Heights*, rejected by readers. Or Kafka, who asked that his manuscripts be burned. Or Van Gogh, who had only one painting sold in his whole life. In science, Copernicus died with the just-printed first copy of his seminal work, *On the Revolutions of the Celestial Spheres*—that proposed that the planets revolved around the sun—beside him on his bed. Rembrandt, who died bankrupt (partly his own fault) in 1669, was accused in 1707, by a highly reputed Dutch painter and art critic, of having "colors that appear to lie like liquid mud on the canvas."[85] A biographer describes how in dying, Rembrandt had the Genesis account of Jacob wrestling with the Angel read to him. Far into the story, Rembrandt slowly put his hand to his eyes and whispered, "And Jacob was left alone."

He recited the passage from the beginning, inserting: "but he did not give in and fought back—ah, yes, he fought back—for such is the will of the Lord—that we shall fight back . . . that we shall wrestle with him until the breaking of the day."

Then instead of Jacob being renamed Israel, he said, "thy name shall be called no more Jacob but Rembrandt."

If one had that kind of calling, I had made every allowance for the lifestyle that produced the work.

In spite of such pictures from the past, however, after Milton's death I was fighting in Charlottesville not to be crushed. As if not a rug but one pole had been pulled out from under me, an irreplaceable one, it seemed.

I learned that the original C. G. Jung Institute, in Küsnacht, a suburb of Zurich—a Swiss German-speaking part of Switzerland—had a program in English. Thinking of applying in March '83, I slept on the question why I deserved admittance "this fall."

In the resulting dream I was with Milton. His girlfriend appeared, holding a baby whom I next carried down a dark passage. Refocusing my question, the baby *took a fall.* Oblivious, I arrived at her home—greeted by her alarmed mother at the front door. Then, frantically retracing my steps, I found the baby.

In a series of puns, the dream pointed to a danger of a last-minute *mis-carriage*. But though I *carried* her, the *expectant* "mother" awaited her *delivery* at the Institute.

Excited, I turned down Hector Kuri's offer—of apprenticing with him in Mexico. And decided to go to Küsnacht in October.

Meanwhile, in March, there was excitement in the air as one of Openway's favorite people, a psychic, Mariah Martin, flew in from Hawaii. I arrived for my appointment in the evening, and when she started by saying she saw me as if on an energy swing, I managed to steer her away from the superficial volatility to the underlying shift that was occurring—the reordering and intention that was playing out. To do this, I merely had to show my awareness of the energy. What I remember most of what she said that evening is "A consciousness is coming toward you"—as if it were actually flying from point A to B.

When I asked about Milton—not mentioning his death—she saw a strong relationship. "But I don't think it can go anywhere," she added. I explained, "No, he's dead." She then said, "He's surrounding you with love."

I wanted her insights into my life purpose. She said, "It's on two levels: (1) on the personality level, you're learning to overcome *the fear* of being strong as a female; (2) on the soul level, you're here to help others *overcome the fear of Enlightenment.*"

At Openway, she was highly trusted, even by the more skeptical like Bob Van de Castle. So I was all set to consider seriously what she said next: "You've been strong and powerful as a male many times. You're here to learn that you can do everything as a female you ever did as a male."

Now two well-respected psychics had told me virtually the same thing.

— 29 —

Charlottesville to Küsnacht

Facing down the confiscation of much of the furniture-sale proceeds, Jan refused to pay rent while the Moroccan bank illegally kept his money. Jailed for a month, he was then informed his visa extension had gone through. Driven to the border, he was to walk across for a passport stamp. But once across was denied reentry. The young Moroccan Abdou got our mini-dachshund out, and Jan and Snoep went to Belgium—never to recoup his manuscripts or belongings, or the money.

In Belgium a physical exam proved him miraculously fit. But while in the hospital he left Snoep with his mother. As they were crossing the street Snoep collapsed, his back legs paralyzed. The vet said the cause was psychological.

Relaying the news, Jan asked me to phone. When anyone said my name, Snoep's ears still perked up. Would I fetch him?

Processing my options, I asked a dream question: "I'm so upset—so emotional, so full of feeling—about my relationship with Jan. Please help me know what to say on the call tomorrow. How should we relate to each other now for the best future development for us both?" I dreamed my room was sinking in water as the result of a fire.

I flew to Belgium, where Jan tried to use the two-day visit to reconcile.

He also wanted us to take Snoep to Holland for a spine operation that might let him walk. Jan thought I'd pay—on my shoestring budget. Pulling on my heartstrings. Nevertheless, I felt guilty.

At the last minute he held back Snoep's passport. I waited to board. Then in a blaze of sunshine he entered the airport, inspired, he said, by two dreams that changed his mind. In one, I was the negative mother to Little Fiss. But then there was the other, in which he saw a beautiful male who impressed him—enough to take the cab to the airport. That, he said, was my animus. He then handed over our cherished Snoep.

Now there was only bleakness ahead. Everything I'd feared became a reality. He was never, in fact, to write again. As he'd seen his family in a Zola-esque light, this was now to become extremely real, for him. The descent would be relentless, an intensity of emptiness. But nothing on earth could assign me to go over there and "stop it." So "the horror" had come. He was going down.

This is what I had tried so hard to prevent. And yet, like someone crying wolf too often, Jan had survived up to this point, and Milton, whom I'd thought invulnerable, had died. So I was done trying to rescue Jan. After all, I could not control destiny and the maneuverings of who lived and who died. Had I had to choose between them on that score, I would have chosen that Milton be spared. So I would focus on what made me the most hopeful and positive now, myself—and this new growth.

Somebody at Openway programmed a computerized numerology system, and we read mine. Based on my birth date and the letters in my name, it detected *major nineteen-year* cycles—the preceding cycle having begun in 1965–66 in New York! According to this chart, a similarly important period was at hand—in even higher intensity. For technical reasons of the dual doubling of "r," the upheaval would associate with "fifty-five."

The prospect of having a sudden infusion of excitement as great as in the New York City days—only, in a different, unknown direction—exhilarated me. It didn't seem possible. I was apprehensive yet open—fearing that I needed help to meet it.

Feeling it would help me in what was to come, I had a couple of additional Lama Sing readings, in July and September 1984, just before leaving for Zurich. In them, I learned more details about issues raised in his first reading. He explained that within a soul group, members were at different levels of consciousness, and each member was vitally important because "the strength, the clarity, and the spiritual attunement [of the group] is equal to that of the least [evolved]." I had asked where was "home." In answer, he replied that my soul grouping was "in a realm of consciousness, that is existence, which is *several dimensions, several spheres of consciousness, removed from the Earth,*" and it tried to "spread its consciousness" between those realms.

The way in which my soul grouping's consciousness was distant from the Earth was in "its ability to accept."

He made no mention of great feats or other signs of mastery, as if the ability to accept (when necessary) signaled an increase in evolution—which, in itself, was a different outlook than any I'd heard. Not that I knew metaphysics. But this shot it up into my peak interest. Did guardian spirits exist? Did everyone have them?

In trying to make sense of certain dreams, I had asked if there was a group project under way. He said yes. Specifically, it associates with the Christ's light.

"And that is"—he defined—"simply the illumination of the universal nature of each soul by the intensification of those forces which relate to this consciousness.

"So it is called the pathway of return unto God, the Christ Consciousness."*

---

* The Christ consciousness is based in the light, love, and truth inside each person, in contrast to the exclusiveness sometimes emphasized in Christianity. For instance, the great Hindu satguru Paramahansa Yogananda, in his *Autobiography*, called a Hindu avatar Babaji the "Yogi-Christ of modern India" (345). In trying to write this footnote, I stumbled across a 2004 book that compiled teachings of Yogananda. In it, this top teacher in the Hindu line interprets the four Gospels according to a unity of religions that is the base of his own work. He says, "A thousand Christs sent to earth would not redeem its people unless they themselves became Christlike by purifying and expanding their individual consciousness." Published fifty-two years after Yogananda's death, it brings together his ideas about the deeper meanings of Jesus's teachings; how they are essentially unified with yoga as a path to oneness with God. In the book he calls the Second Coming the "resurrection of Christ within you." This sort of approach—of inclusiveness—was such a clear basis of my understanding that I was afterwards completely startled whenever hearing this consciousness confused with a religion.

As this could be open to misreading, let me add that "the universal nature of each soul" means that everyone on that level, is ultimately transpersonal—having energy that goes beyond the personal.

I find this helpful definition online: "The transpersonal world is a lateral world, one that covers all in one encompassing moment. It is the way . . . the Tao." This definition adds that "to look outside yourself . . . for recognition and acceptance . . . for a master or teacher . . . for a savior . . . for another to be your authority . . . is to deny the existence of your transpersonal nature."[86]

That said, I hope it's clear that Lama Sing's words refer to a consciousness, which is a very different thing from a religion. As I understand it now, to live the consciousness would mean to live unconditional love. An example might be Gandhi.

Lama Sing said little else about the project other than mentioning "pathway of . . . the Christ consciousness." He said to say more could "abort [my] life purpose." Learning certain information from such a source, he said, could do that. And I had always insisted on finding out things for myself, to forge the qualities from Not Knowing, biting the nails.

He also made clear that if a soul, while on Earth, became individually ready to assist a soul grouping project, then that person was brought in. The thought struck me that this might possibly be happening or about to happen to me.*

* Below is an example of notes taken after a breathwork session at Openway June 2–3. The session made me remember words Milton said once in 1969 in annoyance after—when I sublet his apartment in New York while he went to MacDowell Colony—he returned early, found me in hair curlers with no place else to sleep that night. In *Keep This Quiet*, I wrote, "We got off on the wrong shoe" and stayed in separate rooms. At one point I "told him this relationship made me feel like Sisyphus."

My actual words were "I am not Sisyphus. I am his stone." It was his answer that rose up to haunt me in the breathwork. He paused and grouped his words into perfection: "If you must think of yourself as the Sisyphus stone, the only way I can possibly get rid of you is to pulverize you and let the wind blow you away."

After the breathwork, using Jung's "active imagination," I suddenly associated the wind blowing me away with "gone with the wind," windy Blankenberge, and

I was fully convinced I was heading into a great shift in Zurich. How would I weather and rise up out of something so significant—so long-lasting—as the upheaval in the New York City time frame nineteen years earlier, when I met Hunter, Jan, and Milton: all three? Tingling ran through my veins. It was like being on the tip of an iceberg when the iceberg itself was about to surface. What would it bring? Would I survive it? Master it? I began to pack my bags—staring into a big question mark.

---

a phrase of mine: "waves Olympus high." From here the images transformed—in poetry-length lines, which I am reformatting.

Remembering the Blankenberge parade, I imagined him setting out from Mount Olympus with the torch of freedom—of freedom from Death, A gift to all men, running with that torch. For Death was the torch, and he carried the torch, right to the end of the block. . . .

It defined all logic, but I knew it to be true, know it more than anything else in the world, than any fact of scientific equation explaining life, that there is something beyond death—spiritually and emotionally. In fact, for me, love was BEYOND DEATH.

I realized that "Death was the missing ingredient" in my long-unfinished big book. That I was only a witness, an observer, but "humbly present myself as something that had been dammed, blocked, and that now is UNBLOCKED, For he went to the end of MY BLOCK. That was his death, the end of MY BLOCK. And sent back the news to me."

— 30 —

"White Designs"

Another significant dream showed the charred end of Milton's obituary. I was told me to write the end *verbatim*. This felt like an assignment. A detective story. Something at the end wasn't right. Got reported wrong. I was a reporter. This story I had to report.

As mentioned, when confronting the reality that he hadn't finished his novel or written the poetry he'd expected—and been expected—to write, Milton sometimes quoted from the *Sayings of the Fathers*: "It is not *given* you to complete the task. Neither is it *allowed* you to leave off." He'd said penetratingly, "I can write poems as well as anyone alive. Why don't I?" The public obituary had left that question hanging.

The intricacies below capture me in the act of receiving energy locked into word play—as with Zeus throwing thunderbolts—that uncovered an ambiguity in the words *allowed you, a LOUD U.* I could feel the energy pulsating, as in a voice at the top of its lungs, telling me this was

> Not the End, not A DIEU*
> This is a loudspeaker of the spirit
> a shouter
> *un haut-parleur*†
> This is *IO**
> This is me,

---

* "Adieu" ("good-bye," French); "Dieu" ("God," French)

† "A loudspeaker" (French), a reminder that Milton was "a shouter"; "adieu" in French is an off rhyme with "haut parleur" but pronounced, in English, *uh-D(Y) OO*, rhymes with "a loud U."

Io sol[†]
saying, "We belong on Mt. Olympus together
"We have an appetite for dew"[‡]
It is *not allowed you to leave off*
For this is not adieu
but A LOUD DIEU
Nothing else will do
Nothing else is
A LOUD U

The poetry went on: "Here's the end you were looking for . . . / it is 'A LOUD U.'"

Leaving Charlottesville, I told myself—blind but at warp speed—to make meaning of this death, it hid "buried secrets."

How I could do it, I didn't know. But I predicted that one day—unexpectedly—I would find the unwritten obituary:

just as if these blank pages had held something invisible all
this time. Blanks that were not really blank
Here were
The WHITE DESIGNS

Milton's unfinished novel, "White Designs," drew from the cabalist notion that what *wasn't* written down in the Bible—the white around the Hebrew letters—contained the hidden meaning. Was it possible I was being urged that what wasn't "allowed" him was "allowed" me? A spur if ever there was one. But allowed only if I followed to where this nondeath was leading. Of course, who writes such words is not the personality but the self, the soul, standing, catching the dribblings and the downfalls, holding for dear life onto this "umbilical cord."

---

* "Io" is "I" in Italian, pronounced "eo."

† "Sol" is "sun" in Spanish.

‡ Milton had said this to me.

— 31 —

The Jung Institute Zurich

I arrived in Küsnacht, Switzerland—the small town on Lake Zurich that housed the C. G. Jung Institute—having put my scanty supply of furniture in storage in North Carolina.

An intimate single building, the Institute was warm and welcoming. As I looked at the entrance (at the top of steps) it recalled the door through which the dream mother ran out to receive the baby I carried!

Immediately I was in a world of intuitive and feeling introverts. An intuitive, for instance, does not—when being intuitive—"interpret." An intuitive "knows." This knowing has feeling in it; it is based a lot on sensing. There are ways to develop skill in being accurate, for there is also reverse intuition, which is inaccurate. An intuitive might say, *I have to buy a bed for a guest bedroom, but I don't know why.*

In "A Jungian Analyst Talks about Psychological Types," John Beebe gives examples of the intuitive type. For instance, he talks about the medical training Jung told student Joe Wheelright (later founder of the Jung Institute in San Francisco) he would need, to be an analyst. Beebe writes:

> So Joe Wheelwright tells very funny stories about his training—I guess at Mosley Hospital in London—where he walked into a room on rounds, and the Chief Physician said, "What is that patient suffering from, Wheelwright?" And Wheelwright looked right back, and said, "Oh, he has tuberculosis." The doctor was just furious. He said, "Well, as a matter of fact he does have tuberculosis, but did you put on

> your stethoscope, did you listen to his lungs, did you look at his hands, did you take his pulse, did you look at his skin? No. You just stood across the room and said he has tuberculosis." Joe said that that was how intuition was treated when he was a medical student.[87]

Like Alice coming up out of a hole or falling in, I had never known such a place existed. Here my new intuitive friends understood with amusement what it meant to say, "I know something, but I don't know yet what it is." I attended enthralling classes and made female friends.

It was in the classes that I learned about the "anima woman."

Synchronistically, in November six days before the third anniversary of Milton's death, there was a startling lecture by the astounding Canadian Marion Woodman. The topic made me sit bolt upright in my seat: "The Anima Woman."

Flown in for guest lectures, Woodman, a famous champion of conscious femininity—already the author of *The Owl Was a Baker's Daughter: Obesity, Anorexia Nervosa and the Repressed Feminine and Addiction to Perfection: The Still Unravished Bride*—began to speak. A huge wave of identification—in particular regarding my relationship with Jan—rolled over me.

The inner femininity of a male—the anima—can project herself outward to cause love at first sight, a sense of being meant for each other. Nothing revolutionary here. But Marion went further. The drop of a pin could have been heard inside me as she staked out the parameters of my turf regarding Jan, describing the type of female (myself) who typically received *AND HELD* such projections. The anima woman "can be anything the man wants. She unconsciously hones in on the man's unconscious. She 'really' is that woman with him, and 'that' woman with another—can be anything the man projects." An example is Marilyn Monroe. There are intricate variations in how this plays out.

I realized that in my relationship to Jan, the practice of assisting others to go deep into their unconscious spilled into that category—evidenced by my novel about us, now titled "A Lecture upon the Shadow." Applying Marion's outline, Pouf (myself) was the "anima woman."

The format was visible in the evolution of the characters' names: Mary Lou (me)/Pouf. And Knut Karel (Jan)/Boom. But this ability to go (even disappear) into the unconscious of Jan bound me tightly into the relationship because so much of it took place there, in that murky, borderless land of the unknown—where one can't always distinguish clearly who is who.

All through Romantic literature, Marion said, there is the theme of the love/death marriage, where "love and death dovetail" (which may bring in the "femme fatale"), and many of us are "carrying it from our grandparents."* Love/death dovetailing. I was in further shock at the precision with which I'd followed this blueprint, because by the end of "A Lecture upon the Shadow"—indicating the appalling disintegration in the marriage—I nicknamed the two characters "Dead and Buried" (me being buried).

I felt astounded that when I wrote "A Lecture upon the Shadow," I'd as if put tracing paper over Jung's theories.

I asked Marion to read this book, her lecture seeming its eerie collaborator. I told her I'd written an unconscious study of her topic—that it was "pre-exposure to Jung. In fact, instantly upon

---

* Examples of "carrying the archetype" would be, Marion said, Emily Brontë, who took it as far as she could and then died. Or Emily Dickinson. Or Sylvia Plath and Ted Hughes: she said there was so much electricity in the Plath-Hughes house the roof literally blew off. They couldn't live together and they couldn't live apart. They had "hit into the archetype. The ego takes it on, then goes out to write with it, comes back for recharging." Jung with his mistress Toni Wolff was also an example.

It was said Toni Wolff "had an extraordinary genius for accompanying men—and sometimes women too, in a different way—whose destiny it was to enter the unconscious" (F. G. Robinson, *Love's Story Told: A Life of Henry A. Murray,* 122–123).

Further, many women, said Woodman, had animus issues in anorexia and other eating disorders or addictions. The male, meanwhile, was in his half of the complex. A reemergence of the true feminine principle—extracted from the false animus or mother's power principle—is awakening today.

finishing this little book, I plunged as if by accident into Jung." She had a formidable reputation and was very busy. But she said *perhaps, not yes, not no.* After her next lecture she took it away, having just described (in class) a ritual to release another person. I was riveted. *Should I "turn Milton loose"*?

I went into Zurich November 28, purchased an African brass bowl. In my apartment, using Marion's ritual, I burned Milton's brown scarf, the one tangible thing of his I had. He had bought it for me on a shiveringly cold day in New York as the chill struck my throat and he stopped at a bookie's—the only occasion I ever saw him visit one.

I put the scarf into the bowl, lit a match, and the flame began to crawl up toward the ceiling. As it happened, that very evening Marion was drawn to the manuscript—opened it. And in matching distant tempos, the scarf burned and she read.

I next saw her—leaning on her cane—November 29: the anniversary of Milton's death! As I recorded it in my diary, "Marion Woodman returned my novel (read), liking it—profoundly moved."

Agreeing that it was about the anima female, she said that it went further than she had on some points. I thought she meant that everyone was a shadow or sub-shadow of everyone else. She said, "It's so poetical I don't know if it can be understood now. But in ten years everyone will be able to read it."

So now I knew that the part of my personality in the "karmic bond" with Jan had been an "anima woman" par excellence.

I realized that it was my shadow who married—the "French gypsy" was a good image—and his shadow she'd wed. Shadow places can grow what wants to become conscious, unknown but now constellated truths. Speaking of the *spiritual animus* as a woman's creativity, Marion added, "The creative masculine is born outside the law." For example, she cited Jesus.

Running into her after watching the movie *Amadeus*, I seized the opportunity to ask if there was a Mozart archetype. "*Yes*," she said, "*the child clown*."

About me, on the contrary, Milton had observed, "You're still saying, 'Do your homework, dear, before you can go out and play.'" I felt my inner child provocateur stirring. Considered a "grown-up child," I had probably kept a very extraverted side jailed—always looking through the bars, trying to shout, "Me too!!" That was a bit scary. I felt something click in my belly.

Jung's psychoanalytic theory stresses the goal of individuation—that is, *wholeness*. Jung said that in perceiving and judging, everyone's personality organizes around four tendencies, or types—thinking, feeling, intuition, sensation—with one or two dominant and at least one deeply unconscious, or inferior.

I had my psychological profile tested and was dominant in intuition/thinking. I could now identify that neglected part of me in the Barcelona dream—the shriveled creature that needed cleansing under the fountain—as what Jung, in his typology, labeled my "inferior function." Coming down from the plateau to a *lower* level, I now took to mean from thinking and intuiting—to cleanse the shriveled sensation function.

Synchronistically, November 29 a different lecturer spoke at the Institute on "Confrontation with the Self"—that major part of Jung's work where the Self* is confronted, in my case in a mind-bending initiation. I say that without exaggeration, at least regarding the effect on me.

The way I saw it, I'd written *done, finito* over an area of the unconscious that was unconsciously Jungian. I would now enter a brand-new area of

* Jung defined the Self in the Glossary of *Memories, Dreams, Reflections* (417). It is "the central archetype; the archetype of order; the totality of the personality. Symbolized by circle, square, quaternity, child, mandala, etc." He added that it "embraces not only the conscious but also the unconscious psyche."

Moreover, "The Self is not only the center but also the circumference." He thought it "our life's goal," and from confronting it, we learn our individuality. It was in his confrontation with the unconscious that he learned not only his life's work but also his personal myth.

the unconscious. Psychology would be the Omega, standing on which, through the intuitive structures I'd explored, I would launch myself or more rightly *be* launched by cannon burst into the psychic, the afterlife, the question why we are here and what might be our purpose.

Hemingway had warned that becoming conscious brought drawbacks, could be deadly: In *A Moveable Feast* he said F. Scott Fitzgerald's innate talent was "as natural as the pattern that was made by the dust on a butterfly's wings. At one time he understood it no more than the butterfly did and he did not know when it was brushed or marred." But then he became "conscious of his damaged wings and their construction and he learned to think and could not fly anymore . . . he could only remember when it had been effortless." Milton likewise said he himself knew too much, that it created an "etiquette," restricting a writer's politically incorrect impulses.

The weekend after this scarf burning, I felt awful, remorseful.

To be in company, I attended a crystal workshop, where I met a beautiful one-quarter Cherokee woman with dark, midback-length hair. The South Dakota-born Texan, Jeneane Prevatt (now Jyoti), was advanced in out-of-body experiences (OBEs) and visions. As part of her training, Jyoti was having therapy with some of the most respected Jungian analysts. Meeting her was of major importance in my life.*

As recounted later in her autobiography, *An Angel Called My Name*, she was, at the time we met—around Christmas 1984—a year into an intense kundalini awakening.† She wrote, "Kundalini is a process in which Spirit fuses with matter. A process in which the individual is taken on a journey into the Divine through the body."[88]

---

* With an illustrious career ahead, Jyoti, with her husband, was a founder of the spiritual community Kayumari. She later became Spiritual Director of the Center for Sacred Studies, Traveling Ambassador for the Thirteen Indigenous Grandmothers, and a convener of the Grandmothers Council.

† Kundalini—in Sanskrit "coiled up"—is described, in Eastern belief, as an evolutionary energy system. Or "serpent power." When activated, kundalini moves up the spine to awaken chakras. Chakras are "wheel-like vortices which, according to traditional Indian medicine, are believed to exist in the surface of the subtle body of living beings" (Wikipedia). When completely awakened, the kundalini leads to self-realization. Jung related Kundalini Yoga to developmental phases in higher consciousness.

She added, "The ultimate goal of all paths is union with the Higher Self—the return to the source. The soul (the divine feminine) merges with spirit (the divine masculine), bringing about the wholeness both seek. Each individual journey is unique within itself."[89]

In the chapter "The Induction," she described how from her first Christmas in Küsnacht, December 1983, throughout the next eight years she would experience body restructuring and illness. She knew nothing of kundalini then. Therefore, the book states, "when the visionary experiences began to have physiological manifestations, I became frightened."[90]

She explains, "The archetypal energy was electrifying my field, creating synchronicities that seemed to merge the inner and outer realities. I was like walking around in a dream or waking up in this one we call life. I couldn't tell which!"[91]

In the initial experience of physiological changes, in December 1983, she was on a ski trip. But her right arm "began to ache," she was feverish, her throat sore (though she had no fever). So she stayed behind in the house. As she got worse she lay down. The pain in her arm "mounted in intensity until [she] could barely stand it." Her arm felt "somehow separate from the rest of [her]." She drifted into an altered state.

Then she had a visionary experience: "A great Light, golden and oval in shape, appeared. . . . It hovered above my head and began to shoot a laser of golden light into the top of my head, creating an immense heat that radiated throughout my body. The Light seemed to run into my head, down into the heart region, out through my arm, and completing its cycle back at the saucer of Light. Following the same path, it recycled continuously for several hours. The pain increased to such a high pitch until finally I lost consciousness."

When she woke, all pain was gone and her arm "could lift heavy objects . . . that [she] had not been able to lift before." She asked, "What in the world was happening to me? Was there no one who could help me understand such bizarre happenings?" She quotes Gopi Krishna on kundalini awakenings: "The whole organism now begins to function in a most amazing manner which cannot but strike terror into the stoutest heart. Tossed between the old and yet incompletely built new conscious centre, the subject, unprepared for such a startling development, sees himself losing control of his thoughts and actions."[92]

In June 1985, Jyoti was alone one day in a large classroom at the Institute. I went in. Barely knowing me, on a hunch she invited me to Rome!

I threw the I Ching and fussed about whether to accept. The more confused I was, the more the I Ching reflected the confusion. I ended up going. When booking, she learned that there was only one vacancy in the hotel—we would have to sleep in the same bed—and that the name was "Hotel Homs." She thought something was up.

On the plane she began to speak in what to me were mind-boggling revelations about her journey.-

In suspense about what would happen on our trip, I had the feeling of opportunity reinforced big time when we received our hotel-room keys: 55. "Fifty-five"—in the numerology predictions—equated with my predicted massive upheaval, which, if adhering to nineteen-year cycles, would occur this very year.

I had asked, prayed, thrown the I Ching, for help. The massive upheaval, which I fully expected, felt far too big to master alone—remembering the magnitude of the previous nineteen-year cycle, at the start of which, in 1965–66, I met all three males who dominate this two-book memoir.

Enter Jyoti, soon to be head of Stan and Christina's Grof's Spiritual Emergence Network. She would lend me books, such as *The Autobiography of a Yogi* by Yogananda, which I would set aside till ready.

Soon I would critique the draft of her autobiography. When it finally came out in book form, she was introduced by the well-known psychiatrist and pioneer of the global Human Potential Movement, Claudio Naranjo, as a shaman. In manuscript and in person she would tell me about kundalini. And down the road, Dhyanyogi Madhusudandas-ji, a Kundalini Maha Yoga master who would become my guru—all this keyed to that room number. That is, to my next step, the step I would begin to be initiated into in a few short weeks.

This meeting in Rome set the stage in earnest. Besides the enjoyment of stepping out of the boutique hotel practically into the Piazza di Spagna, I felt the support of a loving person with a huge heart. I was reassured and excited.

At the Sistine Chapel, I stared up at *The Last Judgment* by Michelangelo. Immersed in the recent dreams and experiences, I thought I was looking up at the otherworldly being of white light that a parapsychologist had seen over my head (see page 145). Feeling a deep connection, I bought a post card that years later I would scan for the cover of a book, *The Christ State.*

I also deduced I had magnetism. Walking down the cobblestone streets after she left, I thought it must be that I was being put in a mist of some sort—a blur that made me irresistible—because otherwise I couldn't understand it. I felt the spiritual guidance was creating attractions intentionally and I welcomed an Italian reporter's offer to drive me to far-apart sites: from the Colosseum and the underground jail cell, by legend, of Apostles Peter and Paul, to the Moses statue by Michelangelo in the church of San Pietro in Vincoli (St. Peter in Chains)—which in such a sprawling metropolis is a godsend. In addition, there was a bit of Latin sex thrown in—which, trying to understand my new world, I figured was OK if it started out in the "mist."

Back to Jyoti. To her, this world I was about to enter was not strange. Again at the Jung Institute, I asked her input on cutting ties with Jan. Just afterwards in a class on icons, she left the room.

She reported later that it was as if gorillas (wild emotions) were stomping on her; she had to lie down. At home, she was pulled out of her body through either the head or the feet, whichever location she was not used to exiting through—into an OBE.* So Jyoti was to be

* That night in sleep before talking to her about it, I had a dream that introduced similar situations and information. I was taken to a special building with a light symbol on the door, my "family" home, but I forget the details I remembered then.

a phenomenal meeting—corroborating that I was on the right track. An event was indeed approaching. She dreamed that two babies were in the womb, fully awake. We thought it was hers and mine, our new growth—awake in the womb. How magical, I felt.

Rome had affected me greatly, and I thought a lot about it in terms of my Mars (Rome)-Neptune conjunction.

Before Zurich, I'd asked Edgar Cayce's Association for Research and Enlightenment to prepare my astrology chart. In India, astrology is considered a science, in which the time of birth relates to the karma of the soul. My chart showed a Mars–Neptune conjunction at rare intensity: 24.6.

My life purpose hinged on balancing forceful "Mars" with mystical "Neptune."

In all this new discovery, having realized I was in Küsnacht, Jan made a surprise visit—hobbling sensationally and laboriously on crutches into the Jung Institute, 28 Hornweg; given my Zurich address, hobbling from the tram up the hill to my apartment (which must have been quite a sight)—and I did not open the door, not recognizing the tingling of the bell, having so newly moved from Küsnacht. He chatted with my sophisticated landlords, who told me what a fine person he was. I was glad. But immensely relieved not to have answered the bell.

— 32 —

On Initiations

Well, I have gotten far along into this book, true to the Jefferson Airplane philosophy that "Small things like reasons are put into a jar." But very much reason has emerged.

I discovered sometime back that the closer we stick to what energizes us, the more meaning we find. Because it will erupt "out of nowhere," having waited till we discovered it—or, till, knowing it was there, we deigned to pick it up, express our love for it. So here I am, in my second half of life, about to step into initiations that began in 1985—without safety nets or security devices. In fact, aimed at destabilizing the ego, as in all true initiations; to take me beyond where I had control or even insight; test the bared "first impression," the ability to find my way without markers.

I believe that ability is deep inside everyone, when thrown out of the nest, unable to fly—or into the water without a life jacket. With no one to ask, no one but ourself to turn to and say, *Well, how do we get out of this?* OR, *Well, is this important? Do I want to chuck aside the norm and have a go?* Initiations are like that. Soul-searching. Not for the timid or those holding onto directions left by someone else. But oddly, in the end this kind of discovery ties us to everyone else. It is the Place of Connections, the Natural Location where everything fits in, everyone is a part, and everyone is important.

— 33 —

Confrontation with the Self

An initiation loomed nearer and nearer—the importance of which nothing could overstate.

A September 16, 2009, *New York Times* article reviewed Jung's account of what he called his "confrontation with the unconscious," a period that began in 1913. The author recalled how Jung compared that period to a mescaline experiment, with visions "coming in an 'incessant stream.' He likened them to rocks falling on his head, to thunderstorms, to molten lava. 'I often had to cling to the table,' he recalled, 'so as not to fall apart.'"

The article ventured: "Had he been a psychiatric patient, Jung might well have been told he had a nervous disorder and encouraged to ignore the circus going on in his head. But as a psychiatrist, and one with a decidedly maverick streak, he tried instead to tear down the wall between his rational self and his psyche. For about six years, Jung worked to prevent his conscious mind from blocking out what his unconscious mind wanted to show him."[93]

This great adventure—to let into consciousness what the unconscious wanted to send—is the feat I would now face. If I could go through the upcoming initiation—or confrontation—(which I did), I could step out into new experiences that depended on this framework. My "real" future would be that leprechaun type of "interior telephones" Hunter Thompson once hinted at. I would meet Hunter again.

I will get back into stories. But something comes first. Here the story is pretty solitary. If I said I went on a retreat, it would be true.

Nineteen years before, I met the three Big Guns of my life in my New York period. Supposedly every nineteen years something equally radical happened.

That nineteen-year period had ended. I was standing alone, stripped—for the moment—of the outer male presence. What/whom was I about to meet that would dominate my life for the next nineteen years?

I had separated two archetypes: the "puer" (eternal child) and the "wise old man"—really two halves of each other. And for nineteen years plunged into the consequences.

Emotionally, I'd separated physical attraction from spiritual. (I'd left Hunter a mix of both.) As I stood at this watershed I determined never to divide any person up again, but try to appreciate *every* relationship on the level of *both* physical attraction and the soul.

After so much buildup the initiation that now rushed in could have been anticlimactic but wasn't. It lived up to a "massive upheaval." So I was sitting waiting for a tidal wave, a tsunami, something of major proportions to me, totally transformative, but that could be met positively. The alternative would be somehow to "miss" or "fail" in grasping the opportunity that came every nineteen years. To miss it was unthinkable to me, horrifying. I had tried my best to be ready.

Also, a great spur, having pursued with some devastation the "big book," as it twisted and turned—since 1965!—I found it had some missing component that now showed itself to be my roman à clef character Robert's death (in life as Milton). The imminent Initiation must be some sort of extension or return of the "visitation" I had at seven; the consciousness, let's say, that stood in my body.* But here it was, almost thirty-eight years later. Actually, two nineteen-year cycles later!!!!!

At forty-five I was about to go *into* a consciousness that was rehearsing writing a book for "the audiences of the future," looking up into a stadium, imagining them there. This is obviously the way to work with energy: think of the future as already here. I did not make

---

* As recounted on page 76

any connection between that book and my manuscript. In a way, my books had been an occasion, an opportunity, for the rest to occur. Like always with the unconscious, I am trotting behind. There is something going on here that relates.

So there is a plot NOW in the current memoir to work this connection out somehow—that fact that the completion of the original book was delayed till—or dependent upon?—the return of the consciousness that had stood in me at seven.

Imagine one simple fact removed from your view of reality and the ripples of repercussion, so that you *knew* everything you believed had to be reorganized. Imagine, on the other hand, one simple fact pursued.

— 34 —

Expectancy

A consciousness is a mind space. It has woven-together connections of cause-effect, action-result, qualities and values. What would it be to go into a consciousness? Was it possible?

I still have the index cards. And four little journals, carefully wrapped in faded tan paper: "1985—Initiation Begins." That was September.

The Big Initiation was imminent. Shortly before it began, my dreams played off a passage in *Other Worlds: Space, Superspace, and the Quantum Universe* (Paul Davies), where the author talks about the "Heisenberg loan mechanism" in quantum mechanics.[94] Through that mechanism, if electrons projected at an electric barrier (a "hill") lack energy to get over the *hill* (a field of electric force that slows them down), they can sometimes, by being *lent* energy, *tunnel* though. Obviously, in our macroworld this is impossible, Davies warns; a physical ball cannot (by borrowed energy) tunnel through a physical barrier.*

---

* Ironically earlier, the physicist Evan Harris Walker had a Zen experience of *satori*—a sudden spontaneous expansion of consciousness—that gave him an insight into this very electron tunneling. It happened as Walker strolled through a field across from the University of Maryland campus in 1966—and he spent the rest of his working toward founding a science of consciousness based in the quantum mind. The insight showed him that *electron tunneling* created a condition for nonlocal (QM) effects in the brain synapses.

Similarly, a focus on this tunneling "loan mechanism"—in reading about electrons "borrowing" energy to cross an impossibly difficult barrier—preconditioned me in some way to my Zurich Initiation. To go one step further, formulating his

Ignoring the warning, my dreams ingeniously refocused the issue—to *loans of books from a library.*

Expectancy was building. No longer did a day go by that I didn't sense an approaching massive upheaval. My unconscious was on the alert, receiving signals—sensing, as a Faulkner character might, *Something is going to happen to me.* I loved the expectancy. I trusted it.

In fact, before Zurich, Mariah had warned me at Openway that (because of the high-intensity energy field in Zurich) I should—until further notice—forego alcohol, coffee, and meat. Which I did.

The initiation took me into a level of consciousness.

In the 1990s, closer to 1985 than today, I wrote the following about it:

> To come in *from the unconscious, to rise out of it—as out of the sea, fresh born*—leaves all other routes open. . . .
>
> The situation affected me as a cutting-off line between past and future. It was a virtual watershed, and rightly so. ALL OF THE PRESENT, from that moment on, had to extend—enter into my life and my being—from the narrow straight (like the Straits of Magellan), crossing purposefully and directly, in alignment with (using it as a birth canal) that tiny portion of my life, the initiation (1985 in Zurich).

Quantum Observer Theory *by which anyone who observes anything affects it even from the future,* Walker was, theoretically, saying that his observation (unknown to me) of the tunneling effect could influence me, "lend" me energy.

And in reverse, that my experience (in the future) could backwardsly affect him. Well, I love to play with these possibilities, as now, years later, I feel comfortable with what was, at the time, so unknown and hazardous, seemingly fraught with peril if I took a misstep. And I took missteps aplenty. Later, physicists such as F. David Peat speculated whether, instead of just the convertibility of matter-energy ($E = mc^2$), we should think in terms of "matter-energy and information" (cf., *Pathways of Chance,* 126). Was this principle implied in the dream of the "lending" library?

—35—

Describing the Initiation

In the past I'd meditated briefly, maximum twenty minutes. But as I woke that morning a dream convinced me that something was expected of me. *And that I was being assisted.* So I took this extreme leap of staying in bed, meditating.

Little Snoep watched silently from his pen that faced the bed a few feet away. It took about four and a half hours of suspense while visions of runes and other markers kept prodding me on. Eventually, encouragingly, I saw a hole overhead like the dome of St. Peter's, with hands, including my mother's and father's, pulling me up.

Then in a snap, I broke through. I found myself in a consciousness: a distinct location that if I'd suddenly had a blindfold removed would not be more identifiable. There was silence in the consciousness. I was very impressed with the sense of certainty in the man there, whom I am calling the Initiator.

Now I knew it was possible to "enter a consciousness," and palpably feel it to be "a place."

Inside the atmosphere, a man was writing a book—in an empty stadium—preparing it for the "audiences of the future," going over what he wanted to say. He was not physically writing but mentally checking the content. In the many steps of the stadium were the not-yet-visible crowds. He was sure these readers would be there *in the future* and was projecting their presence into his thought. In the transparency, awareness was easy to pick up. It was all of a piece: drawing his audience in, perhaps in the way that da Vinci was reported to spend innumerable hours on a work *before* starting it.

I had entered a state of consciousness. It was a real "place." It was "where" I broke through at the end of many hours of meditation. A single entity was in the consciousness—as if I'd somehow walked into his mind. I would now get to know this Initiator, who, as in turning a dial, would set my life onto a new course. Just as if he arrived with navigation instruments, he would reorganize the way I saw reality and what was possible.

Insofar as I knew, his book had nothing to do with me. How could it? Later I would guess it was a vast book, written by many people. The scene was overwhelmingly sacred-feeling in the privacy of contemplation. Especially, it felt immensely certain, powerful, as if he knew the future.

It did not occur to me to say, *Ah, there's the man who came into me at seven, calling himself "I."* I had no thoughts, just relief that I was there in the breakthrough, and awe.

It was his intimate conviction, determination, certainty, will to succeed that struck me—the feeling you get when knowing something is identical with what it appears to be.

It would be some years before I had any understanding of the different paths and traditions in East and West, the different routes to higher consciousness. What I am going to say next is complex, but I will try to say it simply.

The most pervasive thing in higher consciousness is a sense of connectedness between all existence: a oneness, a nondual perspective. There are many terms, such as *unity consciousness, cosmic consciousness, liberation.* One person relates most to Lord Shiva or Hanuman or Allah; another speaks of the Ground of Being. At the base of Hinduism is emphasis on the unity of God and the individual soul. These are relationships to the Self—attaining oneness with God, or the Absolute (seeing God in everything, everyone). The Initiator did not make distinctions that excluded any religion or even lack of religion. That said, for this first initiation, I was introduced into the only spiritual teaching I had any personal knowledge of up to that point.

Every person's path is individual. About her learning experiences in one phase, my friend Joyti realized in hindsight that they were rooted in ritual and a ritual is—she quoted Joseph Campbell—"the enactment of a myth." In her case, she said, "One ritual stimulated my Christian mystic side, one spanned the human–spirit divide, while the other enlivened my Cherokee memory."[95] Back to me. I learned from the Initiator and my intuition that I'd been to "the Christ state."

That is, into a consciousness that was in that state, but I'd seen it personalized. It was inhabited. Now, decades later, I might just say it was the Christ consciousness, but then I might come across Swami Krishnananda's statement that there is no such thing as individual consciousness: "It doesn't exist. There is only one consciousness, which is universally present everywhere, and when it appears to be located in a particular point of spatiotemporal context, you call it individuality." So to keep from getting into very deep metaphysics, let me stick closely to this moment, in September 1985.

My experience of this consciousness was of great love and risk-taking. It was my first initiation, of which there would be many different types in the years ahead. How would it set me into a nineteen-year unfolding? Believe me, it did. The new split would be in how to communicate.

The Initiator was operating from a higher awareness but it included, he explained, mass consciousness, right down to the most ordinary. That is, he identified with himself over a spectrum. In saying that, he was planting a seed. It was a difficult concept, which he did not try to teach me in textbook terms. He illustrated and let me figure out what I could at the time. He was not identifying with a single Earth body; yet he had a single sense of "I." This was the beginning of teaching me about different ways to locate "I," which is going to be important in moving from the most rudimentary sense of "I" into an expanded experience of what a single entity might be and some of the rules outside three-dimensional identity.

And if I were to look further at the consciousness he was speaking from, now years later, I might bring out a story told by Bhagawan Yogi Ramsuratkumar about Sri Ramana Maharshi. Someone accosted Sri Ramana Maharshi: "Everyone in this ashram is working and doing jobs. You alone are sitting simply without doing any work. Why don't you do something like others?" Sri Ramana replied, "THERE IS NO OTHERS!"

After telling the story, Yogi Ramsuratkumar asked rhetorically what it meant. He went on:

> When there is no "I," then there is no "you." Only when we separate ourselves as "I" and "you," then there can be a division that some are superior and some are inferior. . . . In our Hinduism, SELF MEANS ONLY OTHERS. OTHERS ARE THE SELF. In truth, there is no such thing called division.
>
> Birds, trees, animals, plants, stone, mud, sea, sky, wind, humans—nothing is separate. Everything is One. That's called God. You and I are part of Him. You are in me, and I'm in you. In an ocean, is there a difference in the waves? Are two sea waves different?[96]

Though it took about four and a half hours to break through that first morning in September, and I had never done anything like it, I stayed with the meditation. Once inside this heightened consciousness, I was very impressed with the snapshot of the Initiator looking up into the empty stadium: his knowledge that the audience would be there, his seriousness composing his thoughts for what he would tell them.

I did not see him in great physical detail. What stayed with me was awareness that he was there, how the space felt, relief that I was able to make it.

So that was my introduction to the Initiator, who would become my teacher for some months, giving me assignments and growth tasks, which I recorded elaborately in gold A4 notebooks I still have. He spoke not a word that first moment in his consciousness.

Everything clear only because he called me to come and intuitively I knew what to do. I knew this situation was far above and beyond anything I'd known to be real before—so how could I not give it my all? See where it led?

Now I was leaving the unconscious, *to some degree*. The wave of What I Believed was collapsing.

Every day I was wakened by music, bars or chords—an instrument sound, a series of notes.* My regimen, prescribed by this spirit Teacher, varied as time passed. Fairly early on, it included fasting. I was told that was to get rid of any dependency. Not right the first day, but soon, I practiced food deprivation by eating only two teaspoons of honey a day and drinking two glasses of water. For a time, I went to the bathroom only twice and practiced sleep deprivation.

A note September 13–14 says, "Slept 12 hours—it's the most exhausted I've been. Even staying awake about 6 days, I felt fine after 4 hours."

How much one forgets in twenty-seven years, but there, in black and white in the gold notebooks, is my record of many assignments (cf. "15 min. quiet meditation," "15 min. Christ meditation to thunder music," "15 min. xxx meditation"), and also I received dreams from him to study together.

And I began to learn something about working in electricity, a specialty of his. I will go into that later.

One day in September, I made a note: "41 ½ kilos"—that's 93 pounds, down from 123.

The reason for the extremeness was that I was *being taught independence from physical drives*—or nonattachment—so that at the drop of a pin or hat I could go anywhere, do anything without needs interfering. The process was severe, but I relished the opportunity to experience what I considered and had been told was a great blessing.

Fasting would remove cellular memories, even the habit of caring about food. He would remove all crutches, even instinctive. To sleep,

---

* These were audible sounds, but not from any physical instrument.

I was to throw away the eye mask, the ear plugs—and not move, not turn over. In dreams he would *plant temptation* (to gorge on food, etc.). Could my unconscious be unprogrammed?

I was expected to react, while asleep, as I did consciously. Both I and my unconscious tried hard not to "fail."

This first stage was purification, which is a standard aspect of initiation. Independence from physical survival drives included sex. But before everyone gasps, there was a logical reason. Anyway, I would learn that a rule applied only for that period. It could be canceled by new circumstances.

Here, the idea was that in physical attraction there is often a high degree of unconsciousness of source. What appeared clearly to be an attraction toward a person might be an unconscious attraction to someone else—spiritually based, thus virtually invisible. More than one might imagine could be at stake. So it would be helpful to learn how this worked. In a society based in materialism, the idea that underlying conditions from other dimensions of ourselves might sometimes hold the key to a particular attraction, or that subtle connections inside situations might hold the real key to them, was not easy to come by. We were more likely to be connecting the dots.

We knew about the role of genes but not yet, to the same degree, that underneath everything were attractions and patterns, just as there were also constellated archetypes. An archetype could be constellated, Jung said—that is, set into motion. Here, in a follow-up, I learned more about how this might be.

My small paralyzed black dachshund was being initiated as well: his diet changed to rice with a plum for seasoning. He loved the plum.

In a one-page summary in September, I mention visions, fasting ("total and semi-: 2 weeks"), meditation exercises to open third eye, studying *Other Worlds*, reading Krishnamurti and studying it with the Initiator, radical-disruption exercises, a Growth Chart, more meditations, initiations, etc.

I look at a sample pulled from a gold notebook for October 24–25, 1985. It narrates how he took me into his consciousness multiple times and what it felt like. Prior to this initiation, I'd never been in such a state. He was trying to teach me to go there and back at will. I was also learning such personal things as that typically because my inferior function was sensation in the Jungian typology, I was attracted to intensity. And that attraction—in league with my inferior sensation—often put me out of touch with my heart.

At the period when I fasted the most (I don't remember for how briefly), with the two teaspoons of honey, two glasses of water/orange tea diet), I stayed inside.

But the Initiator most of all was bringing a sense of purpose. He taught me in terms of archetypes in play that were uplifting or polarizing the planet. Foremost, the archetype of "home." Its positive, symbolical level had the aim of taking the planet into a consciousness more appropriate to the high-tech twenty-first century. But the pull of "home," made literal, would sprout up in many pockets; without our recognizing it as an archetype in play, the drive would have us battling for *physical* homelands with the ferocity that archetypes bring. Exactly what we see today.

He predicted that individual leaders would mistakenly direct this drive toward home to ego levels—with disastrous results—not realizing they were embodying an archetypal energy that had another intent,

The spiritual pull of "going home" to an expanded consciousness that embraced all was a weighty factor in this archetype.

I rethought the dream of my father "going Home" as not only to death but also to a consciousness.

But where taken literally, he predicted in 1985, the energy of the activated archetype would drive wedges between cultures. The intensity would create leaders with a distorted sense of mission that bred a heightened atmosphere: Doomsday, the end of the world.

This prospect was frightening. Symbolically, the positive dynamics went toward overturning our old Earth consciousness, where cultures oceans apart barely knew of each other.

If played out as physical attraction, an archetype of the end of the world risked literally blowing up the planet. But its potential was transformative: to shift the basis of how we lived together into a consciousness that wanted, truly, an equality for all. I could see a miniature kernel of this in my dream of transformation by being held under the fountain. Or the dream of me in a near-death experience after being twirled round and round and flung to the ground by a giant monkey. The planet, to transform, would undergo such archetypal dynamics. He wrote:

> Give them, the living, the energy to bet
> Tell them what the bet is
> so they can choose sides
> Tell them what the sides are
> Tell all this
> to THOSE ALIVE

I did not yet have the integration. I had the pure words, the untarnished, unvarnished poetry, to be received on different levels and sometimes just sift down like music:

> For I was a New Man
> the spirit of the New Man
> the stopped-beating heart of the Old Man
> released rejuvenated in the New Man

And many group missions:

> To go into an experiment
> be pushed to the limit
> and find out what happens
> a discovery, in this way,
> of unknown capabilities in Man*

* The term "Man" meant Male/Female. It's not to be read in gender terms.

What action would it produce
what heart bursting
What was Man capable of
at the outermost limits of the Earth?

The project Earth
To go into unknown territory
What was unknown, unexplored in Man?
For what was known in Man
could not save Man
Perhaps what was unknown
could
To go then into *the shadow*
of Man
And when in the twilight of Man
bring out of the shadow of Man
what was good

He was talking about shadow missions into human potential to wrest out what would successfully bring the planet through this dangerous, necessary dynamics. In a second book, he spelled out the bet. That is, that the positive side of the *archetype of the end of the world* would win.

He said that on three levels my consciousness was equal to his, and on those I was to challenge him. But that on the fourth he was not to be questioned. There, he was the Christ. Perhaps a more sophisticated term to some readers would be "one with the Christ." Or "in unity consciousness." But each path is different—be it through atheism or anything that, in the history of that individual, is timely for growth. So I was in, as Jyoti mentioned of herself, a Christ conscious path, at the time, but—again—that path thought of itself as harbingers of the universality of every single soul.

Another thing I thought fascinating was that he said *there was a new Christ personality coming into being.* This one would not, on the outside, be invulnerable and serious. I later thought how many old structures had been updated in this time period, such as the way Einstein went beyond Newtonian physics. Perhaps one could think of this as similar.

Accordingly, he described a new persona that would often be found in people carrying or potentially carrying this higher consciousness—in sharp contrast to the expected picture. Again, this is not to be read in terms of a religion.

This second *personality*—or exterior—was Mozartean. Reading about the rehearsals for *The Marriage of Figaro*, one sees how he flamboyantly waited till the last evening to write the Overture, then began at midnight, with his wife prodding him with stories if he might fall asleep. Then rushed to the performance, handed the orchestra the sheets—and calmly took his seat at the piano. They played it magnificently.

So in mapping out the arrival of the cosmic, or inner, Christ, he envisaged the energy sometimes presenting itself with a playful, very human outer style but inwardly as firm as ever. Again, though the term "Christ" is associated on the Earth with a religion, it has none of that association here but is a level of pure consciousness centered in love and awareness that can be channeled into any religion. Or stay outside all religions.

From this point on, as Rilke said, I had "met my destiny." I was being initiated deep within. But to draw me in and convince me, he was using Milton, whom I trusted as the sanest, wisest Highest Truth I knew, and my parents, whom I felt never lied.

Nothing, I thought, could be more surreal, more baffling, more a sacred privilege. I did not see physical details of the Initiator with my inner eye, as many people would imagine. He did, a couple of times, take a physical form in my mind; in brief, once I saw Milton as the Lone Ranger in a vision, another time I saw a snatch of a nonwigged "Mozart." And, in dreams—after I left the apartment again—the Initiator sometimes talked to me inside the face of someone I would see that day, whom he wanted me to meet.

I was taught daily by this Initiator for months, including demonstrations that he was there—such as when he made the dates of his incarnations pop onto my green-reading-lamp light bulb. But I didn't have nearly the perspective or emotions about what was happening then I do now. I've said all along that this was a bare glimpse of a nineteen-year project for me—and the introduction intentionally yanked the rug out from under my ego, leaving me swimming in limbo, looking for the sturdiest limbs to catch onto, seeing what didn't break. And much didn't.

I was always afraid his risky projects would fail—because he was "working in the unconscious," a concept I haven't introduced. And I don't know any spiritual teacher who has, to the extent I would when describing how he worked.

Further, they were live experiences, not concepts in the first instance. However, the larger framework, I didn't have. I only had the tunnel vision of what arose out of and was illustrated by experiences as these concepts went into play and I saw what happened. In that period I was "on the inside." As time passed, I had to rely more on my own intuition and awareness. But back then, it felt like an inside perch, as it were—like the little girl, two years old, on her uncle Hunter's lap in the poker game at the start of this memoir. Watching the hand unroll, the cards be played.

I had no idea—from experience—in 1985 that this was the barest sketch of types of multidimensional experiences one might find oneself in by staying open, all the while being as questioning as any skeptic of what in fact was going on, holding on to the fragments of explanation. I watched as the worlds I had not known about breathed and stretched, or shuddered—or shuttered.

This was the hole in the Big Book, that had seemed unable to end: the pathway of standing high enough to see the material marked off, plotted—bringing what had been unconscious into history. In fact, I was shown, it was a hole, or (positively put) potential, in the Earth, something necessary to now include—that the hole in my book was one of the places information was being dropped in.

Eventually I became convinced that genius is in each person (spotlighted in Hunter, Jan, and Milton) at the depth of that soul's individuality.

Genius, I knew, was temperamentally unable not to go first if it knew something, felt something. Each person could go first in their own thing—some one observation, point of view—by looking tenaciously to that original individuality that, without exception, was in each of us, forged from our experience.

It was these kinds of questions, their implications—the structures they demanded—that I turned to. I had to create a place, a mind, a consciousness where "I" made sense to me—now that my ego was uprooted. In the times ahead as I had known only Western teachings, I would have Eastern teachers as well. More initiations would eventually put me into a position from which to initiate others. Who would have thought, certainly not I, that this was the direction my life was taking?

If my highest guide, who had swept like a crop duster into my life, dropping these anti-old-me sprays of new consciousness, was training what he thought of as people in his energy, whose drives touched the hot lava of his intense core, and these were experimenters, no wonder I had been attracted to outsiders, genuine explorers, wresting from the shadow of their own experience future jewels for humankind. As can we all. It would be a new model, a new paradigm, that "do unto others" was suddenly, now "give them your inner expertise, your joy, your self-knowledge"; that truth might be wrapped in different exteriors, that it might not fit the pieces of the puzzle I had before, that the whole jigsaw of life might need reshaping, that courage to be yourself was foremost, that life was at a turning point on Earth again.

The initiation was in 1985. I began to write *Keep This Quiet!* in early 2005, nineteen and a half years later—in response to Hunter's death. Now it's 2012. As I near the end of the second volume, I remember the special circumstances at the start of the writing. Shortly after

Hunter died, when I did my light-body guided meditations, barely awake, lying in bed in the morning with the music playing—before going to the computer—I regularly felt thrills of rippling energy inside me. I called them inner rivulets of light. The memoir was in the early-draft stage. I thought the energy waves were helping set up the writing. I knew the ecstatic experience would not continue forever and I regretted that, but I needed encouragement and this felt like it.

September 25, 2005. I decided to give myself a workshop for my birthday and drove over toward Pittsboro for an event with Kailash Kokopelli, famous for Inner World Music. When Kailash had us meditate while he played a host of instruments—didgeridoo, drums, conchs, rattles, Tibetan singing bowls—that did it. I had an eye-opening ecstatic experience of this rippling light and the sacredness of the body. It was a major understanding of the sacred sensuality of touch.

A loud bang, a flash, an explosion OF CONSCIOUSNESS has set the story down in these conundrums. I believe that this two-part memoir is my response to the cells and heart stuff of HST being blasted into the sky, which was set into motion on this different wavelength of subtle blastoffs by that 1982 dream in which the "Ciao D Hunter" took off in idea, and the realization, the triggered instant, is this.

This is the Ciao D (Chowdy) Hunter, as promised in the dream in 1982, blasting off to honor a portion of two lives, certainly that portion of mine: "You say hello, I say good-bye."

Not that Hunter doesn't have many people remembering him. He does. But I needed to get this off my chest, that the experiences with him were vastly important to me, and they live on in my night skies, and as I lay in bed, preparing what to write in the initial years, 2005–08, I felt so lucky to experience the inner rivulets of light breaking up and bursting inside. What a weird thing to say. Was it true? Gosh. Darn. Was he still doing it over there? Standing outside some cabin in the sky, as it were, and shooting off a gun into the night, and sometimes I felt the repercussions over here. Just as if someone were jiggling my leg in a Trager massage, with the waves shooting from limb to head. Well, others said also that they had a sense of him. So why not me too in my own way?

— 36 —

Jan: Life Lessons

Genius is never afraid to go first

—JAN MENSAERT

I cannot close the book without taking the men who traveled it with me into the present.

Jan remained in Belgium. He was eventually hospitalized a few times, then institutionalized for alcoholism till his death in 1990. We did not divorce but were separated. He stayed there with dignity, committed by his mother, able to leave if he had a place to go where he was "not a danger to himself." He hadn't. In his last years, he repeatedly summoned me to ask me to be sure "The Suicide Mozart" got published.

But that wasn't the end. In 1996 I began to assist in a Flemish museum multimedia retrospective of his writings, drawings, and music—Jan Mensaert: 1937–1990. We prepared for six years with an international cast, particularly psychologists, who branded him a "tension of opposites"; the retrospective lasted April 11–June 10, 2001 and produced an e-book and two music CDs.

Drawing: Orange and Green Nude

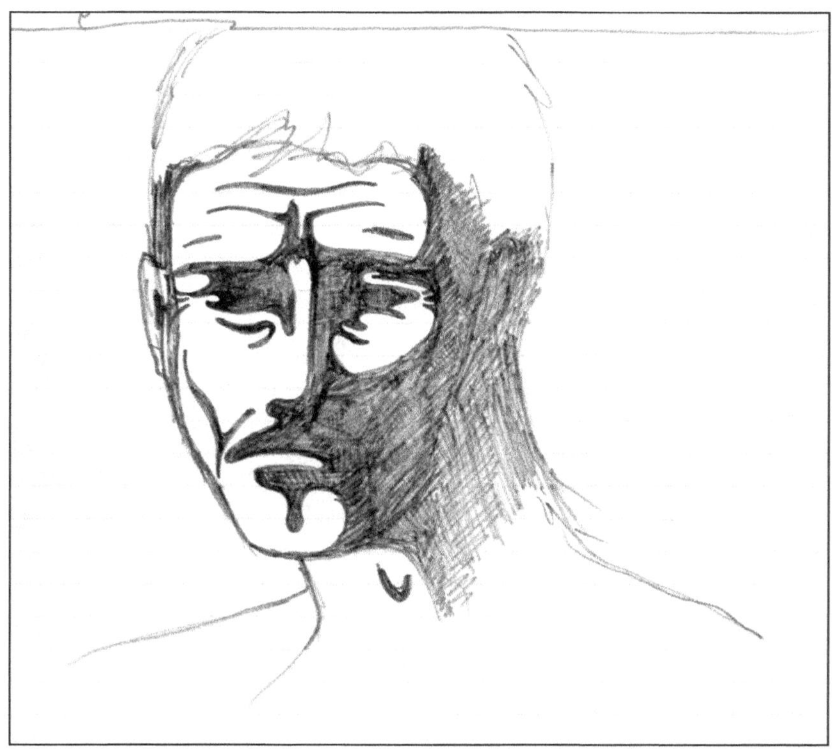

Sketch: Jan Mensaert Self-Portrait

Museum "het Toreke" Exhibit 1996–2001

I joined with the museum, recruiting writers internationally, intent on keeping the retrospective from being sensationalized.

In a live opening-night performance Bruce Wands, a musician/graphic artist, graduate chair of the School of Visual Arts in New York City, played melodies lifted from a thousand out-of-order music sheets in Jan's attic. More importantly to me, I found in my North Carolina storage unit at the last minute—about to give up looking—Jan's thirty-five-year-old reel-to-reel tape recording of "Pretty Margaret" and his "Spanish Dances." There was a high probability it was irretrievably damaged. In his video studio in New Jersey, Bruce and I held our breath as the notes started tumbling on top of each other, at such a fast pace. Bruce asked me if the tempo was accelerated by the machine. No, that was the incredible speed of Jan's playing.

In *Life, Page One* (the "het Toreke" e-book about Jan) Puanani (Pui) Harvey, then president of the New Mexico Society of Jungian Analysts, wrote about his anima. Dr. Harvey said the Anima (soul) archetype, not the Mother archetype, was profoundly wounded in Jan's infancy. Noting the "winds of destruction" gathering over Belgium at his birth in 1937—one year before Europe pressured Czechoslovakia to relinquish a large part of its territory to Hitler, hoping to avoid war—she began: "The remembered nurse fixing the burning cigarette to the toddler's lips to silence his cries becomes the image of a rising collective madness . . . her message: suffer your reality mutely, in silence. . . . turn within to seek other forms of outcry."

She adds that brandishing the fiery cigarette, "like the angel-of-the-flaming-sword forbidding return to Eden," the nurse "initiates the premature intrusion of perverse, unmitigated pain into Jan's childhood, heralding his passage into exile and his precocious entry onto the torturous path of self-discovery and individuation. She is at once the Awakener and Destroyer; a child's paradisiacal world now invaded by the cruel dark feminine."

In the way he played with blocks as a child (building, tearing them down, rebuilding) Harvey finds "archetypal patterns of attachment and loss—patterns of polarities inextricably linked. Jan Mensaert said, 'I have to destroy in order to create.' C. G. Jung said, 'Only that which can destroy itself is truly alive,' illustrating the struggle between these polarities.[97] In time Jan will carve upon his limbs—his self-cutting a symbolic incarnation of the torment of consciously bearing these polarities—creation and destruction—leading into the larger archetypal nexus of Life-and-Death itself."

Of the anima, Harvey wrote, "*Internally*, [she] signifies the deep feminine movement of the Soul." She quotes Jung: the anima "corresponds to the deepest reality in a man. . . . Because she is his greatest danger, she demands from a man his greatest, and if he has it in him she will receive it."[98]

For this particular infant, being burned with a cigarette by the babysitter/nurse left a suspicion of women.

Chris Van de Velde, then supervisor at the Netherlands Academy of Psychotherapy, wrote that for Jan, psyche (soul) was everything. He looked at Jan through the lens of the so-called "Gloria duplux," the way the archetype of the "puer aeternus" (Peter Pan/Eternal Child) and its counterpart, the "senex" (Wise Old Man), work together. Chris wrote that every great artist needs the integration of both: the puer to rebel against boundaries, push into the unknown; the senex to provide structure, order, discipline so as not to become overwhelmed. Also, through the senex he can find the wisdom of the Wise Old Man in himself. This huge tension existed in Jan but was not integrated in his struggle with both extremes, Chris wrote. In the end, the puer, or Eternal Child, won, and the human being failed to become the great artist he had everything in him to be.

However, we know that from Jan's point of view, this had a larger purpose, revealed in "The Suicide Mozart," where Mozart explored his anti-self on Earth in order to find his own replacement on Vegafünf; only that way could he go to the next level of his development, leaving his energy slot filled. For without that he could not abandon post and go to another dimension or universe. That was the fictional story, the woven details, which, Jan believed, were in fact some sort of revelation in story form. So "Mozart was working on his shadow in another dimension," I was to write in *Love in Transition.*

I took the approach that Jan was on some level "unreal," having overridden or turned off his instinct for self-preservation. An extra degree of self-destruction created a war between "two geniuses"—one being a genius at destroying the other.

His infant wound was part of a child-in-danger motif that, according to Jungian James Hillman, begins the myth of the hero: "The Gods single out at an early age those who are to carry consciousness further" (examples: Moses and Hercules).[99] However, Jan was the *unrescued* child in danger.

Another indicator of his personal myth, extrapolated from

Hillman, is that Jan's natural career path into language professor was diverted when he failed a final university exam. So did Gopi Krishna have a similar shove out of a logical career path. But these failures were purposeful—from the "soul exam" perspective. That is, if consciousness research—or better still, the early exploration of patterns—was in the works. And if there was, at least symbolically, such a thing as the "anti-self."

Supposing hypothetically that were true, there would be souls who brought light from the shadow by plummeting it—stopping short of off-limit violations. To be in one's anti-self to investigate its unknown light would involve not knowing how far one could push. Also, like being blindfolded. But suppose these potential, invisible patterns are descending on us. Suppose the ice needed to be broken up so they could have space to land. Suppose . . . I put Jan Mensaert inside these suppositions.

— 37 —

Milton: A Bow

> Blake . . . gave up over and over again . . . But he went on *after* giving up
>
> —Milton Klonsky

In 1991 Wayne State University Press published Milton's collected essays posthumously in *A Discourse on Hip*. The publisher counted solely on his underground status and word of mouth to create a buzz. That didn't happen, but I put piles of the book into select hands, such as of Roberto Sanesi, "one of the most remarkable Italian writers of his generation" (the London *Guardian*).*

Yet readers did discover him. On Amazon, author and critic W. C. Bamberger writes of *A Discourse on Hip*, "Klonsky has become a footnote to modern intellectual history (he is a character in a recent play about Delmore Schwartz, for example), and that's a shame. There are some filler essays, it's true, but more than half are of such brilliance of intellectual wit (or oddity: Klonsky's [wife] left him for Auden—in the poet's single valiant try at a heterosexual relationship) that you will likely find them ineradicable parts of your intellectual cabinet of wonders once you have read them."

---

* Sanesi was a famous poet/critic/translator/professor, friend of pataphysics artists (such as Man Ray), musicians, and directors; winner of Europe's Byron Award and other prizes. As poet in residence at Harvard, he had the audience ringing with applause when he read passionately from his poetry. I met him at a poetry festival in Belgium. Sanesi put Milton's book on his nightstand and sent me a personalized post card of thanks.

Elsewhere, Bamberger observes, "'Klonsky on Blake' parallels 'Kerouac on Benzedrine,' or 'William James on nitrous oxide.' That is, Blake intoxicates Klonsky, helps him look at the world with sustained energy, and from new perspectives."[100]

Milton had, while alive, inspired Chandler Brossard to create a character, Max Glazer, in *Who Walk in Darkness.*

But the "fame" that hit strongest posthumously was what I would call a bitter blow, though probably inadvertent. And I do what I can to correct it here. It was a 2005 play *Klonsky and Schwartz,* by respected playwright Romulus Linney. Linney reportedly got his plot idea when he discovered that it was Klonsky who recovered Schwartz's body from the morgue after it had lain there two days. To Linney this was a shock because why had Milton never mentioned Delmore's name to him (Linney) in the times they met in a bar during the last ten years of Milton's life? So Linney started his play with a piece of mail for Schwartz arriving at Klonsky's door (Schwartz, unbeknownst to the audience, had just died) and built backwards.

Unfortunately, Linney's researcher did not uncover (or Linney ignored) the most relevant facts. One can presume he knew nothing about benefactor Marshall Allen (who had for some time paid Schwartz's bills), because no one still alive knew.

Dwight Macdonald, who gave Milton's eulogy at his wake, was by then gone. Everyone at *Partisan Review* was. Linney speculated that Milton had been a sycophantic adorer, or intimidated protégé, of Schwartz's. At least, that's what reviewers intuited.

Delmore's lines to "Milton" include, "You're a walking penis"—this man by whose total lights, including spiritual, Seymour Krim was so influenced. And from the mouth of the made-up Milton—of whom Anatole Broyard said, "In decades of conversation with him, I can't remember him using a word indifferently"[101]—come such inanities as "My apartment is clean. The track is a national pastime."

Intuited by reviewers as the jealous half of a pair, the made-up Milton is told by Delmore—in an eruption of all caps: "GOD DAMN

YOU, TO HELL WITH YOU!!! THE ONLY REASON ANYBODY WILL REMEMBER YOU IS BECAUSE OF ME!"[102]

Of a vastly different opinion, the beat author Seymour Krim had earlier written, "What it all boiled down to was that of all the writers of my own generation whom I had the opportunity to meet, talk with, buddy with, clash with or even just appreciate through their work—and this includes Mailer, Kerouac, Ginsberg, Bill Goyen, Broyard, Brossard, Jim Jones, Baldwin, all the 35–40 hot shots who are blowing my generation's sound in print—Milt to me was always preeminent, the Number One boy countrywide, the living human, ultra-human soul with by far the greatest potential."[103]

What one learns from this is how history reports its stories—and also how it holds in reserve some unplayed hands.

The play went so far as to set up a (billed-as-true) scene in which the two first met in the Gotham Book Mart—a famous midtown Manhattan bookstore. According to the apocryphal account, Delmore was judging a poetry contest that included Milton's then-unpublished prodigy poem "The End Pocket" (!). Delmore, as one reviewer took it, summarized the poem in a way that "decimates" it. Then magnanimously (but inaccurately) the made-up Delmore tells Klonsky he'll get the poem as well as his "Brighton Beach" essay published—all nonsense.

As Milton recounted in "A Writer's Education" (which was part of his *New York Times Sunday Book Review* obituary), he first met Delmore (along with his good-friend-to-be, poet-critic Allen Tate) at The Cummington School of the Arts, an artist's colony to which Milton—already a published poet—had been accepted on his own merits.

Milton was *not* (as in the play) first published (thanks to Delmore) in the *Hudson Review.* All false. *Hudson Review* cofounder and for fifty-five years editor, Frederick Morgan, made historical corrections that as a byproduct contradict premises in the play—in a letter to me "26 March 1993":

Milton Klonsky—by Robert Johns

Coming back to Milton Klonsky: [William] Arrowsmith and [Fearon] Brown deserve the credit for publishing "The End Pocket" in *Chimera*; I deserve credit for the later things, that were published in *The Hudson Review.* I wrote to him after the war, told him how much I liked "The End Pocket" and asked him to send things to *The Hudson Review.*

I have a letter from Milton Klonsky which I treasure. It's dated April 30, 1954, and in it he says, "I think *The Hudson Review* is the only literary magazine today which maintains the highest literary standards without starch or pomp. I hope it goes on for a long time." We have managed to go on for a long time—I wish Milton Klonsky had been able to do so too.

The apocryphal Milton is at one moment grabbed at the throat by Delmore and—what else?—screams, "HELP! HELP! HELP!" It's just the kind of thing I could never imagine.

I presume none of the play's mischaracterizations were intentional—but were caused by lack of information about the man reputed (in his *Selected Writings* introduction) to hold his personal cards close to the chest.

Yet the play leads a highly reputable reviewer, floundering in the dark of the made-up facts and, as he puts it, Monty Python-like sketches, to write, "His Klonsky has the personality of a little brother, deferring, helping out or beaming with pride." Most bewildering of all, the reviewer writes, "*Unlike his mentor, who is the quintessential highbrow*—with a few weaknesses for sports and money—[Klonsky] is less ambivalent about popular culture or assimilation. His passions, he says proudly, are 'art, blondes, horses, baseball' [italics mine]."[104]

This jars against the (true) fact that Milton taught a course at the City College of New York—on the history of culture!

Authors can write what they wish. But the problem I have here is that the play was presented—heavyweights such as Krim not being around to contradict—as based on facts.

Every step-by-step building of the hypothesis took it further.

Linney has Delmore tell Klonsky to read Blake and adds, "Blake dies poor. That scare you?"[105]

In real life I produced a post card from the New York Public Library in 1966 that said Blake "died twice."

Klonsky immediately told me, "Blake was almost starving at the end of his life."

Me: "But he didn't give up?"

Milton (earnestly): "He gave up *over and over* again. But he went on *after* giving up."

Now that's true dialogue for you.

The playwright puts into Milton's mouth (on the very last evening of Delmore's life, when, in fact, I was out with Milton), such nonsense as, "OHHH! GODDAMNIT! I HATE HIM AND I CAN'T LIVE WITHOUT HIM! DELMORE, STOP! YOU'VE BEEN KILLING ME FOR TWENTY-FIVE YEARS!" (All caps in the script.) Another character says, "You must exorcise each other."[106] In fact, they did meet. Returning to

Sheridan Square in the Village after taking me home, Milton ran into Delmore, who was with a young girlfriend outside the Lion's Head. The two talked. Milton said that at a moment like that, just before death, you're drawn to old friends. And that Delmore, in his disintegrating mental state, "went in and out of lucidity. But there were moments he was completely lucid."

What happened next? In the play, Milton alone knew Delmore was dead. In real life, Marshall Allen was picking up his seedy-hotel tab. When, within hours after running into Milton, Delmore collapsed in the Columbia Hotel hallway with a fatal heart attack, I'm pretty sure Marshall was called. Milton phoned me, the next morning, to tell me what happened. The Delmore Schwartz Papers website of Yale University Library says, "His body went unclaimed at the morgue for two days until friends were alerted to the news."[107] Why the body was unclaimed, I don't know. Probably the two days gave those who knew time to make arrangements with the funeral home on Second Avenue in the East Village.

Marion Magid, senior editor at *Commentary*, asked me—after Milton's death—to write about him: "There was a time," she said, "when New York was known for its talkers. Milton Klonsky was one of them. Call it 'The Milton Klonsky I Knew.'" That essay now sits in the Seymour Krim Collected Papers, University of Iowa Library, MsC367, to help document the friendship of Klonsky and Krim. Klonsky had taught at the Iowa Writer's Workshop. From my essay:

> "I'm famous, not so much for what I've written . . .
> as for the cyclotron of my personality.
> "I'm a teabag, steeped in life."

There is also a wealth of unplumbed material about him in the papers of Malcolm Cowley (who rediscovered Faulkner) and others.

Milton's essay "The Importance of Being Milton" closes with self-discovery. He was in high school; the principal called him in to ask what he wanted to be. Not sure. They shook hands. The principal:

"'You know you're named after John Milton.' No I wasn't." After that he went to the library

> and for the first time opened *Paradise Lost.* The "organ voice" thundered at me: *Of man's first disobedience and the fruit Of that forbidden tree, whose mortal taste Brought death* . . .—and all the words seemed to be sounding at once. . . . But even without understanding why, I couldn't forget that great blind voice, with its oceanic range, broad and powerful enough to be heard across three centuries of time.
>
> . . . As I was deaf to my own name and its meaning, so at last I was identified with Milton, blind to his own image by a kind of visual amnesia. But I don't have to justify myself before you [*Paradise Lost* was written to "justify the ways of God to man"]. Only by accident can we ever find an Eternal Providence in our lives, although, to come down to earth, for our ways to have crossed that way in Brooklyn was a revelation of poetic justice—as if there were any other kind.[108]

— 38 —

Hunter: A Bow

It's like a parachute continuing to open, getting to know you
—Hunter Thompson

Verbally he was just so clever and so quick and so free, and he didn't give a rat's ass about what the repercussions were
—Johnny Depp

Now, at the end of the book, the reader knows much more about Hunter than I did in 1991. And more about me than Hunter did. We'd lived continents apart since 1970. Yet something beckoned in the dark, a buoy, a lantern, a pipe dream. We had to see each other again—at least one last time. Wasn't our past enough? Hadn't the years dimmed that? Hadn't what roared through us when we used to meet died? No, it had not. Yet we were groping in the dark of time that sent us down different paths. How could those paths swerve and wind up in the same spot? It seemed entirely unlikely.

In 1990, I was living in Tienen, Belgium, with a thirty-four-year-old truck driver. I traveled to North Carolina on a visit and passed through New York. Staring down through a picture window at the park on Fifth Avenue, in an old friend's apartment, I took out my old phone book and impulsively dialed Owl Farm. First miracle: the number worked. Hunter turned it on and off. I gave my name to the woman who answered. Miraculously, she said hold on, she was sure Hunter wanted to talk to me.

He was celebrating his exoneration—all charges dropped—in a legal suit that had included five felony charges and three misdemeanors and carried a stiff prison sentence. Though Hunter mentioned having talked about me with Jim Silberman ("Your ears must have been burning," he said) and surprisingly added, "I should have known I'd get into soul searching, talking with you," I had no reason to phone again until the following year, after my boyfriend, Willy Van Luyten, died in a car accident January 6.

Why would that make me phone Hunter? I wanted to talk to people I felt close to, whose conversation was meaningful. So in late January I phoned Hunter. I didn't mention the death. I just wanted the comfort, warmth, stimulation of his voice. Anyway, how was he doing? There was much to catch up on.

Four months later, in May 1991, I would be at Owl Farm.

How this came about: When I phoned in late January 1991 from Belgium, he picked up but was quite upset and barely spoke, he hung up so fast. His live-in girlfriend, Terry Sabonis-Chafee, was—that very minute—walking out. Permanently. He said rather panicked, "It may not be important to you that my lover is leaving. But it is to me." I left him to his devices, he was so clearly consternated and barely knew what he was saying. It was amazing he'd even picked up at all—because he rarely answered the phone. In any case, that shut door—when his girlfriend walked out—literally opened into a bright future for us. Over the phone we began to feel our way through the missing time segments.

When I dared mention my subtle-energy, or psychic, experiences, he said he preferred the word "imagination." He added, "*You talk the craziest of anyone I know.*"

"*I'm not crazier than you,*" I said, aghast.

"No"—he quickly drew the distinction—"but you *talk* crazier."

He said he'd invented an alter ego, Duke, to say things for him while he observed.

My frankness provoked another confidence. He said: "I feel like I'm talking to a naked child." It felt like a compliment.

He suggested we meet flamboyantly in a boat off Key West. Or at Owl Farm, his log cabin home at Woody Creek, Colorado. "I can't figure out why we didn't do this before," he ventured. "Do you know?"

I didn't, I said, though in fact I had some pretty good ideas.

A boat in the waters off Key West—how exciting. I'd spent my summers till eighteen at Island View Shores in our river cottage. I loved water skiing, especially on one leg. But we decided to meet at Owl Farm.

I'd last seen him in New York City, 1969, last had a letter from him in '73. Lifetimes were lived in between.

Such a meeting might be fraught with peril, considering all the water under the dam. But we didn't care. Hunter said, "I'm psyching myself up." (I assumed he meant about what I looked like, at fifty-one.) "Do you still have those long . . . locks?" He actually said "locks"—affectionately. But asked nothing about weight, hair color, or any of that. Neither did I.

His secretary mailed three recent photos and several confrontational/humorous pieces of his correspondence. In one photo, he was at the wheel of his boat. In another in underpants and ski sweater, pointing a gun in the snow outside his ranch. The third was a glamorous face shot—taken in a photo shoot by his friend Alan Becker. I mailed a few of me.

Common sense might predict this was an impossible dream. But Hunter and I thought big. He'd canceled everything, he said, including a possible interview with Gorbachev—adding that it was probably "the ruse of an old girlfriend to get me to Russia."*

I heard the emphasis; he'd cleared the deck.

I know now that his ex-fiancée was in Moscow, where—at some point—he made life miserable, sending, in her words, "raunchy, obscene faxes with naked bodies and swastikas, warning [her] that

* This was inner shorthand, I believe. His former girlfriend was as important as Mikhail Gorbachev, let us say. The interview was code, perhaps, for the idea of a trip to Russia. I'm not clear when the faxes started. In August, months after my trip, she was "pulled in for questioning by the KGB."

[she'd] fallen in with the wrong crowd and that violent overthrow of the Soviet government was a bad idea."

He addressed them to the central telegraph office, where they'd be read before delivery.[109]

It did not occur to me how much he might emotionally have to toe the line to move me up front in his crowded life.

1966. 2005. Now I know the pieces. But not all. I am still collecting them. They are pieces of lives.

My small plane touched down in Aspen in the third week of May 1991. Scouring the tiny airport, I didn't see Hunter

Awkwardly, worriedly, I collected my bags. He was clearly not dodging paparazzi. Now what? At that moment someone barreled through the door. No eyes but mine turned.

Hunter was *much taller than I remembered.* About six feet four. *Heavier than the slim, trim twenty-nine-year-old.*

Swiftly, he lumbered toward me in that walk with the knees turned out, one leg not showing it was shorter. Twenty-two years later—and not visibly surprised—he spotted me at first glance. I did an internal double take as he stood there, towering. One full foot above my head.

Latching onto my bags, he zoomed us out. Hurried us into his notorious, gleaming convertible, the Great Red Shark. The revamped 1970s Chevy Caprice could, with Hunter behind the wheel, wrote Ralph Steadman in *The Joke's Over*, squeeze like liquid through virtually razorblade-wide slits between vehicles!110

We were flying down Highway 82—this now quite balding Gonzo journalist and I, a human bridge back to his prefame years.

He apologized. He was to have been awakened or *kept* awake. But what I remember most clearly is his smile, how it filled a bandwidth between our faces—pouring energy right into me, straight to the heart. Being drawn into the present in intensity inside that smile. So he was speeding along Roaring Fork Valley in the Shark, three miles from Aspen, 7, 815 feet above sea level, and it was not *Fear and Loathing in Las Vegas*. Perhaps it was the anti-*Vegas*. Twenty-four years since my trip to L.A., where we crept off to the Hotel Continental.

No permission asked, he snorted cocaine. Gave a convulsive shiver. Then was back like before, as if he'd accommodated every shift of the substance that entered his body, allowed some in, not absorbed the rest—perfectly sober and lucid. There were no bats on the horizon. There was the same charming person; no "drug taking hold" but himself phenomenally *right there*, a person I was overly relaxed beside just like before.

This was the notorious, famed Hunter, the new Hunter I didn't know close up. In fact, living in Morocco and then Europe, I hadn't realized that he really was hounded by paparazzi or how huge his following was—and that he had a growing reputation as "the Hunterfigure," a totally outrageous prankster/shocker who might do anything that got attention or crushed the hapless victim of his antics and blasphemies. And that he also imbibed a growing list of drugs, most notably having begun sniffing cocaine in 1975, just after my exit, when, investigating Sigmund Freud, he finally tried it. Freud used it against depression and pain, mostly without repercussions, unlike those he recommended it to. But it was also the Hunter I had grown up on "way back when."

Committing a cardinal sin, I asked, "Do you *have* to do that?"

But I saw no gibbering maniac, not a wild terrifying driver. He is answering *why.* He turns his head, looks right into my eyes with a sparkle in his, a bit of mischief, that winning, charming smile that spreads wide into the creases. It is as if the smile is capturing all the focus so that nothing else can be felt—only the feeling that emotes presence, frankness, that says, *This is me, take it or leave it.*

Actually, here was the same person who'd loved the Jefferson Airplane song: "This is my life, I'm satisfied, so watch it, babe, don't try to keep me tied. . . . Why not throw your life in with mine?" It is now 1991. And all our lives had shoved themselves between those days when we were young, he not famous, me not in any way a mystic, not having experienced anyone's death, which now I had; both of us novelists then, which in a sense neither of us was now. He answered—unquestionably creating a wavelength I joined him on—not concerned to get my approval. Dimpling. "*It's not what you HAVE to do, Margaret. It's what you WANT to do.*"

He suggests getting reacquainted at the upscale Hotel Jerome bar/restaurant—catch the Lakers game—drink margaritas, nibble guacamole, my favorites!! We sat at a table. Again, no heads turned. He'd protected this encounter solicitously. Told *no one*, he said. Had he told anyone, *reporters would have been at the airport in droves.*

I was heart and soul plunged into hopes. Fifty years after my birth, he fifty-three—our lives ahead of us, though it would take a lot of adjustment to bring two such dissimilar people into one point of time and extend it, make our lifestyles accommodate our attraction, having found each other again after many adventures along the way. And yet this relationship for both of us survived, stayed possible. We were going to try it.

He more convinced than I, I think, but more reckless. To not see each other for twenty-two years while barreling at high speed in opposite directions might send chills down the noblest, gamest, most *up for it* adventurer or romantic. After all, there were such things as habits that might cramp us, cause us to buck. So far, we were melding, grooving. Stolen away in a private enclave. A hot, simmering feeling, appraising glances, passion lurking around the corner.

Was the red "Ciao de Hunter" that kept reappearing on my palm in a dream, every time it washed away, *this moment*?

A phone was brought to the table. His assistant, Deborah Fuller, wanted to go over things before leaving us alone.

I do not remember how fast he drove to the farm, though speed was in the mind-boggling readjustments both of us were making, the turn of the time dial backwards, then forwards, and then in modulations; the excitement, the passion of having dropped our worlds to meet.

At his "fortified compound," eight thousand feet up in the Rockies—where peacocks strutted—I stepped across the threshold.

Since MacDowell Colony I'd fantasized about log cabins. Yellow dandelions dotted green grass. In the picturesque rustic background a satellite dish nestled.

Purposefully carrying my bags, he led past the sign on his front door: "Abandon all hope, ye who enter here." Words inscribed at the entrance to hell in the *Inferno*, which midway in life Dante was guided through successfully. As a teenager Hunter painted "gates to hell" on his bedroom floor.[111]

He headed past the kitchen counter—where his typewriter perched at the ready—straight into his bedroom. Without a word he deposited the suitcases on the floor. *Hot damn! We don't have to wade through that awkward bit.*

No question where I wanted to sleep. Just acting on what he thought self-evident. I was relieved he was so natural, that he matter of factly figured out the only possible place for the bags.

That over, we conferred with Deborah, who seemed charming—highly competent, responsible, a lifesaver for him.

Hot damn again! Entirely alone with a magazine deadline imminent, we settled in. Admiring each other, breathing in the air of being together, a hand running down my back—things like that but the bedroom reserved for later (knowing full well it would be there), we sat happily at the kitchen counter, back in the groove. Hunter assumed, rightly, I would thrill to the possibility, so long withheld, of sharpening my mind on any text he came up with. Being that I was highly intuitive, I took it for granted when he made decisions silently. It set my imagination going, trying to follow the thread of unspoken conversation.

Hunter was fully acquainted with this side of me. He had said in 1966, "You're a leprechaun. You come and go. You go off and answer some inner telephone, and then you come back till it rings again. . . . [O]n the phone I thought you were giddy. It seemed like you couldn't finish a subject . . . but you fill in the gaps with vibrations."

I had jotted this comment down and written beside it: "Perfect characterization. *He* talks with vibrations."

His fingers over the keys, Hunter told me *to keep him focused*—if he wandered *off subject.* So I took up my seat, nose to nose—electricity rustling underneath. A computer had just arrived, which he didn't use. He had the TV news on, the sound off.

"Your farm is quite a communications nerve center, isn't? You've got just about every communication device known to man. How many televisions do you have?" an interviewer once asked him.

"HST: I try, yes. Oh, four, five around the room. It's great to have them side by side for various time zones. You have a sense of being on top of the world."[112]

Absorbed at the Typewriter

From 1985 to 1989 he'd been a columnist for the *San Francisco Examiner*—producing *Generation of Swine: Tales of Shame and Degradation in the '80s* (1988). *Songs of the Doomed* (1989) followed. In the '80s to research a piece for *Playboy,* he'd been the so-called Night Manager of the O'Farrell Brothers' sex club in San Francisco. A girlfriend helped him stay focused.

None of which I knew. But I did know that he was ready to write as ever.

Faxes sped to the machine (I'd never sent a fax, and unknown to us, none went out: I didn't push "send"!). We rode in the Great Red Shark to the Woody Creek Tavern to eat. There he bought my friend Jyoti (who had phoned and he picked up, teasing her) and me each a T-shirt that said, "Part of the Legend."

In his twenties he'd confessed to me that people often disappointed him. Not this time, let's hope. For us both. A *New York Times* article by Michael Slackman later noted that in moments "Mr. Thompson let the public in on the point"—which was, "he seemed to suggest, not really about guns and drugs, and tearing up the pavement and planting grass, but about grabbing public attention to focus on the failures of leadership, *the hypocrisy in society*" (italics added).

So, relative to my life I was enchanted by a fireball. And when he was wrong or hurtful, the important thing to me was that you knew where you stood. I called it unconditional Authentic Self-Portrayal, no matter the consequences, instinctively. It may be wrong. *But it is not hypocritical.*

At Owl Farm

— 39 —

Hunter Cont'd.

We were in the living room in the evening. Hunter had made a few romantic remarks. But we had focused on the deadline-facing article. I remember, though, laughing to myself when he inadvertently pulled out of a drawer a cardboard cartoon warning against BJs. Looking at the paper, he'd said to himself in a deadpan manner, like W. C. Fields, "I don't think that applies here."

In the living room he put on music. I did not pay attention to the words till he mumbled that they were for me.

I perked up my ears. I was sure the country singer professed to have been waiting for a particular woman, always loved her.* But it was the kind of thing where your emotions have jet lag; time is frozen; you're hearing on two levels (one, you know what was said; the other, you can't believe it) while you ask yourself: *did he really say it?* My emotions were arguing: *no, he didn't OR it doesn't mean what you think*—contradicting with *yes, it does.* It came so fast. I had to race from hope to fact, to "it's here, now," to "what do I do????"

I pointed out that I was *sure* he'd been in love during all those years.

He said *yes, "But you have to understand about time."*

He was admitting all the love affairs that were real, obviously, not backing away. But never mind. He had always loved me if you understand "about time." Thrills ran up my legs. At least our lives would have this rounding out (no matter if only as in *Casablanca*).

An angle into time was like a tuning fork. A missing angle *reflavored everything*. Perhaps he meant that time held experiences in

* Come to think about it, it might have been Utah Phillips's "I Think of You."

layers. I thought it incredibly wise. I will mention a lipstick tube. Details would be quite inappropriate. I hear "simply the best." The lipstick tube in his large hand approaching my breast, we withdraw the light from the living room floor and leave the reader to his or her voluptuous, tender imagination.

Unfortunately, because of what came next it's hard to draw the curtain here. The rules of propriety and modesty are counteracted by the distortion if I keep the rest to myself.

But first, I have to bring back in Willy. A charismatic truck driver with whom I'd lived three years, he had died in an automobile accident at age thirty-five January 6, only *four months before.* Hunter knew nothing of him.

After his death, Willy had, according to witnesses who felt his presence, seemed to "go down phone wires" to create a situation something like in the film *Ghost,* where newly departed Patrick Swayze hangs around Demi Moore, though in Willy's case not because of having been murdered.

And that's just the first page of the high spirit energy that I felt was always around me, often planning interventions—particularly those recent months.

Going back into the room: Hunter effortlessly created an orgasm in me—which wasn't the easiest thing, in general, to do. No problem with him, in the slightest. But—of all the crazy things—my throat began to tremble, the first sign, I well knew, of kundalini kriyas. Now, during kriyas, you have no control over the area the prana (energy) goes into, because the whole purpose is to destroy blocks—in breakthroughs.

It went for my throat, which threatened to make the rest of me tremble. That's because the energy running up the spine pierces and awakens chakras or prepares the way for that to occur. My experience of kriyas had been on a few occasions when they shook a block out of an arm or a leg, sending waves of energy through me into a room. Talk about awkward.

With the kriyas in my throat, I would have no control over what

I said. "The naked child" would have the floor, literally. The emotion left me speechless.

Hunter had shot me into opening the throat chakra. I suppose he would have been intrigued and fascinated with the situation he'd created, had I told him. Therefore, if I make it sound like I was holding back, the opposite is true. Also, obviously he no doubt was feeling the prana, as it could not be confined inside one person.

However, what happened at this point set up a fluke. For some reason, having romantically, elaborately, totally satisfied me, precipitating the kriyas, or shaking in my throat, which I was trying to conceal, he didn't continue the very intense sex. As said, I was speechless, trying to hide the shaking because I didn't want to spoil the perfect mood or seem too odd. Kundalini can and did heighten sexual feeling and can create what is sometimes called cosmic orgasms, stimulating cellular response in the whole body, not to mention bliss. There was no way Hunter didn't know I'd had an orgasm, though I was not yelling or speaking. The feeling I sensed traveling back and forth between us was huge and I had no doubt it was for him too.

I expected things to continue. But he headed us for the bedroom and there instantly popped a sleeping pill. I didn't know this habit. The pill was fast acting. As he swallowed it—before I could react—he said it was a good thing he was taking it "because of what I feel like doing to you."

What? Go ahead, I wanted to shout. Too late.

I absorbed the shock. And fell into an untroubled, cuddly sleep.

Next: wonderful morning. I can see Hunter preparing a hearty breakfast—including cinnamon toast—with Wild Turkey and cocaine. "Do you know what you're doing?" I asked about the coke—committing a mortal sin. But he didn't shout.

Yes, he said; *he monitored it*: recently he noticed he was taking too much and cut back.

He was a glutton for writing (around me, anyway). At the kitchen-counter typewriter he twirled his hands with the Dire Straits music, his fingers curled like loose fists. He got rhythms into his hands, from his hands into his brain, in twirling his fists. He was absorbing the music the way he absorbed the chemicals, letting it pour through his body, into his hands—that twirled, then came down on the keys.

Hunter was imaginative in life as on book pages. Courtly, stunningly original. In his car on a hilltop, we reenacted his high school parking days.

The visit flew toward a culmination, which would have happened on the hilltop except that I suddenly had to pee. This was (though it doesn't seem possible, so jam-packed and intense everything was) just the next day, Day 2.

In the early evening, he sat at his IBM Selectric typewriter. His legs hurt from poor circulation. With some trepidation I asked to feel his energy field; I'd learned aura healing in a two-year Basic Applications of Psychodynamics course (in Brussels three hours a week). He said yes.

I wasn't prepared for what I felt. Putting my hands into the energy around him, I felt a time bomb field. Or volcanic air space. No wonder he had to shoot off guns to get the intensity out of his body, which he was to do that very night.

A little warning bell went off in my head. I tried to shussh it—the implications of walking in an energy field this strong but *externalized*. I had seen highly energized fields. There could be archetypes in them, sending pulsing, exploding attractions smashing far and wide. But I didn't let all this information/sensation sink in. I halted it.

I told myself perhaps that was just the field he was used to, always *about to explode*. Keeping that voice of awareness inside me quiet.

Would he like to get into altered states *without drugs*? I asked.

HST: "It would save me a lot of money."

He had an ultrapure ¼ LSD dose he hoped I'd take in the evening while he took ¾. I knew that LSD, unlike cocaine, was supposed to cleanse "the doors of perception" without necessarily feeding the ego. I'd never tried it, though Jan had, with me there, twice. After leaving him, I'd thrown myself into Holotropic Breathwork, or "nonordinary states without drugs." And my psychodynamics work in Belgium created an altered state through meditation. So we were quite a funny duo on that score, not to mention that I perceived I'd kept contact with two people after they died. And was about to have a spirit initiation again in the '90s that was just starting. Also, I knew quite a lot about indigenous rituals and had even attended several all-night Native American Church teepee ceremonies, where peyote was the sacrament, and participated in a sacred Brazilian indigenous church ceremony that used the psychoactive ayahuasca. Yet I didn't get to tell Hunter this.

I was embarrassed to admit that in view of my spiritual initiations and how sensitive I was, plus having entered mystical states without drugs, I was concerned to keep my mind clear—because (I worried) if I took the risk of messing up my energy, who knew how long it might stay that way? It wasn't that I was afraid to take LSD with Hunter (it could have been fun) but that I didn't know what kind of risk it would be for me; I didn't know if I could still "channel" and other things I took for granted. Anyway, why rock the boat? Hunter, of course, thought differently. He wanted to initiate me—see what happened.

At this point, the phone rang with a dinner invitation. "You decide," he said. Why did I not say *stay in?*

Idiotically, I answered let's go. As if being alone—at that instant—were not what I wanted. Right then and up till now, he'd not been Duke, his alter ego. He'd been Hunter.

The field I'd felt with my hands was so intensely volatile it was like a walking cosmic primordial soup, a quark-gluon plasma, the aftermath of the Big Bang, when worlds are created. It was as if I were at the threshold of consciousness about it, carrying it no further than a tight ball of astonishment, with many emotions and possible responses carefully packed inside—turbulent, bustling, jostling, seemingly ready for a giant emission. I thought, *It could not mean what it seems to. Obviously he can handle it.*

At the local store he leapt out to buy champagne. Not telling me exactly what he had planned, but I could imagine. What an evening.

Obviously, we would complete part two of the night before, even if kundalini tried to horn in.

However, at the restaurant parking lot a man hurried to intercept him, whispering. Hunter later told me he knew he was "in trouble" at that moment.

Inside, a woman I didn't particularly notice sat casually at his side. I felt unthreatened. They had a history. I didn't know. And now she'd temporarily returned to Woody Creek unannounced. Uh-oh.

I could hear her insist he "go out with" her. I assumed—wouldn't anyone?—she meant some obscure day. Not here, now, from this table. She kept insisting. He later admitted he thought—as she pounced in hushed tones—no one else could hear.

I heard, "Are you married again?" He must have felt this was the craziest development, that he could never in his wildest dreams have conjured it up. But his face remained static. I got no suggestion of foreboding or need to take action; I was in a discussion with one of his friends, who was saying to me, "I know you must be a good [friend of Hunter's] because you survived."

But then, suddenly one of the two—I think the woman—headed toward the back of the room. In a moment the other followed. There were some pictures on the walls. Not much else. What was back there? Rest rooms? An exit door? It was so fast. As total disbelief raged inside me everyone at the table started apologizing for him, saying how wrong this escapade was. I sat—my hands tied—as the dream overturned. I stayed seated there, watching the seconds tick.

The impossible was happening. It was not conceivable.

He returned and—him ahead, me pounding him with the information that *I knew*—we left. Amazingly, he hadn't suspected that he'd been obvious. Maybe he thought I trusted him so much that betrayal would never cross my mind. I don't know what might have happened had I kept my mouth shut. The worst was in the open. Suddenly a giant wave of difficulty rolled in, in what had looked like clear sailing. I just knew the unthinkable had occurred and I didn't know how to turn the tide.

I too was an old flame. Now I believe the energy field in various variations encompassed all that, that night. Two old flames. I think that's what he meant about "time." But why now? What the heck. To go out with her was something at least part of him "wanted to do." The other part might have been wringing his hands.

He'd had that moment of foresight—in the parking lot—*this was big, heavy, an earthquake.* He might have told himself he could just pick back up—no one the worse—not listening to the part of him that knew better. Or not caring. Living in the moment, one second of passion before the next.

I knew, however, having heard every word, that she took the initiative.

So the blast-off champagne evening was asphyxiated. I imagined we could retrieve the dusted-off bright spark, because what such a scene usually does is take away trust. *But Hunter inspired trust;* I still felt I knew where I stood. Besides, I found the incident, in a perverse way, united us, as I was confrontational and *he did not hide,* not pretend, not deny but took the blow squarely on the chin, admitting regret and attraction, apologizing *for the rudeness only* but no more than his emotions said to, apologizing even more, perhaps, to his self.

He had played out his philosophy of doing what you "wanted to" without comparing it to something else you also wanted to do. And yet, if all these experiences can have validity, intent, and passion—*at the same time*—it cannot be *at the exact same restaurant table.*

Back at the ranch Hunter took the LSD. I didn't take my ¼ though I did puff a bit of a joint.

Yet another friend—unexpectedly—dropped in and stayed for hours to say good-bye *before leaving for five years.* Four hours of that exhausted my patience. I kept wishing for him to leave. In a photo at 4:00 a.m. shot by the friend. Hunter looked bright, sharp, happy—pleased, with his large arm resting on my shoulder. It's the only picture I have of us together. I love his casual at-homeness, his arm resting there on my shoulder as if it belonged. That beautiful face is the Hunter I know.

Hunter and Margaret

That night ended in his pool. We devoured raw oysters he expertly pried open poolside with a primitive can opener, his feet dangling in the water. I stripped and swam. Then he got in too. On the overhead screen a soft-porn video played—about a Caesar and his sister. Hunter thought it was the most erotic movie ever made.

But there was no way to resurrect the spark. I left two days later, he to go to Louisville because his mother was ill. At least, that's what he said. It was not the fact.

Earlier, I had the date I left Woody Creek wrong. Newfound notes tell me that arriving with a one-way ticket (projected stay TBD), I stayed one week.

The next (last) evening, Hunter drove off alone. Back in the wee hours he stumbled upon Mae West/Cary Grant, *I'm No Angel.* I tried to stay awake—as Mae West beckoned, "ya better come up and see me." But soon went to bed with a plane to catch.

Up the next midday in the living room in his favorite chair, he took the copy of *Songs of the Doomed* I handed him. I had no autographed book. Now he did the job up proudly, like saying "Here's one for old times." Or "Here's looking at you, kid." *Or here's the champagne in another form, what I wanted to recall, bring to life, tell you.*

He took out a felt marker—twice murmuring aloud that the evening was "not what I planned: I bought champagne"—while in large silver letters that spanned both inside covers he wrote:

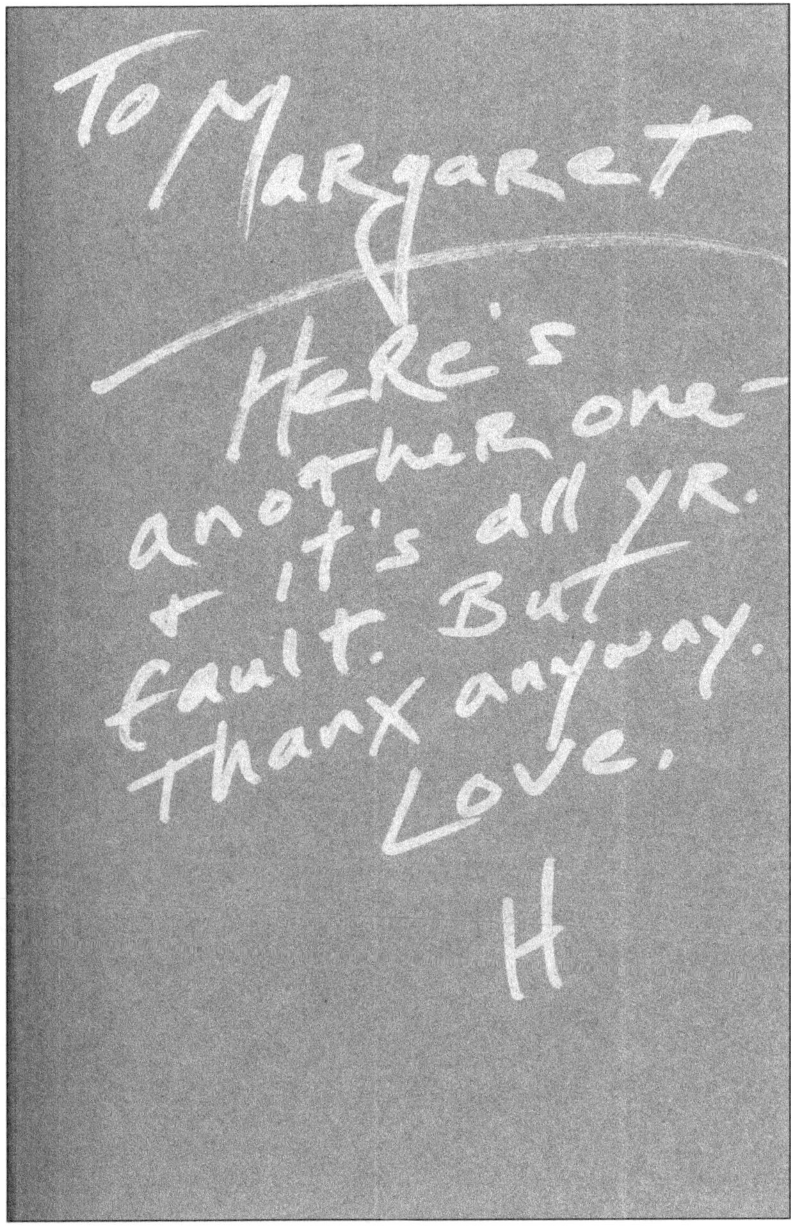

HST
Hunter
Owl Farm ~ May 20 '91

He smiled up at me. I smiled at him.

I remember him seated in that chair, signing in that translucent lettering, saying cryptically—aloud, "I know where I made my mistake." Mentioning that he'd felt a warning in the parking lot.

Surely, this was not the end. Surely, though, that honeymoon first arrival without a care in the world or anything but the unknown to climb up over was past. Who ever knew Hunter to mind a challenge? As he said, it never got too weird for him. And myself? That was May 20, '91. To be continued. (It is February 20, 2006.)

After he passed over I realized he was saying something. Of course, he didn't plan it. What sort of oaf would? Was there more to it to fall back on someday when I perhaps read a fact? To know where to draw the line short of treachery, in case I began adding up suspicions?

I was ready to forgive. Where his attention and heart were (in time) was for him to know. Anyway, I left with no idea what would come next, no official breakup, no official status at all, him sitting in that chair yards away from where fourteen years later he would shoot himself in the mouth.

What did he mean, "I know where I made my mistake"? Years went by, and I hadn't a clue. Now I think I know. He had "psyched [himself] up" for the physical changes. But what about aging in another way?

Also, perhaps this was what some people call "the hunterfigure."

But I had met the intuitive guy who internalized his reactions, in 1967—underneath the one who externalized them in wild pranks. He was both. He said so. But few people, I believe, followed his internal discussions with himself, which endeared him to me.

Back in Belgium in early September I received two snapshots from "H.S.T., Box 220." If there was a letter, I've lost it. In one photo a round sun set. High to the left hung a flying object that one would say if one said such things, was a silver UFO—opposite a shooting star. The other was of the perfectly round moon visible through a V opening in darkened foliage.

We lost contact. Then in 1992 in a poetry festival in Sibiu, Romania, I was to read a poem. Shortly beforehand suddenly I sensed—in one moment—that I was connecting with someone powerfully, electrically.

In that inspiration, I wrote Hunter the oddest letter I ever mailed him, perhaps the weirdest he ever got: about the existence of "Jesus" and "Magdalene" cells, how he and I had one of those cells. How we used to "swim in electricity baths." Who knows what he thought? I hope he destroyed it. I meant it, of course. In the atmosphere of spirit committees, which I was in. And the growing interest in multidimensional energy I was beginning to explore.

I asked him: "Do you remember when you said it was like a parachute continuing to open, getting to know me?" I told him the mistake he kept referring to was mine, not his—that I'd felt the beginnings of kundalini in the living room. An excerpt reads:

> Also, earlier when you were massaging my back so uninhibitedly and playing music, I picked up signals and wondered did I dare believe them? But what I have to explain is that in the living room right in the beginning I felt my throat begin to shake as if it had something to say. And I suspected the energy would go all over my body, as [I'd experienced] in kundalini [but never before in the throat]. I had just remet you after 22 years. I thought: It might be too strong. What's he going to think?

The letter made sense in the background of my initiations and frequent kundalini episodes.* In the latter, the familiar picture is of someone who sits and the energy goes straight up from the lowest chakra to the top of the head. But I'd proceeded in stages since the

---

* For a definition of kundalini, see pages 150, 176. In Hindu belief, kundalini is the divine source of energy in every human being. It is initially dormant, turned downwards at the base of the spine. If activated, it moves upward, awakening chakras: internal energy systems. When it reaches the crown of the head, it leads to unity consciousness. It has been studied by yogis for thousands of years. I go into this in my next book. The effect it has is quite beyond any individual control.

Zurich Initiation. And that's a long story that makes sense if someone walked with me from 1986 to 1991. Hunter hadn't. We'd barely broken the ice on it.

Soon, I would organize a Belgian workshop for the Kundalini Maha Yoga master Dhyanyogi-ji, in India, and receive shaktipat, or energy transfer, into that lineage. So, in the background was this great guru. Hunter's friend David Pierce, as recounted in the first volume of this memoir, had back in the day exited California—left Hunter—to become a leader of Swami Muktananda's entourage for several years. Hunter had friends that covered a wide spectrum.

I'd flown out of Aspen to Jyoti's in California in May 1991, then back to Belgium—then returned to California in September for three months—subletting space at Jyoti's. At that time, in the fall of 1991 in Colorado, Hunter wrote "Fear and Loathing in Elko."

I would call this really slapstick as the rubber band stretched and the two trajectories moved apart, yet both fueled in a flood of writing. The letter, I wrote—and finally mailed—in the summer of 1992.

It crossed with his arriving note. Bundled into a *Rolling Stone* issue—mailed mistakenly *to California*—belatedly forwarded.

It was waiting in Belgium in early October, when I got back from reading in the Romanian poetry festival. Opening it, what did I find? Hunter at his best. He invited me confidently, tersely, cutting to the chase, to meet him "in Little Rock on election night."

I stop and laugh hilariously. Could any comedian, any trickster, any Gonzo conflict inciter, plan anything more far-fetched, star-crossed, more embarrassing, more open-ended?? And then watch the players try to squirm out of it or embrace it.

Hunter wrote that I was "*just the person I need.*"

I took it to mean needed in Little Rock on election night.

Margaret 1991

I will never forget this man who put soul shimmer into politics. Initially baffled as to what to reply (I was beginning a new relationship), I dawdled a few days. Then, in explaining my lateness, I left a long answering-machine message, saying a lot I never had in response to what he'd said through the song that first evening. Saying "I've always loved you," as the song had. A mechanical voice interrupted: "End of tape, call back later." Or was it Hunter, disguised, breaking in as the speaker phone broadcast the too-personal message and in the kitchen people listened, maybe a new girlfriend—an awkward moment? The Prankster salvaging a prank? I thought so.*

It was only through historian Douglas Brinkley that I learned, as he graciously told me, that Hunter did not forget. He remembered. Always grateful for the *Hell's Angels* work, and more than that, he kept the emotional tie to the end of his life—silent albeit. THANX, DOC.

* Later publications make this likely the case.

I needed to see the twenty-odd-years-later Hunter, rekindle that fire, watch him in his now-famous attire, and so we close on that:

My voyage with
an old alchemist's key
to decipher here
what it really means
when the mate to Faust turns out to be
the one voyaging with
ME-
FIST*
O

* If anyone doesn't know, Hunter is known for the logo of a fist. The reference here is to Faust and Margaret in Goethe's epic. "Faust" means "fist" (German). So to end on an outrageous note.

"I know," Thompson once told me, "that I will be back around. You get your assignment in the great hall. It's like going to court. Your name is called, and you go to stand in front of the judges, in the great hall of karma. And you get your judgment in the form of your next assignment. Who knows?" he said. "I might be back as a three-legged dog on a Navajo Indian reservation. But I don't think that will happen

—Robert Chalmers

Appended Letters

In 1997, after the publication of *The Proud Highway,* his first letters collection, for shock effect—not having been included—I mailed back to Hunter some of his original *Hell's Angels*–period letters to me, in bright orange-gold. Also, a few photocopies. I didn't realize then that a lot of these letters were not in his archive, as he had not carbon copied them. Many were handwritten or written on both sides.

I wrote, "They brought the you from then back so vividly, and I think they would for anyone. In fact, you have a book to be made from this if you wanted it, and I would find it really exciting to be part of that, if you wanted. . . . [They have] a natural built-in humor." Or, I added, he could just have fun reminiscing. He didn't respond.

May 14, I mailed some version of the communication below with one of my books—in which there was one measly footnote about him. An extract went:

> I was rather overwhelmed, to tell the truth, to find myself eliminated, supposedly, from all existence in your early days. But as you yourself noted, this was not a conclusive representation. There were many friends in the same boat. However, I am most partial to the collection of letters I myself have, and even the tribute to you that they offer and the personality and dreams that come through. Also the humor nonending. And the characterization of you that is completely uncensored and yet as appealing as any restructured or invented one. I have said this before. I am sure these letters are destined for survival someday, in the general understanding of how these things turn out. Probably I will not even be around then, but they will. . . .

Most of all, I hope you are happy. And also that you are still healthy. I wondered it, all the more, as it is that time—sixty and all. So here, looking back, I hope you will find one of the best friends you ever had. As I find that, looking back, and always believed it. I hope you will always sing, "This is my life. I'm satisfied.". . .

If ever you have a hunch you want to say something to me, or give me any kind of assignment or whatever, you know that I am someone you will be able to count on. No? I would like to think that you think so. Are you well? (once again). How did you manage? (next question).

In the next book of letters, he included me with a bang. Not that I even discovered the second collection till 2005! Too late. I would have loved to write a thank-you.

Lunevillelaan 46
3300 Tienen, Belgium
Oct. 11, 1997

Dear Hunter,

Here are some more photos. I hope that you will enjoy and be intrigued by the pink form, which I thought initially must be a reflection of something on the ground (a hologram image) but which has appeared rather repeatedly. I always liked mysteries.

Speaking of mysteries, HOW ARE YOU? I hope you are enjoying the "cult hero" state—AND ANYTIME you want me to do something (within reason or otherwise), I will do my best.

I have sometimes missed our conversations & communications (ENTER CHANGES?). Your books (2) are in my living room, and the prose

stark
poetic
gripping

can always make me laugh. And sense the courage.
A big courage to carry.

M

e-mail: Oct. 21–Nov. 21: marharr@sibiu.ro

Afternote: Descending the Stairs

So not really knowing how I did it, starting book one of this memoir with the idea of having "my personal myth" run invisibly through the pages, I began with the scene of me—after climbing out of my crib, aged about two—walking/crawling down stairs to the living room. There, I saw a secret hand in play. A poker game. Sitting on my uncle Hunter's lap as he showed me his hand. Naturally, I broke a parental rule to get there.

I ended up this book without realizing it till now in another ground-floor living room, but there I was. Hunter in front of me. Is it another version of the same thing? A poker hand in play? I had a lot of steps to walk down: steps that encompassed the distances and translations of who we are on many levels. Yes, my soul wanted that task.

I had these lessons under my belt. Like a knife to protect me. I was prepared. I walked a few steps further down. No mirror to see what I looked like.

Notes

Abbreviation: After the first entry, *Fear and Loathing in Las Vegas and Other Stories* is abbreviated FFLV.

1. Wenner and Seymour, *Gonzo*, 102–103.
2. Thompson, *Gonzo Letters* 2: 216.
3. Thompson, "Kentucky Derby," in *Fear and Loathing in Las Vegas and Other Stories*, 269.
4. Vetter, *Playboy* interview: "Hunter Thompson."
5. McKeen, *Outlaw Journalist*, 146.
6. Thompson, "Kentucky Derby," in *FFLV*, 271–272.
7. Thompson, "A Conversation on Ralph Steadman and His Book, *America*, with Dr. Hunter S. Thompson," in The Great Shark Hunt, 112.
8. Rosenbaum, "Hunter Thompson, William Kennedy, the America's Cup and Me."
9. Alpert (Ram Dass), http://www.linda-goodman.com/ubb/Forum3/HTML/002252.html.
10. "Richard Alpert (Ram Dass) on Psilocybin," YouTube.
11. Thompson, "A Conversation on Ralph Steadman and His Book, *America*, 117.
12. Thompson, "Freak Power in the Rockies," in *The Great Shark Hunt*, 160.
13. Thompson, *Kingdom of Fear*, 95.
14. Klonsky, "Down in the Village," 36
15. Ibid., 43.
16. Krim, "*From Two Teachers—Nuts, Two Human Beings!" in Views of a Nearsighted Cannoneer*, 226, 229–31.
17. Ibid., 230.

18. Feehan, "Reconsidering the Legend of Raoul Duke on the 40th Anniversary of Fear and Loathing in Las Vegas."
19. Thompson, Gonzo Letters 2:434.
20. Hodgson and Guest, "My Crazy, Hazy Days with the Late, Great Godfather of Gonzo."
21. Thompson, *Fear and Loathing: On the Campaign Trail '72*, 1–2.
22. Ibid., 15.
23. Thompson, *Gonzo Letters* 2: 334.
24. Ibid., 216.
25. Thompson, *On the Campaign Trail*, 7.
26. Thompson, *Gonzo Letters* 2:216.
27. Wenner, et al. Hunter S. Thompson tribute issue in *Rolling Stone*, 57.
28. Steadman, *The Joke's Over*, 62.
29. Ibid., 71.
30. Thompson, *Fear and Loathing in Las Vegas*, in *FFLV*, 23, 24.
31. Steadman, *The Joke's Over*, 75.
32. Thompson, "Jacket Copy for *Fear and Loathing in Las Vegas*," in *FFLV*, 213.
33. O'Rourke, interview with Hunter Thompson: "Fear and Loathing at 25."
34. Hahn, "Writing on the Wall: An Interview with Hunter S. Thompson."
35. Wenner and Seymour, Gonzo: T*he Life of Hunter S. Thompson*, 88–89.
36. Thompson, *On the Campaign Trail*, 233–34.
37. Wenner and Seymour, *Gonzo*, 89.
38. Isherwood, *Diaries: 1939–1960*, 392.
39. Based on Margaret A. Harrell, "A Lecture upon the Shadow," 105–06.
40. Ibid., 90–92.
41. Ibid., 112–13.

42. Seligson, review of *Fear and Loathing: On the Campaign Trail '72.*
43. Thompson, "Memo from the Sports Desk & Rude Notes from a Decompression Chamber in Miami," in *The Great Shark Hunt*, 247–248.
44. Klonsky, "Art & Life," 116.
45. Ibid., 160–61.
46. Ibid., 188.
47. Woo, obituary of Tillie Olsen, *L.A. Times*, January 4, 2007.
48. Turow, review of *Yonnondio.*
49. Olsen, *Silences*, viii.
50. Kafka, *Diaries*, 341, 352, 353.
51. Ibid., 49.
52. McKeen, "Doing Time on the Proud Highway."
53. Thompson, *Gonzo Letters* 2:623.
54. Thompson, *Kingdom of Fear,* 195–96.
55. Thompson, *Gonzo Letters* 2:626.
56. Ibid., 649–650.
57. McLemee, "Sometimes a Pipe Wrench Fight Is a Thing of Beauty."
58. Klonsky, Introduction to *Speaking Pictures*, 1.
59. Based on Margaret A. Harrell, "A Lecture upon the Shadow."
60. Klonsky, "W. B.4 : or, The Seer Seen by His Own Vision," 7–8.
61. Klonsky, Introduction to *Blake's Dante*, 6.
62. Harrell, *Love in Transition* 2: 164.
63. Fein, The Media Business. "Head of Summit Books Is Said to Be Leaving."
64. Krim, "From *Two Teachers—Nuts, Two Human Beings!*" in *Nearsighted Cannoneer*, 228.
65. Jung, *Man and His Symbols*, 4.
66. Ibid., 5.
67. Ibid., 63.
68. *Mozart en Belgique (Mozart in Belgium)*, 20.
69. Ibid., 21.

70. Mensaert, "The Suicide Mozart," 64, 73.
71. Shechner, Introduction to *A Discourse on Hip: Selected Writings*, 32.
72. Klonsky, "A Writer's Education," 45.
73. Jung, *Basic Writings*, 166.
74. Ibid., 173.
75. Finch, director, *Fear and Loathing on the Road to Hollywood.*
76. Broyard, obituary of Milton Klonsky, *New York Times Sunday Book Review.*
77. White, *The Unobstructed Universe*, 17–18, 20.
78. Ibid., 11–13.
79. Ibid., 31.
80. Redwood, interview with Stanislav Grof.
81. Grof, "Stan Grof about his LSD Experience," YouTube.
82. Grof, interview with Helena Norberg-Hodge.
83. Campbell, "Hector."
84. Campbell, *Group Dreaming: Dreams to the Tenth Power*, 110.
85. Willem van Loon and Johannis van Loon, *R.v.R: The Life and Times of Rembrandt van Rijn*, 567–68.
86. Wynter and Tulk, "Transpersonal: A Definition of Humanity."
87. Arraj, "A Jungian Analyst Talks about Psychological Types: A Visit with John Beebe."
88. Jyoti, *An Angel Called My Name*, xxxiii.
89. Ibid., 44.
90. Ibid., 46–47.
91. Ibid., 48.
92. Ibid., 46–47
93. Corbett, "The Holy Grail of the Unconscious."
94. Davies, *Other Worlds*, 80.
95. Jyoti, *An Angel Called My Name*, 63.
96. Sadasivam, "How Yogi Ramsuratkumar Shattered Ayn Rand."
97. Jung, *The Collected Works*, XII, *Psychology and Alchemy,* par. 93. Quoted in Puanani Harvey, "Until the Destroyer of All Things Comes," in *Life, Page One.*

98. Jung, *The Collected Works*, IX ii: *Aion: Researches into the Phenomenology of the Self*, par. 845. Quoted in Puanani Harvey, "Until the Destroyer of All Things Comes."
99. Hillman, Commentary, in *Kundalini: The Evolutionary Energy in Man*, 43–44.
100. Bamberger, "On Klonsky on Blake," in Zoamorphosis: The Blake 2.0 Blog.
101. Broyard, obituary of Milton Klonsky.
102. Linney, *Klonsky and Schwartz*, 15.
103. Krim, "From *Two Teachers—Nuts, Two Human Beings!*" in *Nearsighted Cannoneer*, 250.
104. Zinoman, review of *Klonsky and Schwartz*.
105. Linney, *Klonsky and Schwartz*, 23.
106. Ibid., 41.
107. Wheeler, *Guide to the Delmore Schwartz Papers*.
108. Klonsky, "The Importance of Being Milton," in *A Discourse on Hip*, 80.
109. Wenner and Seymour, *Gonzo*, 293.
110. Steadman, *The Joke's Over*, 355–358.
111. McKeen, *Outlaw Journalist*, 1.
112. Johnston, "An Unpublished Interview with Hunter S. Thompson."

Works Cited

Hunter S. Thompson Books in order of publication

Hell's Angels: The Strange and Terrible Saga of the Outlaw Motorcycle Gangs. New York: Random House, 1967.

Fear and Loathing in Las Vegas: A Savage Journey to the Heart of the American Dream. New York: Random House, 1971. Originally published in *Rolling Stone* #95, November 11, 1971, and #96, November 25, 1971.

Fear and Loathing: On the Campaign Trail '72. San Francisco: Straight Arrow Books, 1973. Reprint. New York: Warner Books, 2006.

The Great Shark Hunt: Strange Tales from a Strange Time. Gonzo Papers Vol. 1. New York: Summit Books, 1979. Reprint. New York: Simon & Schuster, 2003.

Songs of the Doomed: More Notes on the Death of the American Dream. Gonzo Papers Vol. 3. New York: Summit Books, 1990.

Fear and Loathing in Las Vegas and Other American Stories. New York: Modern Library, 1996.

The Proud Highway: Saga of a Desperate Southern Gentleman, 1955–1967. The Fear and Loathing Letters Vol. 1. Edited by Douglas Brinkley. London: Bloomsbury Publishing Plc., 1997.

Fear and Loathing in America: The Brutal Odyssey of an Outlaw Journalist, 1968–1976. The Gonzo Letters Vol. 2. Edited by Douglas Brinkley. New York: Simon & Schuster, 2000.

Kingdom of Fear: Loathsome Secrets of a Star-Crossed Child in the Final Days of the American Century. New York: Simon & Schuster, 2003.

Hunter S. Thompson Articles in order of publication

"The Temptations of Jean-Claude Killy." *Scanlan's Monthly*, March 1970. Reprinted in *The Great Shark Hunt*, 77–96.

"The Kentucky Derby Is Decadent and Depraved." *Scanlan's Monthly*, June 1970. Reprinted in F*ear and Loathing in Las Vegas and Other Stories*, 263–283.

"The Battle of Aspen: Freak Power in the Rockies." *Rolling Stone* #67, October 1, 1970. Reprinted in *The Great Shark Hunt*, 151–74.

"Strange Rumblings in Aztlan." *Rolling Stone* #81, April 29, 1971. Reprinted in *The Great Shark Hunt*, 119–51.

"Memo from the *Sports Desk & Rude Notes from a Decompression Chamber in Miami*." *Rolling Stone* #140, August 2, 1973. Reprinted in *The Great Shark Hunt*, 238–48.

"A Conversation on Ralph Steadman and His Book, *America*, with Dr. Hunter S. Thompson." Introduction to *America*. San Francisco: Straight Arrow Books, 1974. Reprinted in *The Great Shark Hunt*, 111–19.

"Jacket Copy for *Fear & Loathing in Las Vegas: A Savage Journey to the Heart of the American Dream*." *The Great Shark Hunt*, 1979. Reprinted in *Fear and Loathing in Las Vegas and Other American Stories*, 207–15.

Hunter S. Thompson Interviews in order of appearance

Vetter, Craig. "Hunter Thompson: A Freewheeling Conversation with the Outlaw Journalist and Only Man Alive to Ride with Both Richard Nixon and the Hell's Angels." *Playboy*, November 1974. http://www.playboy.com/playground/view/playboy-interview-hunter-s-thompson.

McKeen, William. "Doing Time on the Proud Highway: A 1990 Interview with Hunter S. Thompson." http://www.williammckeen.com/Hunter_S._Thompson_Interview.html.

Originally in McKeen. *Hunter S. Thompson* (Twayne's United States Author Series). New York: Twayne Pub, 1991.

O'Rourke, P. J. "Fear and Loathing at 25—Thompson Reflects on the Addictive Properties of Professional Journalism." *Rolling Stone*, November 28, 1996. http://plagiarismbeginsathome.wordpress.com/2008/06/24/fear-and-loathing-at-25-thompson-reflects-on-the-addictive-properties-of-professional-journalism-by-pj-orourke-nov-28-1996/.

Hahn, Matthew. "Writing on the Wall: An Interview with Hunter S. Thompson." *Atlantic*, August 26, 1997. http://www.theatlantic.com/past/docs/unbound/graffiti/hunter.htm.

Johnston, Ian. "An Unpublished Interview with Hunter S. Thompson." *Quietus*, February 17, 2011. http://thequietus.com/articles/05707-hunter-s-thompson-interview.

Miscellaneous

Finch, Nigel, director. *Fear and Loathing on the Road to Hollywood* (*Fear and Loathing in Gonzovision*). BBC Omnibus documentary, 1978. http://www.wilderutopia.com/performance/literary/gonzovision-1970s-hunter-s-thompson-on-the-american-dream/.

Bibliography of Other Authors

Alpert, Richard. "Richard Alpert (Ram Dass) on Psilocybin." YouTube.

———. Quoted at http://www.linda-goodman.com/ubb/Forum3/HTML/002252.html.

Arraj, Jim. "A Jungian Analyst Talks about Psychological Types: A Visit with John Beebe." http://www.innerexplorations.com/catpsy/a.htm.

Bamberger, W. C. "On Klonsky on Blake." Zoamorphosis: The

Blake 2.0 Blog, December 10, 2010. http://zoamorphosis.com/2010/12/on-klonsky-on-blake/.

Brinkley, Douglas. Editor's Note to Hunter S. Thompson letters, *Fear and Loathing in America*, xiv–xxii.

Broyard, Anatole. Obituary of Milton Klonsky. *New York Times Sunday Book Review*, March 7, 1982.

Campbell, Jean. *Group Dreaming: Dreams to the Tenth Power.* Norfolk VA: Wordminder Press, 2006.

———. "Hector." From *Life's Little Book of Magic*. http://es-es.facebook.com/permalink.php?story_fbid=262199210520736&id=334676919878265.

Chalmers, Robert. "Hunter S. Thompson: Fear & Mourning." Original British *GQ* version, September 2005. http://www.gq-magazine.co.uk/entertainment/articles/2011-11/24/hunter-s-thompson-funeral-death/viewgallery/9#./9?&_suid=13440969201110512788630976 0705. The abridged, archived "Fear and Mourning" does not contain the quote in the *Keep **This** Quiet Too!* epigraph.

Corbett, Sara. "The Holy Grail of the Unconscious." *New York Times*, September 16, 2009. http://www.nytimes.com/2009/09/20/magazine/20jung-t.html?pagewanted=1&_r=1.

Davies, Paul. *Other Worlds: Space, Superspace, and the Quantum Universe.* New York: Touchstone, 1980.

De Haas, Fons, and Irene Smets, et al. *Mozart en Belgique: Un enfant prodige traverse les Pays-Bas méridionaux, 1763–1766* (French). Antwerp, Belgium: Fonds Mercator, 1990,

Feehan, Rory. "Reconsidering the Legend of Raoul Duke on the 40th Anniversary of Fear and Loathing in Las Vegas," November 11, 2011. http://totallygonzo.org/2011/11/11/reconsidering-the-legend-of-raoul-duke-on-the-40th-anniversary-of-fear-and-loathing-in-las-vegas/.

Fein, Esther B. "The Media Business: Head of Summit Books Is Said to Be Leaving." *New York Times*, October 30, 1991.

Flynn, Martin. "Scanlan's Issue 1: Hunter S. Thompson, Jean-Claude Killy." http://hstbooks.org/hst-scanlans/.

Grof, Stanislav. Interview with Helena Norberg-Hodge. "New Paradigm Thinking in the Life Sciences: Psychology and Consciousness Research." *ReVision*, Vol. 9, no. 1, summer/fall 1986, 56–57. Reprinted as "Atheism in Psychology: Psychoanalyst Stanislav Grof on True Spirituality & Atheism." http://www.atheisms.info/atheisms/grof.html.

———. "Stan Grof about his LSD Experience." YouTube. Basel, March 2008. http://www.youtube.com/watch?v=5ig3eU_oDS0.

Harrell, Margaret A. "A Lecture upon the Shadow." In manuscript.

———. *Love in Transition: Voyage of Ulysses—Letters to Penelope*. Vol. 2. Sibiu, Romania: Hermann Press, 1996.

Harvey, Puanani. "Till the Destroyer of All Things Comes. In Jan Mensaert, et al., *Life, Page One*, 35–38. Tienen, Belgium: Museum "het Toreke," 2001.

Hillman, James. Commentary. In Gopi Krishna, *Kundalini: The Evolutionary Energy in Man.* Boston: Shambhala, 1997.

Hodgson, Martin, and Katy Guest. "My Crazy, Hazy Days with the Late, Great Godfather of Gonzo." Review of *The Joke's Over. The Independent*, August 20, 2006. http://www.independent.co.uk/news/media/my-crazy-hazy-days-with-the-late-great-godfather-of-gonzo-412652.html.

Isherwood, Christopher. *Diaries: 1939–1960.* New York: Harper Perennial, 1998 (also in *Lost Years: A Memoir 1945–1951*. New York: HarperCollins, 2000).

Jung, Carl Gustav. *The Basic Writings of C. G. Jung*. Edited by Violet Staub de Laszlo. New York: Modern Library, 1959.

———. *The Collected Works*, IX ii. Aion: *Researches into the Phenomenology of the Self.* 2nd ed. Princeton NJ: Princeton University Press, 1969.

———. *The Collected Works*, XII, *Psychology and Alchemy*. 2nd ed. London: Routledge, 1968.

——— et al. *Man and His Symbols*. New York: Picador, 1978.

———. *Memories, Dreams, Reflections*. London: Fontana Press, 1993.

Jyoti (Jeneane Prevatt). *An Angel Called My Name: A Story of a Transformational Energy That Lives in the Body*. Prague: DharmaGaia Publishing, 1998.

Kafka, *Diaries, 1910–1923* (Schocken Classic Series). New York: Schocken, 1988.

Klonsky, Milton. "The Importance of Being Milton: That Talent Which Is Death to Hide." *Commentary* 14:4 (October 1952). Reprinted in *A Discourse on Hip: Selected Writings of Milton Klonsky*, 70–80. Edited by Ted Solotaroff. Detroit: Wayne State Univ. Press, 1991.

———. "Mc^{2}Luhan's Message, *or*: Which Way Did the Second Coming Went?" *New American Review* #2 (January 1968).

———. "Down in the Village: A Discourse on Hip. Or, Watch Out for the Cynosure." *New American Review* #13 (1971).

———. "Art & Life: A Menippean Paean to the Flea; or, Did Dostoevsky Kill Trotsky?" *American Review* #20 (April 1974).

———. Introduction to *Speaking Pictures: A Gallery of Pictorial Poetry from the Sixteenth Century to the Present.* Edited by Milton Klonsky. New York: Harmony Books, 1975.

———. "W. B.^{4}: or, The Seer Seen by His Own Vision." Introduction to *William Blake: The Seer and His Visions*. Edited by Milton Klonsky. New York: Harmony Books, 1977.

———. Introduction to *Blake's Dante: The Complete Illustrations to the Divine Comedy.* Edited by Milton Klonsky. New York: Harmony Books, 1980.

———. "A Writer's Education." *New York Times Sunday Book Review*, March 7, 1982. Reprinted in *A Discourse on Hip: Selected Writings of Milton Klonsky*, 42–46; part of his obituary.

———. *A Discourse on Hip: Selected Writings of Milton Klonsky*. Edited by Mark Shechner. Detroit: Wayne State University Press, 1991.

Krim, Seymour. "From *Two Teachers—Nuts, Two Human Beings!*" A short version appeared in *Views of a Nearsighted Cannoneer,* 1961. Expanded in *Views of a Nearsighted Cannoneer,* 226–56. Foreword: Norman Mailer. New York: E. P. Dutton, 1968. Reprinted as "Milton Klonsky" in *What's This Cat's Story? The Best of Seymour Krim.* St. Paul: MN. Paragon House, 1991, and in Mark Cohen, *Missing a Beat: The Rants and Regrets of Seymour Krim*, 2010.

Linney, Romulus. *Klonsky and Schwartz.* New York: Dramatists Play Service, 2006.

Madhusudandas-ji, Shri Dhyanyogi. *Shakti: An Introduction to Kundalini Maha Yoga.* Rev. 2nd ed. Antioch CA: Dhyanyoga Centers, 2000.

McKeen William. *Outlaw Journalist: The Life and Times of Hunter S. Thompson.* New York: W. W. Norton & Co., 2008.

McLemee, Scott. "Sometimes a Pipe Wrench Fight Is a Thing of Beauty." Quick Study: Scott McLemee on books, ideas & trash-culture ephemera—an ArtsJournal Weblog. http://www.artsjournal.com/quickstudy/2008/11/pipe_wrench_fight.html.

Mensaert, Jan. "The Suicide Mozart." In Manuscript. Tienen, Belgium: Museum "het Toreke." Excerpted in Mensaert, et al. *Life, Page One.*

———, et al. *Life, Page One.* International editing coordinator, Margaret A. Harrell. Tienen, Belgium: Museum "het Toreke," 2001. In conjunction with the exhibit titled Jan Mensaert: 1937–1990, sponsored by Director Staf Thomas.

Nichols, John. "Hunter Thompson's Political Genius," *Nation*, February 22, '05. http://www.thenation.com/blog/hunter-thompsons-political-genius.

Olsen, Tillie. *Silences.* New York: Delacorte Press/Seymour Lawrence, 1978. Reprint. New York: Feminist Press at Cuny, 2003.

Pauli, Wolfang. "Modern Examples of Background Physics." In Wolfgang Pauli and Carl Jung. *Atom and Archetype: The Pauli/Jung Letters 1932–1958.* London: Routledge, 2001.

Peat, David. *Pathways of Chance.* Pari, Italy: Pari Publishing, 2005.

Redwood, Daniel. "Frontiers of the Mind." Interview with Stanislav Grof." http://www.healthy.net/scr/interview.aspx?Id=200.

Reed, Bill. *A Fine Romance: My Lifelong Affair with Jazz Singing and Singers.* Los Angeles: Cellar Door Books, 2009.

Rosenbaum, Ron. "Hunter Thompson, William Kennedy, the America's Cup and Me: A Belated Requiem." October 5, 2006. http://ronrosenbaumwriter.wordpress.com/?s=Hunter+thompson.

Sadasivam, Manivannan. "How Yogi Ramsuratkumar Shattered Ayn Rand." http://manivannansmirror.blogspot.com/2010_10_01_archive.html.

Seligson, Tom. Review of *Fear and Loathing: On the Campaign Trail '72*. *New York Times*, July 15, 1973. http://www.nytimes.com/1973/07/15/books/thompson-1973-trail.html.

Shechner, Mark. Introduction to *A Discourse on Hip: Selected Writings of Milton Klonsky*.

Smith, Patti. "The Crowded Mind of Johnny Depp." *Vanity Fair*, Feb. 2011. http://www.vanityfair.com/hollywood/features/2011/01/johnny-depp-201101.

Steadman, Ralph. *The Joke's Over: Bruised Memories: Gonzo, Hunter S. Thompson, and Me*. New York: Harcourt, 2006.

Time magazine, March 25, 1946. "Temptations of St. Anthony." http://www.time.com/time/magazine/article/0,9171,888158,00.html.

Turow, Scott. Review of *Yonnondio*. *Ploughshares*. http://www.pshares.org/read/article-detail.cfm?intArticleID=244.

Van de Velde, Chris. "Van vol ledigheid naar volledigheid" ("From Full Emptiness to Completeness"). In *Life, Page One*, 63–72. Tienen, Belgium: Museum "het Toreke," 2001.

Van Loon, Henrik Willem, and Johannis van Loon. *R. v. R.—The Life and Times of Rembrandt van Rijn*. New York: Horace Liveright, 1930.

Van Ruysbeek, E. *De Standaard*, March 1971. Also a lecture, "Poetical Afternoon," at Ghent, Belgium, March 1971.

Wenner, Jann S., et al. *Rolling Stone* #970 (Hunter S. Thompson tribute issue), March 24, 2005, 57.

Wenner, Jann S., and Corey Seymour. *Gonzo: The Life of Hunter S. Thompson*. New York: Little, Brown & Co., 2007.

Wheeler, Molly. Guide to the Delmore Schwartz Papers. http://drs.library.yale.edu:8083/fedora/get/beinecke:schwartz/PDF.

White, Stewart Edward. *The Unobstructed Universe: An Unparalleled Detailed Report of Life after Death*. New York. E. P. Dutton, 1940.

Woo, Elaine. "Tillie Olsen, 94, author, known for a slim output of raw, powerful works." *Los Angeles Times*, January 4, 2007. http://articles.latimes.com/2007/jan/04/local/me-olsen4.

Wynter, Christopher, and Fiona Tulk. "Transpersonal: A Definition of Humanity." http://www.transpersonal.com.au/about/transpersonal-definition.htm.

Yogananda, Paramahansa. *Autobiography of a Yogi.* 11th ed. Los Angeles: Self-Realization Fellowship, 1984.

———. *The Second Coming of Christ: The Resurrection of the Christ within You.* Los Angeles Self-Realization Fellowship Publishers, 2004. http://bookstore.yogananda-srf.org/The-Second-Coming-of-Christ-p357.html.

Zinoman, Jason. Theater review of *Klonsky and Schwartz:* "Protégé Inspired and Intimidated by Delmore Schwartz. *New York Times*, December 7, 2005. http://theater.nytimes.com/2005/12/07/theater/reviews/07klon.html?pagewanted=print.

Acknowledgments

I would like to acknowledge and thank Douglas Brinkley, the literary executor of the Hunter Thompson Estate, for permission to reprint letters from Hunter S. Thompson to me.

Thanks to those who particularly supported *Keep This Quiet*! Notably, Doug Brinkley, William McKeen, Martin Flynn, Ron Whitehead, Nick Storm, Rory Feehan, Kevin Ring, Mary Paul Thomas, Kim Thompson, the Chatham Community Library. And to those who contributed content to it: Jim Silberman, Bill Kennedy, Paul Krassner, David Pierce, Rosalie Sorrels, and Oscar Acosta. Also to Lumena Atherton, creator of the book website.

A huge thanks to those who assisted with *Keep **This** Quiet Too!* They include Virginia P. Williams, who read every word multiple times untiringly, and Frank Despriet, Martin Flynn, Chris Van de Velde, Mary Paul Thomas, and Noel Lang Baucom, who read the entire manuscript. As well, Russell D. Park and Helen Titchen Beeth, who read parts. Their comments and editing marks were a tremendous help. Also, thanks to the expert editing of Alice Osborn. And to my long-time publisher, Didi-Ionel Cenuşer. Special gratitude to Hunter's friend the photographer and cinematographer Alan Becker of Aspen for Hunter's cover photo, taken in 1991. And to Director Staf Thomas, of "het Toreke" museum, which houses the Jan Mensaert collection. The museum provided a CD of corrected decades-old slides. I am deeply grateful to Gaelyn Larrick, the cover designer, Darlene Swanson, for the interior design work, and Bram Larrick for the original interior design model. Finally, appreciation to the contributors to "Life, Page One" from whom I excerpted. And loving thanks to Hans, my mini-dachshund, who lay peacefully in the room while I typed. With memories of my full-sized dachshund, Snoepie, who began the memoir journey with me, and of my mini-dachshund Snoep, who shared the Morocco–Zurich adventures.

Artwork Credits

Hunter S. Thompson: illustrations (signatures)

Jan Mensaert: drawings, slides

Milton Klonsky: handwritten poem

Harrie Spelmans ("het Toreke"): scans of Jan Mensaert portfolio

Robert Johns: Milton Klonsky portrait

Alan Becker: HST cover image

Margaret A. Harrell copy edited Hunter S. Thompson's first book, *Hell's Angels*, at Random House. HST acknowledged her in *Gonzo Letters* 2. Years after Random House she became the author of the *Love in Transition: Voyage of Ulysses—Letters to Penelope* nonfiction series, including *Toward a Philosophy of Perception.* Also of *Marking Time with Faulkner* and volume 1 of this series, *Keep This Quiet!* Between 1996 and 2001, she was international editing coordinator for a "het Toreke" (Belgium) museum exhibit on Jan Mensaert. Since 1995 she has been in Marquis *Who's Who in the World* and similar publications, including *Who's Who in American Art* for cloud photography. Since returning to the States in 2001 she has taught personal-growth, guided-meditation courses through "the light body." She earned a BA from Duke University (magna cum laude, Honors and Distinction in History) and MA from Columbia University (contemporary literature) and studied postgraduate at the C. G. Jung Institute, Zurich. For more, visit http://www.hunterthompsonnewbook.com, http://www.cloudgiclee.com, or http://www.lightangel.net.